A Voyage to New Holland

The English Voyage of Discovery
to the South Seas in 1699

A Voyage to New Holland

The English Voyage of Discovery to the South Seas in 1699

William Dampier

Edited with an introduction by James Spencer

ALAN SUTTON
1981

Published in Great Britain by
Alan Sutton Publishing Limited
17a Brunswick Road
Gloucester GL1 1HG

This edition first published 1981

British Library Cataloguing in Publication Data

Dampier, William
 A Voyage to New Holland
 1. Roebuck *(Ship)*
 2. Pacific Ocean — Exploring expeditions
 I. Title
 910'.09164   G420.R/

 ISBN 0-904387-75-5

Typesetting and origination by
Alan Sutton Publishing Limited.
Photoset Caslon 12/14
Printed in Great Britain
by Redwood Burn Limited
Trowbridge

CONTENTS

ACKNOWLEDGEMENTS

The Editor wishes to thank those learned organisations and informed indi-viduals who have generously given time-consuming assistance, direction and advice in the production of this book. Particular graditude is conveyed to:

Royal Geographical Society, London
National Maritime Museum, London
Public Record Office, London
The British Library, London
Curator of the Herbaria, Oxford University
Oxford University Press, *Dictionary of National Biography*, for permission to take quotations
The Government of Western Australia

Thanks are also especially due to Mr. N.J. Jones for the maps reproduced in the Introduction, and the staff of Alan Sutton Publishing Ltd. for work beyond normal call of duty.

Editor's Note

A Voyage to New Holland was originally published in two parts by James Knapton, London; the first in 1703, the second in 1709. The text for this book is taken from the complete 1729 edition where the two parts were incorporated into one volume. The early eighteenth-century prose, punctuation and spelling emphasize the essential character of the work and for this reason little editorial alteration has been made to the original.

Throughout the text, Dampier makes various references to his previous works *A New Voyage Round the World* (Vol. I) and *Voyages and Descriptions* (Vol. II). In this publication the 1729 inter-volume page cross-references are omitted.

James Spencer is a Fellow of the Royal Geographical Society and previously served as an officer in the District Administration of Papua New Guinea, prior to and following that Country's Independence.

MAPS AND ILLUSTRATIONS

Introduction

The sources of the illustrations are indicated and grateful acknowledgement is made to those organisations or persons concerned in granting permission to reproduce their material.

A Voyage to New Holland

These illustrations are taken from engravings published in a copy of the 1729 edition belonging to the editor. All the plates are reproduced with the exception of one which does not relate to the 1699 expedition.

INTRODUCTION

William Dampier 1651–1715 — variously described as English navigator, hydrographer, writer, naturalist and pirate — stands alone between the explorers of the Elizabethan period and those of the mid-eighteenth century. He circumnavigated the globe three times and, with outstanding powers of description, accurately recorded a wide spectrum of the events and natural phenomena observed during many diverse voyages. From the somewhat materialistic nature of his ships' immediate commissions, confined with rough company or isolated in an atmosphere often poisoned by poor relations with the crew, he wrote with a new scientific enlightenment. The resultant journals had a powerful contemporary influence, inspiring the literary circles and the natural scientists of late seventeenth-century Britain. As pioneer for the first English initiative into the Pacific since the era of Drake, his detailed records and surveys paved the way for those voyagers such as Wallis, Bougainville, Carteret, Cook and Flinders who were to follow.

The effect upon the British nation as a whole was no less impressive. Dampier's books were best-sellers, they caught the imagination of the public and aroused interest in Pacific exploration. The formation of the South Sea Company in 1711, although eventuating in the disastrous 'bubble' a decade later, gives some indication of the fire that his writings had helped to fuel. The Pacific historian Rear-Admiral Burney wrote of Dampier:

> It is not easy to name another voyager or traveller who has given more useful information to the world; to whom the merchant and mariner are so much indebted; or who has communicated his information in a more unembarrassed and intelligible a manner. And this he has done in a style perfectly unassuming, equally free from affectation and from the most distant appearance of invention.

One hundred years after Dampier's death, his work continued as a valuable

reference, recommended by such notables as Howe and Nelson. At the end
of the nineteenth century Professor Sir J.K. Laughton comments in the
Dictionary of National Biography:

> In their clear, easy, homely, common-sense style, his writings are
> almost classical; his surveys and charts, making allowance for the
> imperfections of the age, are most highly commendable, and his
> dogged determination to keep and preserve his journal through all
> hardships, dangers, and adverse circumstances, is beyond all praise.

The late Poet Laureate, John Masefield, observed how Dampier's style of
writing provided both charm and excitement, enabling the reader to possess
imaginatively the experiences of a varied and wild life. Today, *A Voyage to
New Holland*, gives not only an absorbing account of discovery, but a vivid
record of a seventeenth-century sea passage, with lively descriptions of the
lands, the peoples, the flora and fauna.

LIFE OF WILLIAM DAMPIER

Born and baptised — 1651 in East Coker, near Yeovil, Somerset, England;
son of George and Ann Dampier, tenant farmers. It is known that he had an
elder brother George and that both parents died in his early youth. He
completed some education at a nearby grammar school before going to sea on
a Weymouth Trader in 1669. The first voyage to Newfoundland established
a strong dislike of extreme cold and he was to confine subsequent voyages to
the tropics, going next as a seaman aboard an East Indiaman to Java.
Returning to Britain at the outbreak of the 1672 Dutch war, he served on
the *Royal Prince*, flagship of Sir Edward Spragge, and took part in the
engagements of 28 May and 4 June 1673. Soon after, he was hospitalised
and eventually returned home to stay with relatives.

While convalescing in England, Dampier accepted the offer of his late
father's landlord, Squire Helyar, to work as agent on Helyar's sugar
plantation in Jamaica. Employment on the estate was a disappointment, he
moved to another plantation but by the end of nine months had returned to
sea, engaging aboard various West Indies trading vessels in the Caribbean.
During his voyages and travels from this period, until his return from New
Guinea in 1701, he went to great lengths in maintaining an accurate journal
of observations, preserving the manuscripts by keeping them in lengths of

bamboo sealed with wax.

From Jamaica in August 1675, a round voyage to the Bay of Campeche, Yucatan was commenced contact being made with the bands of British logwood-cutters and casual buccaneers of that area. Once back in Jamaica, Dampier immediately made a return to the Yucatan, trading and working with the lumber-men there for some two years. He went back to England briefly in August 1678 and married a girl by the name of Judith, 'out of the household of the Duchess of Grafton'. In the spring of 1679 he sailed for Jamaica again, leaving Judith at Arlington House. By the end of that year he had sold his immediate trading cargo and purchased some land in Dorset with the intention of returning to England, but at the last moment embarked upon a short trading mission. One thing led to another and instead of a return to Dorset as a landowner, a career in buccaneering was adopted. Judith fades from the picture at this stage and is not mentioned again except in instructions to receive his salary 1698.

Beginning in December 1679, he took part in the sack of Portobelo, and with the buccaneers Watling, Sharp, Sawkins, Coxon and Cook crossed the Darien Isthmus to start sea-borne raiding south into the Pacific to Juan Fernandez Island. After a hazardous return voyage up the western South American coast, the overland crossing of the Darien was again successfully negotiated during 1681. The next year was spent 'cruising' the Caribbean, eventually ending up in Virginia. Dampier comments on these buccaneering pursuits as being undertaken 'more to indulge my curiosity than to get wealth'. While taking a share of the work and fighting he appears to have remained aloof from the ships' companies, following instead the pursuit of knowledge in these not wholly conducive circumstances.

From Chesapeak Bay 1683, he joined Captain Cook, an acquaintance who intended to undertake a privateering voyage to the Pacific. However, their ship the *Revenge,* was too small for the project in hand and this necessitated a search being mounted for a more suitable craft. A Danish slaver was eventually seized off the Sierra Leone coast and the captured vessel, renamed the *Bachelors' Delight,* was then headed to the Pacific, by way of Cape Horn, to raid the shores of Chile and Peru. Later, following Captain Cook's death, the *Bachelors' Delight* was joined by other buccaneer vessels, among them the *Cygnet,* a ship commanded by a Captain Swan. When this force parted company in August 1685, Dampier transferred to the *Cygnet* for a voyage to western Mexico and from there across the Pacific to Guam. During this crossing provisions ran so low that the crew had proposed eating the ship's officers, starting with the captain. Dampier records: 'This made Captain Swan say to me after our arrival at Guam, *"Ah! Dampier, you would have made them but a poor meal;"* for I was as lean as the captain was lusty and fleshy.'

The *Cygnet* continued to the Philippines where command was taken over by Read, a crewman, after the marooning of Captain Swan and thirty-six others at Mindanao. An erratic course was followed to Siam, China, back to South-East Asia and eventually, after gale-force winds, to the north-west coast of Australia, coming ashore in January 1688 near the Buccaneer Archipelago in Lat. 16° 15' S. This was the first recorded British vessel to make landfall on the Australian coast. Dampier eventually left the *Cygnet* at the Nicobar Islands in May 1688, immediately undertaking a stormy five-day journey aboard a small canoe to arrive exhausted in Sumatra. From there, following a serious illness, he embarked on trading voyages toTonkin, Malacca and India, before taking the post of master-gunner at the fort of Benkulen in Sumatra. Escaping from the fort where the Governor had attempted to detain him, Dampier returned to England via Cape Town, arriving off Deal in September 1691. His only possessions were his journal manuscripts and a tattooed slave called Prince Jeoly, a Meangis Islander, whom Dampier had obtained in Benkulen. Jeoly was exhibited to provide a livelihood in England before being sold and subsequently dying of smallpox at Oxford.

For the next five years there appears no activity of note before the publication of his first book *A New Voyage Round the World* in 1697. It was dedicated to Charles Montagu, later Earl of Halifax, at that time Chancellor of the Exchequer and President of the Royal Society. The book had immediate success, running quickly into four editions. The publishers, encouraged by the reception, requested him to write a further volume covering material not included in the first work. As a result, a second volume *Voyages and Descriptions,* was published in 1699, being dedicated to the Earl of Orford, then Lord High Admiral of England. This book contained a section entitled *Discourse of Trade Winds* which, with its charts and drafts, established his reputation as a leading hydrographer. Dampier was given a Customs Service post in 1697, but with the surge of interest in West Indies and Pacific trade he was examined by the Council of Trade and Plantations on various maritime initiatives then being considered. One such plan was the ill-fated Scottish undertaking to establish a trading colony on the Darien Isthmus. There were further calls for consultation on matters such as navigation in the Indian Ocean and on the problem of piracy. The sudden turn in fortune brought Dampier to the attention of the Royal Society and the Admiralty from where, on Montagu's recommendation, he was deputed to lead a voyage of exploration to the South Seas. Little account was taken of the fact that he had no experience of command and this was later to expose a flaw in his abilities, to the detriment of himself and the expedition.

The voyage to investigate New Holland, Terra Australis and New Guinea was undertaken in the *Roebuck*, a ship that caused constant anxiety in respect to sea-worthiness once in the antipodes. A violent personality clash between Dampier and the ship's lieutenant made for a bad start and a near mutiny. The recalcitrant crew weakened by scurvy and fever, together with the ship's pinnace becoming unserviceable, led to the expedition's enforced return while on the north-east coast of New Guinea. The condition of the *Roebuck's* hull continued to deteriorate on the voyage home, with an uncontrollable leak developing off Ascension Island where she sank on the 24 February 1701. The crew got ashore and lived off turtles and goats until rescued and taken to Britain by a passing English squadron of four ships in April of that year. Though this expedition had its failures and shortcomings, it was not without considerable achievement.

Once home Dampier had to face court-martial charges for loss of the ship, the circumstances of boatswain Norwood's death, and the alleged ill-treatment of Lieutenant Fisher. Cleared of the first two charges, he was found guilty of the latter, fined three years' pay and declared unfit to command any of Her Majesty's ships. The court made its findings in 1702, but less than a year later he was called to an audience with Queen Anne, ushered into her presence by the Lord High Admiral, on his imminent departure for a privateering expedition to the Pacific. The first part of his book *Voyage to New Holland* was published at that time.

This new privateering venture to the Pacific in 1703 during the Spanish Succession War, gave him command of the twenty-six gun *St. George* and orders over the *Cinque Ports,* a sixteen gun vessel sailing in company. With uncertain pay incentive to the crews and at the best of times the captain being but nominally in charge, he was unable to maintain order and cohesion. He was later accused of being an irresolute and overbearing commander, but whatever the truth or falsehood in the allegations arising from this none too satisfactory episode it appears that leadership did not entirely suit Dampier. However, while the conduct of some of the engagements with the French and Spanish may have been over-cautious, the charge of cowardice laid upon him seems inappropriate, for his mettle on previous or subsequent occasions was not called in question. He apparently intended to use good navigation and surprise as a means to obtaining prizes and was disinclined to undertake heavy fighting with the small calibre armaments available.

Briefly, the ships on this voyage rounded the Horn to refit at Juan Fernandez Island where disaffection and disagreement amongst the crews set in. Dampier managed to talk them out of a mutiny and rallied them for the proposed raiding action up the South American coast. The first engagement with a French ship was unsuccessful and though prizes were taken on the journey north, the attack on the town Santa Maria, fell through. At this stage the *Cinque Ports* returned south, later to founder, and Clipperton, Dampier's mate, defected with a prize ship taking with him crew members and provisions. Now ill-equipped, the *St. George* failed in an attempt to overcome the Spanish Manila galleon, said to be loaded with pieces of eight. There was a further defection of the crew after which, with less than thirty men, Dampier seemed to have better fortune. He sacked the settlement of Puna, took a Spanish vessel and abandoning the dilapidated *St. George* to founder, sailed across the Pacific to Batavia, Java. Here he was seized by the Dutch authorities but managed to extricate himself and make a return to Britain in 1707. A critical account of this privateering venture was written by William Funnell, a crew member of the *St. George*. Dampier responded by publishing a *Vindication*, which in fact did little to absolve his somewhat tarnished reputation.

Whatever the failures of the *St. George* mission, enthusiasm for privateering was by no means dead. A new expedition was fitted out with the ships *Duke* and *Duchess*. Captain Woodes-Rogers was given command, with Dampier, now aged fifty-six, appointed as pilot and adviser. Before departure on this commission Dampier must have submitted for publication the manuscript of *A Continuation of a Voyage to New Holland*, for the book was brought out in 1709.

The *Duke* and *Duchess* sailed in August 1708, rounded the Horn and called at Juan Fernandez Island before proceeding up the South American coast taking prizes. The town of Guayaquil was sacked and the smaller of the two Manila galleons captured after a hard fight off the Gulf of California. The expedition with its gains then crossed the Pacific to Guam, refitting at Batavia and returning to Europe via the Cape of Good Hope. Arrival in the Thames during October 1711 was greeted with acclaim and celebration, for the prizes and booty were then valued at over £170,000. The voyage was considered a major success, towards which Dampier's expert navigation and counsel had played a vital role. Woodes-Rogers reported that the name of Dampier alone was sufficient to strike terror into the hearts of all Spaniards in the West Indies.

William Dampier lived latterly in Coleman Street, Old Jewry, London until his death in March 1715, aged sixty-three; 'diseased and weak in body, but of sound and perfect mind'. The place of burial is unrecorded. Prize money from his last voyage was not shared out until 1719, but he appears to have been able to receive various substantial advances and credits. His will left nine-tenths of the estate to a cousin, Grace Mercer of London, who had looked after him in the latter years. The remaining one-tenth was left to the surviving brother George, residing in Dorset. No chronicles of the *St. George* or Woodes-Rogers voyages were left by Dampier. However, Woodes-Rogers wrote an account of the 1708 expedition in *A Cruising Voyage Round the World* published in 1712. Some historians suggest it likely that Dampier took a hand in the Woodes-Rogers book.

In the main fields of achievement as observer, chronicler, hydrographer and navigator, Dampier was held in the highest regard by British, Dutch, French and Spanish contemporaries. Even following generations dubbed him 'the Cook of a former age'. Sir Hans Sloane, who succeeded Sir Isaac Newton as President of the Royal Society, collected Dampier's journals. These records were also closely studied by Sir Robert Southwell. But apart from the scientists, merchants and colonialists, Dampier provided the writers of that period with ample 'copy'. He dined with Samuel Pepys and John Evelyn. Coleridge described him as, 'a man of exquisite refinement of mind', and it is probably through this association that much of the background for the poem *The Ancient Mariner* was furnished. Similarly, Jonathan Swift relied heavily upon Dampier's chronicles for the work *Gulliver's Travels*. Further material for romance lay in the marooning of Alexander Selkirk on Juan Fernandez Island, at Selkirk's own request, from the ship *Cinque Ports* during Dampier's expedition of 1703. It was over four years later when Dampier returned as pilot of the *Duke* with Woodes-Rogers that Selkirk was eventually relieved from his lonely sojourn. Daniel Defoe took this event as the theme for the classic *Robinson Crusoe*.

Various sources have described Dampier as being blunt, resolute, modest, exact, skilful, intelligent and courageous. Antithetically there also appeared to be a morose and less stable side to his nature which surfaced when the burden of command was assumed. Some evidence of these opposing facets of character is provided both in the court-martial statements following the *Roebuck* voyage of 1699 and in William Funnell's account of the 1703 privateering mission. Possibly a harsh lifetime at sea and the strong sense of disappointment at not achieving greater success exacerbated Dampier's inner conflicts; but through the pen he maintained a balanced, humane and questing spirit in his best tradition of sailor-scientist.

HISTORICAL SETTING 1699 – VOYAGE TO NEW HOLLAND

In the first decade of the sixteenth century the Portuguese had begun their discovery of South-East Asia and the Western Pacific. At the same time the Spaniards commenced their Pacific enterprise, firstly from Panama and South America and from there to link with their base in the Philippines. Though Elizabethan England had shown interest in the South Seas following Sir Francis Drake's voyage of 1577, the Spaniards became increasingly established in the region by their occupation of the Central and South American Pacific sea-board.

During the following century the wars and unrest in Europe had tended to polarise English discovery, trading and colonial effort towards the consolidation of interests in North America, the West Indies and India. The lucrative South-East Asia Spice Islands trade was left largely to the Netherlands, Portugal and Spain. The better established these three nations became, the more difficult it was for England to undertake an official initiative into the Pacific without either encountering an enemy or arousing the trading jealousy of an ally. The only scope available in this situation was for the roving buccaneer and it was in such a role that Dampier had obtained his experience of the region.

By the end of the seventeenth century a number of factors culminated in generating a renewed English interest in the Pacific. The Dutch wars had come to an end, William of Orange was on the English throne and the

Dutch had become joint allies with England against the French and Spanish rivals. An exhausting war with France came to an uneasy truce in 1697. Meanwhile, the King of Spain, Carlos II, was about to die, leaving no direct heir. The maritime nations of Europe were, therefore, looking to the fate of the Spanish colonial empire, much of it real estate fronting onto the Pacific. Dutch expansionist policy in the Pacific Ocean lost its momentum on the death of the Dutch East Indies Governor-General Van Dieman in 1645, and good relations between England and Portugal, established since 1640, were shortly to be ratified by a treaty of alliance. Developing French and even Scottish activity in the South Sea gave a spur to English endeavour in the area, and therefore, in the brief period of peace before 1701 when Europe was again to become embroiled in war, Dampier's expedition was mounted. The Great South Sea, it was felt, was the coming theatre of enterprise.

While these few years of peace provided the suitable political environment for Dampier's voyage, there was also at this time a renaissance of intellectual attention towards the study of scientific subjects. The Royal Society, with its highly influential membership, lent a strong impetus to the need for collection of new specimens and for the observance and recording of natural phenomena. By this means it was hoped that development of the sciences would be facilitated and that fresh channels for research could be identified. Dampier's earlier journals had already introduced the dimensions of study and observation as rewarding aspects to be derived from overseas exploration. These same journals had focused English attention upon the Pacific as being the most promising region for productive discovery.

The map following this paragraph illustrates the approximate routes of relevant navigators in the Terra Australis/New Guinea region, prior to Dampier's voyage of 1699; excluding his own brief visit in 1688. Although it may appear that substantial coverage had already been achieved in the region, in fact the previous discoveries had been made by England's competitors. Therefore, much of the information would have been either unobtainable in Britain or confused with other conflicting evidence and legend. Maps drawn from alleged Portuguese visits to Terra Australis in the sixteenth century afforded only another aspect of unsubstantiated conjecture. No reliance could have been placed on any of the charts available, and the course taken by Torres between New Guinea and Australia was certainly unknown in England at that time. New Guinea was believed to be the northern extension of Terra Australis while New Holland constituted the western half of the continent. It was evident that the Dutch had terminated their immediate commercial prospecting interests in New Holland by the mid-seventeenth century, largely because of the forbidding reports of the country made by their navigators visiting the northern and western coasts. The need for ships to water and reprovision, together with the lure of profitable trade with fertile tropical lands, tended to draw a seventeenth-century voyager's exploratory attention towards the north of the region and New Guinea.

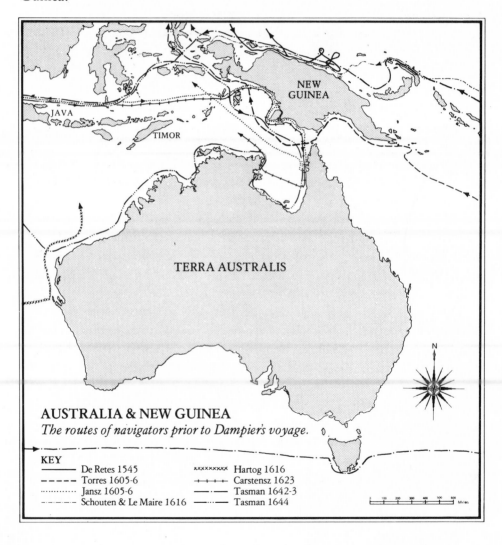

AUSTRALIA & NEW GUINEA
The routes of navigators prior to Dampier's voyage.

KEY

——— De Retes 1545	xxxxxxxx Hartog 1616
– – – – Torres 1605-6	+++++ Carstensz 1623
·········· Jansz 1605-6	—·— Tasman 1642-3
–··–··– Schouten & Le Maire 1616	—··— Tasman 1644

THE VOYAGE 1699

After the publication of Dampier's book *A New Voyage Round the World* in 1697, the author was invited by the Lord High Admiral of England, the Earl of Orford, to undertake a voyage of exploration. The objective was to be of a geographical and scientific nature, virtually the first of its kind, with the Admiralty being particularly interested in what lay to the south-east of the Dutch East Indies. There was also a strong emphasis towards finding new openings for trade and commerce. Dampier's written response to the undertaking read:

> . . . but as there is no larger tract of land hitherto undiscovered than the Terra Australis (if that vast space surrounding the South Pole, and extend so far into the warmer climate be a continued land, as a great deal of it is known to be) so 'tis reasonable to conceive that so great a part of the world is not without very valuable commodities to encourage the discovery. . . . An attempt upon the unknown tracts of that part of the world has this to recommend it, that none of our European neighbours can think themselves injured thereby: nor shall we need to interfere with any of them even in the passage thither. . . .

He asked for two ships, and sufficient pay and gratuity for the crew to prevent them turning pirate. In March 1698 the vessel *Jolly Prize* was offered for the expedition, a ship which he turned down as unfit for the service intended. Following this the 290 ton *Roebuck* was then allocated by the Admiralty, Dampier joining her as captain in the autumn of 1698, having supervised the fitting out initially at Deptford.

The most suitable approach route to the expedition's objective was at first thought to be from the west via Cape Horn. But owing to delays in fitting out the *Roebuck*, Dampier was obliged to sail east via the Cape of Good Hope, the Horn route being too hazardous in winter. It was planned to head for northern Australia and from there to New Guinea, working round to that island's north coast and investigating other islands on the way for spices or opportunity for trade. At that time in England not a great deal was known about the extent of Dutch and Portugeuse interests and settlements in the East Indies. The Dutch in particular had generally opposed exploration in the area of what was virtually their Spice Islands trade monopoly. So in addition to discovery, Dampier had an important intelligence undertaking in the South-East Asia archipelago and beyond. Eventually the aim was to continue east along the New Guinea north coast, then south to chart the eastern sea-board of Australia. The return voyage was to be negotiated via the Horn.

Dampier's correspondence prior to departure indicates that he considered it a possibility that Terra Australis might be a continuous land mass from the Antarctic regions to New Guinea. Although he was aware of various aspects of Tasman's voyage of 1642 and had some of Tasman's charts with him, it is not clear just how well these were understood in England. While the extent of Tasman's discoveries was published in the various Dutch atlases of the period, it was common practice to suppress or even alter details that were of particular value to the Dutch East India Company. In the opening pages of the second book of the *Roebuck's* voyage, not published until 1709, Dampier does mention the passage south of Australia. He writes that this route was not selected because it meant undertaking the journey in the winter period with an exhausted crew and that it was felt more worthwhile discoveries could be made in the warmer more northerly parts of the country. As previously stated, the Torres Strait between Australia and New Guinea, located in 1606, was unknown in England; in fact Tasman, after his voyage of 1644, was of the view that Australia was joined to New Guinea.

The instructions for the voyage, dated 30 November 1698, gave directions to proceed to the Cape of Good Hope, 'and from thence to stretch away towards New Holland, and then to New Guinea and Terra Australis'. Permission was given to steer any other course, but Dampier was reminded to take especial care to use his best endeavours to discover any such things as might tend to the good of the nation, to take specimens, and bring home any natives 'willing to come along'. During the voyage an exact journal of the proceedings and of all things remarkable was to be kept. Special care was to be taken not to annoy the King's subjects or allies en route, but rather to give them what assistance possible. The captain was also given power to discharge any mutinous and disorderly hands aboard any King's ship that might be met with.

The expedition, in view of the undertaking, was poorly equipped, and manned with an inferior crew. Dampier did not get a second ship nor the extra men that he had requested. The ship's officers were of little help to him, providing nothing to make up for his own deficiencies or for his lack of experience in commanding any previous ship, let alone a King's ship.

Complaints were made of the ship's master, describing him as a 'very old man' incapable of performing a long voyage, and the appointed boatswain, not keen to go on the expedition, had to be later dismissed the ship for pilfering stores. The ship's carpenter was incompetent and ill-equipped. Worse, Dampier and the first lieutenant, George Fisher, took a strong dislike to each other and were quarrelling openly before they had even put to sea. Dampier was suspicious of the allegiance of the crew and had been warned of mutiny, he believed that Fisher was behind the discontent. Fisher, for his part, saw himself as a naval officer with the misfortune of having an ex-pirate as a captain, 'an Old Pyrating Dog' with, he conjectured, intentions to run away with the King's ship. They countermanded each others orders, openly abused one another and both alleged that the other was inciting the crew. Their disputes became more violent once at sea until eventually a scuffle developed: Dampier struck Fisher with a cane and had the lieutenant confined to his cabin in irons.

Mutiny appeared to be imminent and Dampier took to sleeping on the quarter-deck where he had all the ship's small arms brought. The proposed Brazilian port of call was changed at this point from Pernambuco to Bahia where it was known support could be provided by the guns of the fort, should the crew attempt to purloin the ship. Once at Bahia, Fisher was consigned to the Governor for custody, along with a servant, four months' provisions and instructions for the lieutenant to be sent to Lisbon and there to be passed to His Majesty's envoy for repatriation to England. Dampier advised the Admiralty of this action, briefly enumerating in a letter the difficulties encountered with Fisher and providing supporting evidence. No charges or informations were laid, for, as Dampier had already told the Admiralty, he was 'much a stranger to His Majesty's Service'. After provisioning the *Roebuck* at Bahia he departed east for the long haul to New Holland, the problem solved until his return to England, thinking no doubt that if the expedition was a success all would be forgiven.

Fisher in due course returned to England and immediately set about laying a case against Dampier, generally preparing the ground for a court-martial pending his captain's return. Meanwhile more effective authority seems to have been exercised on the ship once Fisher was gone, although it was not the end of dissension among the crew. Of the disputes with Fisher, the difficulties with the ship's company and the death of John Norwood while confined to quarters, Dampier makes no mention in this book, except for oblique reference.

The *Roebuck* approached the west coast of Australia sighting land on the 1 August 1699 in Lat. 27°S, after a direct passage east from Brazil. Once on the Australian coast a northerly course was followed to Shark Bay and on to the Dampier Archipelago, searching for fresh provisions and water. Surveys and observations were effected as the ship sailed north and a landing was made in the vicinity of Roebuck Bay for a number of days. Here a concentrated search for water proved largely unsuccessful; therefore, with a crew now seriously weakened by a long voyage, the expedition was forced away to Babao, West Timor, where a refit was carried out and the ship revictualled.

Continuing the voyage, a route to the west of the Arafura Sea was selected, indicating an intention to adhere to the original plan of plying to the east along the northern New Guinea coast. This was duly facilitated by working round Cape Mabo on the north-west tip of New Guinea during February 1700. However, Dampier reflects upon the likelihood of a strait, somewhere between New Holland and New Guinea, providing a passage into the Great South Sea. Once to the north of New Guinea a long run east into the Pacific was achieved, picking up with the north-west coast of what is now New Ireland to follow that shoreline to the south-east, breaking completely new ground. Dampier charted the coast and nearby atolls to the east and south of New Ireland and New Britain, but thinking the channel dividing these two main islands only a bay, St. George's Bay, he called both islands what he concluded to be a single landmass, New Britain. St. George's Bay was to become St. George's Channel, after a survey conducted by Captain Philip Carteret over sixty years later.

The expedition continued to navigate west along the New Britain south coast, thereby discovering the strait that lies between New Britain and mainland New Guinea. Once this position had been reached the ship should have been turned away south-east again, to make for the east coast of Terra Australis, if the original objective was to be accomplished. In fact the westerly route, back up the north New Guinea coast was maintained. Dampier gives an account of the circumstances that resolved him on continuing westwards from New Britain in the preface to this book. The narrative of the *Continuation* also refers to the unseaworthiness of the ship's pinnace at that stage. Passing through the uncharted New Guinea islands the strong currents, calms and sudden storms typical to the area would have been encountered. The coasts were hostile, provisions were scarce, the seas

The *Roebuck* under attack in Slinger's Bay, New Ireland.
From a French 19th century engraving.
'*they began to fling stones at us as fast as they could, being provided with engines
for that purpose*'

there bristle with reefs, and being without a good auxiliary boat for sounding, towing or bringing on water, he was taking a serious risk. Another point for concern lay in the poor condition of the *Roebuck's* hull, making it unlikely that she would survive the damage of striking a reef; nor, incidentally, had the carpenter sufficient ability to make good the necessary repairs, were such an emergency to occur. Seventy years later, when Cook was off the Great Barrier Reef, heavy reliance was placed upon the pinnace to prevent the *Endeavour* being washed on to the 'deadly wall of coral'. In the event, *Endeavour* was holed and the carpenters saved the day; but in Dampier's case, the carpenter was to be instrumental in eventually losing the ship.

For the *Roebuck* a westerly return course was therefore pursued. The New Guinea Rai and North Coasts were charted and a string of islands named, including: Sir George Rooke Island (Umboi Is), Long Island (Arop Is), Crown Island (Lotin Is), Sir Robert Rich Island (Bagabag Is), Dampier Island (Karkar Is), and Burning Island (Manam Is). This impressive and beautiful part of the world, with its steep volcanic islands rich with luxuriant tropical vegetation, remains much as it was when first seen from the deck of the *Roebuck*. Dampier, if he returned today, would recognise his discoveries with their smoking summits set against the high coastal ranges of the mainland.

The westerly bearing was followed past New Guinea and then south-west into the South-East Asian archipelago. There, after investigating a number of islands, a sweep south, to the west of Australia was made, before eventually making sail to Batavia, Java, to effect a refit for the journey home. Despite Dampier's anxiety over the condition of the ship's hull, an uneventful passage was made to the Cape of Good Hope before the *Roebuck* sprung a leak off Ascension Island. The carpenter and the hands at the pumps worked against the flow of water in vain. The ship was steered to the shore and the valuables taken off before she finally sank. Dampier complains that of the supplies and items sent to the beach, 'great part of it was stolen away, before I came ashore; and many of my books and papers lost'. However, he seems to have retained sufficient to enable him to draw up his charts and this comprehensive book with its illustrations. Botanical specimens were also saved from the *Roebuck,* and some sixty-three of them are still preserved in the Sheradian Herbarium at Oxford. A number of these plant specimens are referred to in the appendix to the third volume of

John Ray's *Historia Plantarum* published in 1704. Others are figured in Leonard Plunkenet's work *The Amaltheum Botanicum* of 1705.

The crew of the *Roebuck* were in due course picked up from Ascension Island by a squadron of passing English ships, thereby making their return to Britain. Having survived the rigours of voyage, disease and shipwreck, Dampier was immediately faced with court-martial to answer charges brought by Lieutenant Fisher. The court was held on board HMS *Royal Sovereign* at Spithead on the 8 June 1702, the President being Admiral of the Fleet, Sir George Rooke. William Dampier was found guilty of 'very hard and cruel usages towards Lieutenant Fisher'. He was fined all his pay for the previous three years, with the court also being of the opinion that Captain Dampier was not a fit person to be employed as commander of any of *Her Majesty's ships. Dampier's leadership of the expedition has ever since been open to censure. Certainly, good relations with the ship's company may have appeared wanting; but his resolve to persevere and his resourcefulness in carrying out a demanding voyage with a small and reluctant crew, no first lieutenant, an unreliable master, an incompetent carpenter and a rapidly deteriorating ship, was no small achievement.

The relevance of the voyage's exploratory accomplishment has also been questioned. In the narrow sense of new lands charted, the contribution to the map of the world may have been small; but for the first time a deeper scientific dimension had been incorporated. This aspect alone lent a special significance to the voyage to New Holland. It must also be recalled that no reliable investigations of the Western Pacific had been made by English navigators for some one hundred years. The reports and charts of that area received from other competing European maritime nations would, for obvious reasons, omit matters of particular interest or advantage. At last, England, in Dampier, had her own man on the spot. His return from the Western Pacific and the tabling of his report was, therefore, extremely important to the nation, not only from a strategic and commercial point of view, but as a stimulant to the growing scientific awareness then resurgent in Britain. Rear-Admiral Burney in his work *A Chronological History of the Discoveries in the South Sea* stated: 'To the credit of Dampier it is to be remarked, that although the ship foundered, the purpose of the voyage was

* William III died March 1702, leaving the English throne to Queen Anne.

not thereby defeated. He fully performed the service on which he was sent, and rendered his account, and both in an able manner'.

INFLUENCES BEFORE AND AFTER

Ever since Mendana's sixteenth-century Pacific voyages, there was a popularly held belief that the potential for wealthy trade commodities, gold in particular, lay in the tropical islands to the immediate north and north-east of Terra Australis. Dampier himself seems to have been influenced by these views and subsequent enterprise by the French shows that they too had this theory in mind. It is of consequence to record that in England, proposals for an early follow-up to Dampier's voyage suggested exploring the Solomon Islands and New Britain more thoroughly, rather than going to the Terra Australis east coast region missed out by the 1699 expedition. Later there were schemes devised by both the French and the British to establish settlements in the area of New Britain.

New Holland was generally confirmed as being arid and inhospitable. Presumably, it might be reasonably concluded by a seventeenth-century navigator that the same latitudes on the unknown eastern coast of Terra Australis might turn out to be of a similar nature, with the resultant risk to satisfactorily reprovisioning there. The sixteenth-century Portuguese term for this uncharted eastern shore was the Dangerous Coast, which had an ominous ring. It may have been thoughts such as these, together with the poor condition in general of the *Roebuck* and her crew, that resolved Dampier on continuing a return home west after coasting New Britain. To follow south to Terra Australis as originally intended, with the prospect of a long easterly Pacific crossing to the Horn, would have included the strong possibility of taking the expedition into oblivion.

A common criticism of ships' captains undertaking exploratory assignments in New Guinea waters was that they did not better explore the land with shore parties. Dampier, apart from the unseaworthiness of his ship's pinnace, found his reception by the inhabitants uncertain to say the least. Subsequent voyagers to New Guinea learnt that the ambushing of their shore parties by hostile indigenous people was a common and very real hazard. Captain Owen Stanley of HMS *Rattlesnake* in 1849, was reluctant to go ashore any more than necessary in this region. Similarly, the crew of HMS *Challenger* in the 1870s found it impossible to land on parts of the island because of the antagonistic reception from the inhabitants.

To conclude, if William Dampier made only a 'small' impression upon the Great South Sea by his voyage in the *Roebuck,* that vast unknown area was at least better geographically delineated on its western approaches. The book *A Voyage to New Holland* was the first English attempt to chronicle the region's ethnography and natural history, thereby establishing a basis for applying a methodical and scientific dimension to exploration work on the more appropriately equipped expeditions that were to follow. A start had been made, giving Britain a lead which was to be held and built on. While Cook and Flinders largely completed the outline of Terra Australis, it was left to other expeditions, over a long period to conclude the map of New Guinea.

THE SHIP AND CREW

The *Roebuck*	—	Built at Wapping, fifth rate 26 gun capacity
		Refitted at Deptford 1698
		Length — 96 ft
		Beam — 25 ft
		Tonnage — 290
		Guns — 12 Dampier asked for 20
		Crew — 50 Dampier asked for 70
		Provisioned — 20 months
The Officers	—	Captain William Dampier
		Master John Hughes
		Lieutenant George Fisher
		Mates R. Chadwick
		John Knight
		Gunner Philip Paine
		Doctor William Borthwick
		Clerk James Brand
		Boatswain John Norwood

SUMMARY OF VOYAGE

Departed the Downs, England	14 January 1699
Canary Islands	30 January 1699
Cape Verde Islands	February 1699

Bahia (Salvador) Brazil	March/April 1699
Off Cape of Good Hope	June 1699
New Holland (Western Australia)	August 1699
Timor (*Refit*)	October/December 1699
South-West New Guinea	January 1700
Cape Mabo, North-West New Guinea	4 February 1700
New Britain	March 1700
Return Cape Mabo, North-West New Guinea	18 April 1700
Batavia, (Djakarta) Java (*Refit*)	July/October 1700
Cape of Good Hope	December 1700/January 1701
St. Helena	February 1701
Roebuck developed a leak off Ascension Island	22 February 1701
Roebuck sank off Ascension Island	24 February 1701
Crew of *Roebuck* picked up by English Squadron visiting Ascension Island	3 April 1701

J.S.

Captain William Dampier painted by T. Murray 1698

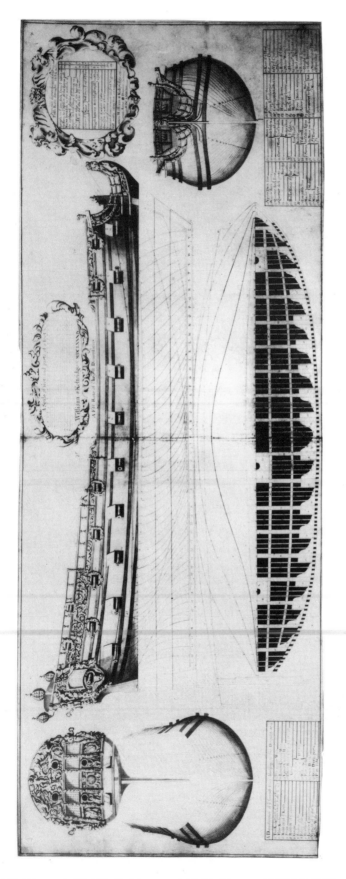

A thirty-two gun fifth-rate vessel of 1684. Probably the closest surviving plan in size and type of ship to the smaller twenty-six gun *Roebuck*

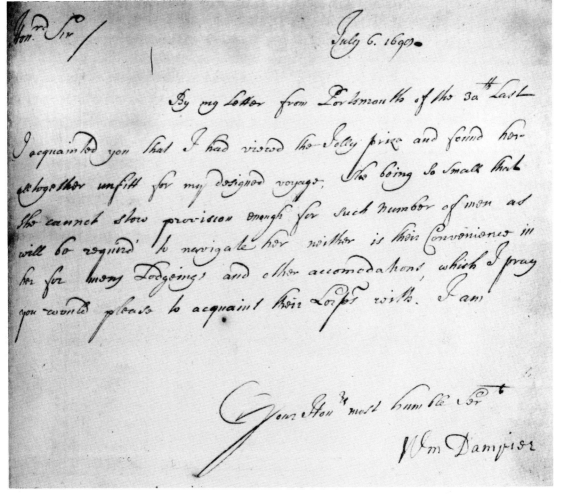

Dampier's letter to the Admiralty after inspecting *Jolly Prize*, 6 July 1698
'*found her alltogether unfitt . . . . being so small that she cannot stow provision enough for such number of men as will be required to navigate her neither is their convenience in her for many lodgings and other accomodations*'

A corner of Shark Bay, Western Australia. Dampier's area of landfall in New Holland '*the mouth of this sound, which I call'd Shark's Bay, lies in about 25°S. lat*'

Dampier's letter to the Admiralty prior to the *Roebuck's* departure, 31 December 1698.
In fact a sudden wind change prevented sailing until 14 January 1699
'now unmoring in order to sayle having the wind att NW by N'

SOME NEW GUINEA DISCOVERIES 1700

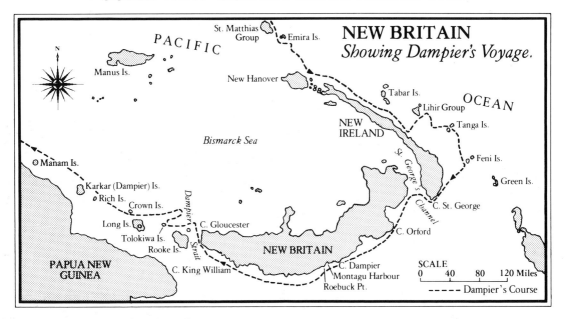

NEW BRITAIN
Showing Dampier's Voyage.

PACIFIC

St. Matthias Group

Emira Is.

Manus Is.

New Hanover

Tabar Is.

Lihir Group

OCEAN

Tanga Is.

NEW IRELAND

Bismarck Sea

St. George's Channel

Feni Is.

Green Is.

Manam Is.

Karkar (Dampier) Is.

Rich Is.

Crown Is.

Dampier Strait

C. St. George

Long Is.

Tolokiwa Is.

C. Gloucester

C. Orford

Rooke Is.

NEW BRITAIN

PAPUA NEW GUINEA

C. King William

C. Dampier

Montagu Harbour

Roebuck Pt.

SCALE
0   40   80   120 Miles

- - - - Dampier's Course

Above

A present-day map illustrating some of the main features in the area of New Britain where Dampier made discoveries in 1700. Many of the names given to islands, bays and capes by Dampier to honour his patrons, are still in current usage.

Volcanic features on the coast of New Britain
'this island which I called Nova-Britannia, has about 4° of latitude'

Sailing canoe
'saw also among these islands small vessels with sails'

A coastal village, Long Island *'a high hill at each end; this I named Long Island'*

Karkar or Dampier Island in the distance, viewed from the mainland
'high, full of fair trees and spots of green savannahs'

Manam Island *'sending forth a great smoak at once'*

Turning a turtle, Long Island *'English count the green turtle very extraordinary food'*

A

VOYAGE

TO

NEW-HOLLAND, &c.

In the YEAR 1699.

Wherein are defcribed,

The *Canary*-Iflands, the Ifles of *Mayo* and St. *Jago.*
The Bay of *All-Saints*, with the Forts and Town
of *Babia* in *Brazil.* Cape *Salvadore.* The Winds
on the *Brafilian* Coaft. *Abroblo* Shoals. A Table
of all the *Variations* obferv'd in this Voyage. Occurrences near the Cape of *Good-Hope.* The
Courfe to *New-Holland. Shark*'s Bay. The Ifles
and Coaft, *&c.* of *New-Holland.*

Their Inhabitants, Manners, Cuftoms, Trade, *&c.*
Their Harbours, Soil, Beafts, Birds, Fifh, *&c.*
Trees, Plants, Fruits, *&c.*

Illuftrated with feveral MAPs and DRAUGHTS: Alfo divers
Birds, Fifhes and Plants not found in this Part of the
World, Curioufly Ingraven on Copper-Plates.

By Captain WILLIAM DAMPIER.

The THIRD EDITION.

LONDON,

Printed for JAMES *and* JOHN KNAPTON, at the
Crown in St. *Paul's* Church-Yard. MDCCXXIX.

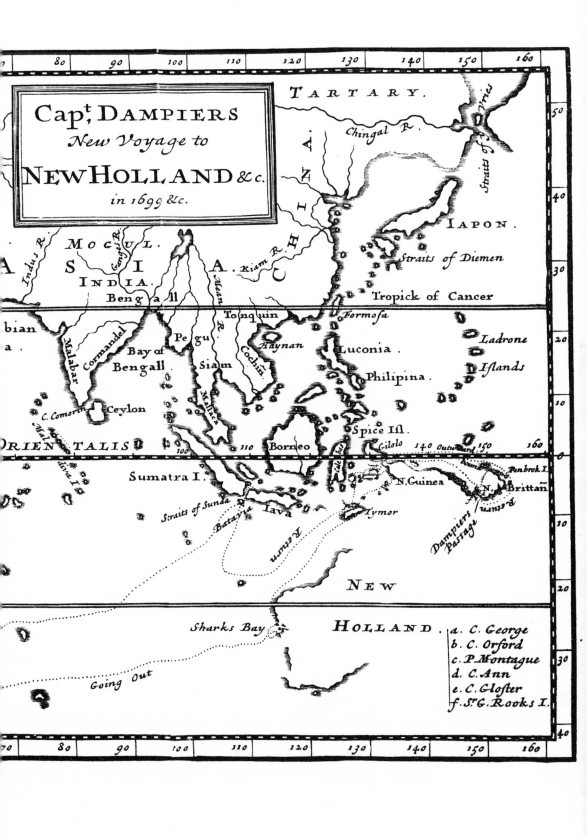

Capt. DAMPIERS
New Voyage to
NEW HOLLAND &c.
in 1699 &c.

TARTARY.

Chingal R.

Straits of J. Vries

CHINA.

IAPON.

Straits of Diemen

Kiam R.

Tropick of Cancer

ASIA.

MOGUL.

INDIA.

Indus R.

Ganges R.

Benga ll

Tonquin

Formosa

Ladrone

Islands

Malabar

Cormandel

Pegu

Haynan

Luconia .

Bay of
Bengall

Siam

Cochin

Philipina .

C. Comorin

Ceylon

Malacca

Spice Isl.

Cilolo

Outward

ORIENTALIS

Borneo

Sumatra I.

N. Guinea

Penbrok I.

N. Brittañ

Straits of Sunda

Batavia

Iava

Tymor

Dampiers Passage

Return

Return

NEW

Sharks Bay

HOLLAND .

a. C. George
b. C. Orford
c. P. Montague
d. C. Ann
e. C. Gloster
f. Sr G. Rooks I.

Going Out

To the Right Honourable
THOMAS, EARL OF PEMBROKE
Lord President of Her Majesty's Most Honourable Privy-Council,

My Lord,

The honour I had of being employ'd in the Service of his late Majesty of Illustrious Memory, at the time when Your Lordship presided at the Admiralty, gives me the Boldness to ask Your Protection of the following Papers. They consist of some Remarks made upon very distant Climates, which I should have the Vanity to think altogether new, could I persuade my self they had escap'd Your Lordship's Knowledge. However I have been so cautious of publishing any thing in my whole Book that is generally known, that I have deny'd my self the Pleasure of paying the due Honours to Your Lordship's Name in the Dedication. I am asham'd, my Lord, to offer You so imperfect a Present, having not time to set down all the Memoirs of my last Voyage: But as the particular Service I have now undertaken, hinders me from finishing this Volume, so I hope it will give me an Opportunity of paying my Respects to Your Lordship in a new one.

The World is apt to judge of every thing by the Success; and whoever has ill Fortune will hardly be allow'd a good Name. This, my Lord, was my Unhappiness in my late Expedition in the *Roe-Buck*, which founder'd thro' perfect Age near the Island of Ascension. I suffer'd extreamly in my Reputation by that Misfortune; tho' I comfort my self with the Thoughts, that my Enemies cou'd not charge any Neglect upon me. And since I have the Honour to be acquitted by your Lordship's Judgment, I should be very humble not to value my self upon so compleat a Vindication. This, and a World of other Favours, which I have been so happy as to receive from Your Lordship's Goodness, do engage me to be with an everlasting Respect,

My Lord,
Your Lordship's
Most Faithful and
Obedient Servant,
WILL. DAMPIER.

THE PREFACE

The favourable Reception my two former Volumes of Voyages and Descriptions have already met with in the World, gives me Reason to hope, That notwithstanding the Objections which have been raised against me by prejudiced Persons, this Third Volume likewise may in some measure be acceptable to Candid and Impartial Readers, who are curious to know the Nature of the Inhabitants, Animals, Plants, Soil, &c. in those distant Countries, which have either seldom or not at all been visited by any Europeans.

It has almost always been the Fate of those who have made new Discoveries, to be disesteemed and slightly spoken of, by such as either have had no true Relish and Value for the Things themselves that are discovered, or have had some Prejudice against the Persons by whom the Discoveries were made. It would be vain therefore and unreasonable in me to expect to escape the Censure of all, or to hope for better Treatment than far Worthier Persons have met with before me. But this Satisfaction I am sure of having, that the Things themselves in the Discovery of which I have been imployed, are most worthy of our diligentest Search and Inquiry; being the various and wonderful Works of God in different Parts of the World: And however unfit a Person I may be in other respects to have undertaken this Task, yet at least I have given a faithful Account, and have found some Things undiscovered by any before, and which may at least be some Assistance and Direction to better qualified Persons who shall come after me.

It has been objected against me by some, that my Accounts and Descriptions of Things are dry and jejune not filled with variety of pleasant Matter, to divert and gratify the Curious Reader. How far this is true, I must leave to the World to judge. But if I have been exactly and strictly careful to give only True Relations and Descriptions of Things (as I am sure I have;) and if my Descriptions be such as may be of use not only to my self (which I have already in good measure experienced) but also to others in future Voyages; and likewise to such Readers at home as are more desirous of a Plain and Just Account of the true Nature and State of the Things described, than of a Polite and Rhetorical Narrative: I hope all the Defects in my Stile, will meet with an easy and ready Pardon.

Others have taxed me with borrowing from other Men's Journals; and with Insufficiency, as if I was not my self the Author of what I write, but published Things digested and drawn up by others. As to the first Part of this Objection, I assure the Reader, I have taken nothing from any Man without mentioning his Name, except some very few Relations and particular Observations received from credible Persons who desired not to be named; and these I have always expressly distinguished in my Books, from what I relate as of my own observing. And as to the latter; I think it so far from being a Diminution to one of my Education and Employment, to have what I write, Revised and Corrected by Friends; that on the contrary, the best and most eminent Authors are not ashamed to own the same Thing, and look upon it as an Advantage.

Lastly, I know there are some who are apt to slight my Accounts and Descriptions of Things, as if it was an easie Matter and of little or no Difficulty to do all that I have done, to visit little more than the Coasts of unknown Countries, and make short and imperfect Observations of Things only near the Shore. But whoever is experienced in these Matters, or considers Things impartially, will be of a very different Opinion. And any one who is sensible, how backward and refractory the Seamen are apt to be in long Voyages when they know not whither they are going, how ignorant they are of the Nature of the Winds and the shifting Seasons of the Monsoons, and how little even the Officers themselves generally are skilled in the Variation of the Needle and the Use of the Azimuth Compass; besides the Hazard of all outward Accidents in strange and unknown Seas: Any one, I say, who is sensible of these Difficulties, will be much more pleased at the Discoveries and Observations I have been able to make, than displeased with me, that I did not make more.

Thus much I thought necessary to premise in my own Vindication, against the Objections that have been made to my former Performances. But not to trouble the Reader any further with Matters of this Nature; what I have more to offer, shall be only in relation to the following Voyage.

For the better apprehending the Course of this Voyage, and the Situation of the Places mentioned in it, I have here, as in the former Volumes, caused a Map to be Ingraven, with a prick'd Line, representing to the Eye the whole Thread of the Voyage at one View; besides Draughts and Figures of particular Places, to make the Descriptions I have given of them more intelligible and useful.

Moreover, which I had not the opportunity of doing in my former Voyages; having now had in the Ship with me a Person skill'd in Drawing, I have by this means been enabled, for the greater Satisfaction of the Curious Reader, to present him with exact Cuts and Figures of several of the principal and most remarkable of those Birds, Beasts, Fishes and Plants, which are described in the following Narrative; and also of several, which not being able to give any better or so good an Account of, as by causing them to be exactly Ingraven, the Reader will not find any further Description of them, but only that they were found in such or such particular Countries. The Plants themselves are in the Hands of the Ingenious* Dr. Woodward. I could have caused many others to be drawn in like manner, but that I resolved to confine my self to such only, as had some very remarkable difference in the Shape of their principal Parts from any that are found in Europe. I have besides several Birds and Fishes ready drawn, which I could not put into the present Volume, because they were found in Countries, to the Description whereof the following Narrative does not reach. For, being obliged to prepare for another Voyage, sooner than I at first expected; I have not been able to continue the ensuing Narrative any further than to my Departure from the Coast of New Holland. But, if it please God that I return again safe, the Reader may expect a Continuation of this Voyage from my departure from New Holland, till the foundring of my Ship near the Island of Ascension.

In the mean time, to make the Narrative in some measure compleat, I shall here add a Summary Abstract of the latter part of the Voyage, whereof I have not had time to draw out of my Journals a full and particular Account at large. Departing therefore from the Coast of New Holland in the beginning of September, 1699 we arrived at Timor, Sept. 15. and anchored off that Island. On the 24th we obtain'd a small Supply of fresh Water from the Governor of a Dutch Fort and Factory there; we found also there a Portuguese Settlement, and were kindly treated by them. On the 3d of

* Dr. J. Woodward: 1665-1728. Botanist and council member of the Royal Society.

December we arrived on the Coast of New Guinea; where we found good fresh Water, and had Commerce with the Inhabitants of a certain Island call'd Pulo-Sabuti. After which, passing to the Northward, we ranged along the Coast to the Eastermost Part of New Guinea; which I found does not join to the main Land of New Guinea, but is an Island, as I have described it in my Map, and call'd it New-Britain.

It is probable this Island may afford many rich Commodities, and the Natives may be easily brought to Commerce. But the many Difficulties I at this time met with, the want of Convenience to clean my Ship, the fewness of my Men, their Desire to hasten home, and the Danger of continuing in these Circumstances in Seas where the Shoals and Coasts were utterly unknown, and must be searched out with much Caution and length of Time; hindred me from prosecuting any further at present my intended Search. What I have been able to do in this Matter for the Publick Service, will, I hope, be candidly receiv'd; and no Difficulties shall discourage me from endeavouring to promote the same End, whenever I have an Opportunity put into my Hands.

May 18. in our Return, we arrived at Timor. June 21, we past by part of the Island Java. July 4, we anchored in Batavia-Road; and I went ashore, visited the Dutch General, and desired the Privilege of buying Provisions that I wanted, which was granted me. In this Road we lay till the 17th of October following; when, having fitted the Ship, recruited my self with Provisions, filled all my Water, and the Season of the Year for returning towards Europe being come; I set Sail from Batavia, and on the 19th of December made the Cape of Good Hope; whence departing Jan. 11, we made the Island of Santa Hellena on the 31st; and February the 21st, the Island of Ascension; near to which my Ship, having sprung a Leak which could not be stopped, foundered at Sea; with much difficulty we got ashore, where we liv'd on Goats and Turtle; and on the 26th of February found, to our great Comfort, on the S.E. Side of a high Mountain, about half a Mile from its Top, a Spring of fresh Water. I returned to England in the *Canterbury* East-India-Ship. For which wonderful Deliverance from so many and great Dangers, I think my self bound to return continual Thanks to Almighty God; whose Divine Providence if it shall please to bring me safe again to my Native Country from my present intended Voyage; I hope to publish a particular Account of all the material Things I observed in the several Places which I have now but barely mentioned.

PART I

THE CONTENTS

CHAP. I

The A.'s departure from the Downs. A Caution to those who sail in the
Channel. His Arrival at the Canary-Islands. Santa Cruz in Teneriffe; the
Road and Town, and Spanish Wreck. Laguna T. Lake and Country; and
Oratavia T. and Road. Of the Wines and other Commodities of Teneriffe,
&c. and the Governors at Laguna and Santa Cruz. Of the Winds in these
Seas. The A's Arrival at Mayo. Of the C. Verd Islands; its Salt-pond,
compar'd with that of Salt Tortuga; its Trade for Salt, and Frape-boats. Its
Vegetables, Silk-Cotton, &c. Its Soil, and Towns; its Guinea-Hen's, and
other Fowls, Beasts, and Fish. Of the Sea-Turtles, &c. laying in the Wet
Season, Of the Natives, their Trade and Livelihood. The A.'s Arrival at J.
St. Jago; Proga, and St. Jago Town. Of the Inhabitants, and their Com-
modities. Of the Custard-Apple, St. Jago Road. J. Fogo.

CHAP. II

The A.'s Deliberation on the Sequel of his Voyage, and Departure from St.
Jago. His Course, and the Winds, &c. in crossing the Line. He stands
away for the Bay of All-Saints in Brazil; and why. His arrival on that Coast
and in the Bay. Of the several Forts, the Road, Situation, Town, and
Buildings of Bahia. Of its Governour, Ships and Merchants; and
Commodities to and from Europe. Claying of Sugar. The Season for the
European Ships, and Coire Cables: Of their Guinea-trade, and of the Coast-
ing-trade, and Whale-killing. Of the Inhabitants of Bahia; their carrying in
Hammocks: Their Artificers, Crane for Goods, and Negro-Slaves. Of the
Country about Bahia, its Soil and Product. Its Timber-trees; the Sapiera,

Vermiatico, Commesserie, Guitteba, Serrie, and Mangroves. The Bastard-Coco, its Nuts and Cables; and the Silk-Cotton-trees. The Brasilian Fruits, Oranges, &c. Of the Sour-sops, Cashew's, and Jennipah's. Of their peculiar Fruits, Arisah's, Mericasah's, Petango's, Petumbo's Mungaroo's, Muckishaw's, Ingwa's, Otees, and Musteran de Ova's. Of the Palm-berries, Physick-nuts, Mendibee's, &c. and their Roots and Herbs, &c. Of their Wild-Fowl, Maccaw's, Parrots, &c. The Yemma, Carrion-Crow and Chattering-crow, Bill-bird, Curreso, Turtle-dove and Wild-pigeons; the Jenetee, Clocking-hen, Crab-catcher, Galden, and black Heron: The Ducks, Widgeon and Teal; and Ostriges to the Southward, and of the Dun-ghil-fowls. Of their Cattle, Horses, &c. Leopards and Tiger's. Of their Serpents; the Rattle-Snake, small Green-Snake. Amphisbæna, small Black and small Grey-Snake; the great Land, and the great Water-Snake; and of the Water-dog. Of their Sea-fish and Turtle; and of St. Paul's Town.

CHAP. III

The A.'s Stay and Business at Bahia: Of the Winds, and Seasons of the Year there. His departure for N. Holland. C. Salvadore. The Winds on the Brasilian Coast; and Abrohlo Shoal; Fish, and Birds: The Shear-water Bird, and Cooking of Sharks. Excessive number of Birds about a dead Whale; Of the Pintado Bird, and the Petrel, &c. Of a Bird that shews the C. of G. Hope to be near: Of the Sea-reckonings, and Variations: And a Table of all the Variations observ'd in this Voyage. Occurrences near the Cape; and the A.'s passing by it. Of the Westerly Winds beyond it: A Storm, and its Presages. The A.'s Course to N. Holland; and Signs of approaching it. Another Abrohlo Shole and Storm, and the A.'s Arrival on part of N. Holland. That part describ'd, and Shark's Bay, where he first anchors. Of the Land there, Vegetables, Birds, &c. A particular sort of Guano: Fish, and beautiful Shells; Turtle, large Shark, and Water-Serpents. The A.'s removing to another part of N. Holland: Dolphins, Whales, and more Sea-Serpents: And of a Passage or Streight suspected here: Of the Vegetables, Birds, and Fish. He anchors on a third Part of N. Holland, and digs Wells, but brackish. Of the Inhabitants there, and great Tides, the Vegetables and Animals, &c.

A Voyage to Terra Australis

CHAP. I

I Sail'd from the Downs early on Saturday, Jan. 14. 1699. with a fair
Wind, in his Majesty's Ship the *Roe-buck*; carrying but 12 Guns in this
Voyage, and 50 Men and Boys, with 20 Month's Provision. We had several
of the King's Ships in Company, bound for Spit-head and Plimouth; and by
Noon we were off Dungeness. We parted from them that Night, and stood
down the Channel, but found our selves next Morning nearer the French
Coast than we expected; C. de Hague bearing S.E. and by E. 6L. There
were many other Ships, some nearer, some farther off the French Coast,
who all seem'd to have gone nearer to it than they thought they should. My
Master, who was somewhat troubled at it at first, was not displeas'd however
to find that he had Company in his Mistake: Which, as I have heard, is a
very common one, and fatal to many Ships. The Occasion of it is the not
allowing for the Change of the Variation since the making of the Charts;
which *Captain Hally has observ'd to be very considerable. I shall refer the
Reader to his own Account of it which he caus'd to be publish'd in a single
Sheet of Paper, purposely for a Caution to such as pass to and fro the
English Channel. And my own Experience thus confirming to me the Use-
fulness of such a Caution, I was willing to take this Occasion of helping
towards the making it the more publick.

Not to trouble the Reader with every Day's Run, nor with the Winds or
Weather (but only in the remoter Parts, where it may be more particularly
useful) standing away from C. la Hague, we made the Start about 5 that
Afternoon; which being the last Land we saw of England, we reckon'd our

---

* E. Halley 1656–1742. Astronomer-Royal.

An. 1699   Departure from thence: Tho' we had rather have taken it from the Lizard, if the hazy Weather would have suffer'd us to have seen it.

The first Land we saw after we were out of the Channel was C. Finisterre, which we made on the 19th; and on the 28th made Lancerota, one of the Canary Islands; of which, and of Allegrance, another of them, I have here given the Sights, as they both appeard to us at two several Bearings and Distances. [Table I. N°. 1, 2.]

We were now standing away for the Island Teneriffe, where I intended to take in some Wine and Brandy for my Voyage. On Sunday, half an hour past 3 in the Afternoon, we made the Island, and crouded in with all our Sails till 5; when the N.E. Point of the Isle bore W.S.W. dist. 7 Leagues: But being then so far off that I could not expect to get in before Night, I lay by till next Morning, deliberating whether I should put in at Santa Cruz, or at Oratavia, the one on the E. the other on the W. side of the Island; which lies mostly North and South; and these are the principal Ports on each Side. I chose Santa Cruz as the better Harbour (especially at this Time of the Year) and as best furnish'd with that Sort of Wine which I had occasion to take in for my Voyage: So there I come to an Anchor Jan. 30th, in 33 Fathom-water, black slimy Ground; about half a Mile from the Shore; from which Distance I took the Sight of the Town [Table I. N°.3.]

In the Road, Ships must ride in 30, 40, or 50 Fathom-water, not above half a Mile from the Shore at farthest: And if there are many Ships, they must ride close one by another. The Shore is generally high Land, and in most Places steep too. This Road lies so open to the East, that Winds from that Side make a great Swell, and very bad going ashore in Boats: The Ships that ride here are then often forced to put to Sea, and sometimes to cut or slip their Anchors, not being able to weigh them. The best and smoothest Landing is in a small sandy Cove, about a Mile to the N.E. of the Road, where there is good Water, with which Ships that lade here are supply'd; and many Times Ships that lade at Oratavia, which is the chief Port for Trade, send their Boats hither for Water. That is a worse Port for Westerly than this is for Easterly Winds; and then all Ships that are there put to Sea. Between this Watering-place and Santa Cruz are two little Forts; which with some Batteries scatter'd along the Coast command the Road. Santa Cruz its self is a small unwalled Town fronting the Sea, guarded with two other Forts to secure the Road. There are about 200 Houses in the Town, all two Stories high, strongly built with Stone, and covered with Pantile. It hath

Table I   Canary Iſlands

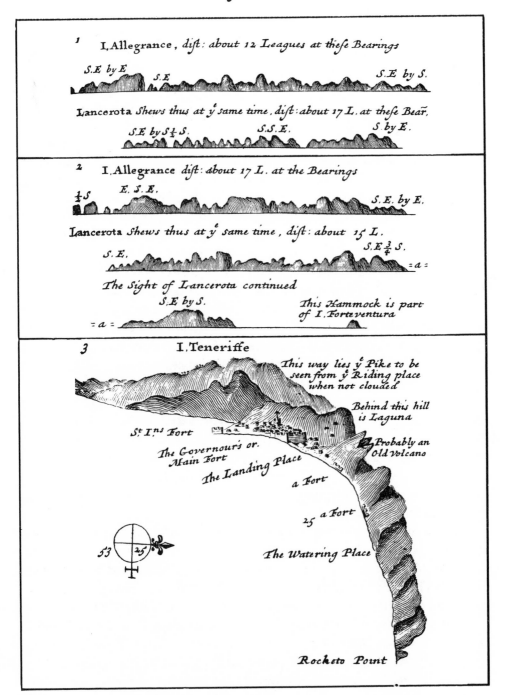

1   I. Allegrance, *diſt: about 12 Leagues at theſe Bearings*

S.E by E   S.E   S.E by S.

Lancerota ſhews thus at y̓ same time, diſt: about 17 L. at theſe Bear.

S.E by S¼ S.   S.S.E.   S by E.

2   I. Allegrance *diſt: about 17 L. at the Bearings*

¼ S   E.S.E.   S.E. by E.

Lancerota ſhews thus at y̓ same time, diſt: about 15 L.

S.E.   S.E ¾ S.   = a =

The Sight of Lancerota continued

S.E by S.   This Hammock is part
= a =   of I. Forteventura

3   I. Teneriffe

This way lies y̓ Pike to be
seen from y̓ Riding place
when not clouded

Behind this hill
is Laguna

S.t I.ns Fort

The Governour's or.
Main Fort   Probably an
Old Volcano

The Landing Place

a Fort

25   a Fort

The Watering Place

53   25

Rocketo Point

two Convents and one Church, which are the best Buildings in the Town. The Forts here could not secure the Spanish Galleons from Admiral Blake, tho' they hall'd in close under the main Fort. Many of the Inhabitants that are now living remember that Action; in which the English batter'd the Town, and did it much Damage; and the marks of the Shot still remain in the Fort-Walls. The Wrecks of the Galleons that were burnt here, lie in 15 Fathom-water: And 'tis said that most of the Plate lies there, tho' some of it was hastily carried ashore at Blake's coming in Sight.

Soon after I had anchor'd I went ashore here to the Governour of the Town, who receiv'd me very kindly, and invited me to dine with him the next Day. I return'd on Board in the Evening, and went ashore again with two of my Officers the next Morning; hoping to get up the Hill Time enough to see Laguna, the principal Town, and to be back again to dine with the Governour of Santa Cruz; for I was told that Laguna was but 3 Miles off. The Road is all the way up a pretty steep Hill; yet not so steep but that Carts go up and down laden. There are Publick Houses scattering by the Way-side, where we got some Wine. The Land on each Side seemed to be but rocky and dry; yet in many Places we saw Spots of green flourishing Corn. At farther Distances there were small Vineyards by the Sides of the Mountains, intermixt with Abundance of waste rocky Land, unfit for Cultivation, which afforded only Dildo-bushes. It was about 7 or 8 in the Morning when we set out from Santa Cruz; and it being fair clear Weather, the Sun shone very bright and warmed us sufficiently before we got to the City Laguna; which we reached about 10 a Clock, all sweaty and tired, and were glad to refresh our selves with a little Wine in a sorry Tipling-house: But we soon found out one of the English Merchants that resided here; who entertained us handsomely at Dinner, and in the Afternoon shew'd us the Town.

Laguna is a pretty large well-compacted Town, and makes a very agreeable Prospect. It stands part of it against a Hill, and part in a Level. The Houses have mostly strong Walls built with Stone and covered with Pantile. They are not uniform, yet they appear pleasant enough. There are many fair Buildings; among which are 2 Parish-Churches, 2 Nunneries, an Hospital, 4 Convents, and some Chapels; besides many Gentlemens Houses. The Convents are those of St. Austin, St. Dominick, St. Francis, and St. Diego. The two Churches have pretty high square Steeples, which top the rest of the Buildings. The Streets are not regular, yet they are mostly spacious and pretty handsome; and near the middle of the Town is a large Parade, which has good Buildings about it. There is a strong Prison on one Side of it; near which is a large Conduit of good Water, that supplies all the Town. They have many Gardens which are set round with Oranges, Limes, and other Fruits: In the middle of which are Pot-herbs, Sallading, Flowers, &c. And indeed, if the Inhabitants were curious this way, they might have very pleasant Gardens: For as the Town stands high from the Sea, on the Brow of a Plain that is all open to the East, and hath consequently the Benefit of the true Trade-wind, which blows here, and is most commonly fair; so there are seldom wanting at this Town, brisk, cooling, and refreshing Breezes all the Day.

On the Back of the Town there is a large Plain of 3 or 4 Leagues in length and 2 Miles wide, producing a thick kindly Sort of Grass, which lookt green and very pleasant when I was there, like our Meadows in England in the Spring. On the East-side of this Plain, very near the Back of the Town, there is a natural Lake or Pond of fresh Water. It is about half a Mile in Circumference; but being stagnant, 'tis only us'd for Cattle to drink of. In the Winter-time several Sorts of wild Fowl resort hither affording Plenty of Game to the Inhabitants of Laguna. This city is called Laguna from hence; for that Word in Spanish signifies a Lake or Pond. The Plain is bounded on the W. the N.W. and the S.W. with high steep Hills; as high above this Plain as this is above the Sea; and 'tis from the Foot of one of these Mountains that the Water of the Conduit which supplies the Town, is conveyed over the Plain, in Troughs of Stone rais'd upon Pillars. And, indeed, considering the Situation of the Town, its large Prospect to the East (for from hence you see the Grand Canary), its Gardens, cool Arbors, pleasant Plain, green Fields, the Pond and Aqueduct, and its refreshing Breezes; it is a very delightful Dwelling, especially for such as have not Business that calls them far and often from Home: For the Island being generally mountainous, steep and craggy, full of Risings and Fallings, 'tis very troublesome Travelling up and down in it, unless in the Cool of the Mornings and Evenings: And Mules and Asses are most us'd by them, both for Riding and Carriage, as fittest for the stony, uneven Roads.

Beyond the Mountains, on the S.W. side, still further up, you may see from the Town and Plain a small peeked Hill, overlooking the rest. This is that which is called the Pike of Teneriffe, so much noted for its Heighth: But we saw it here at so great a Disadvantage, by Reason of the Nearness of the adjacent Mountains to us, that it looked inconsiderable in Respect to its Fame.

The true Malmesy Wine grows in this Island; and this here is said to be the best of its Kind in the World. Here is also Canary-Wine, and Verdona, or Green-wine. The Canary grows chiefly on the West-side of the Island; and therefore is commonly sent to Oratavia; which being the chief Sea-port for Trade in the island, the principal English Merchants reside there, with their Consul; because we have a great Trade for this Wine. I was told, that that Town is bigger than Laguna; that it has but one Church, but many Convents: That the Port is but ordinary at best, and is very bad when the N.W. Winds blow. These Norwesters give notice of their Coming, by a great Sea that tumbles in on the Shore for some Time before they come, and by a black Sky in the N. W. Upon these Signs Ships either get up their Anchors, or slip their Cables and put to Sea, and ply off and on till the Weather is over. Sometimes they are forced to do so 2 or 3 Times before they can take in their Lading; which 'tis hard to do here in the fairest Weather: And for fresh Water, they send, as I have said, to Santa Cruz. Verdona is green, strong-bodied Wine, harsher and sharper than Canary. 'Tis not so much esteemed in Europe, but is exported to the West-Indies, and will keep best in hot Countries; for which Reason I touch'd here to take in some of it for my Voyage. This Sort of Wine is made chiefly on the East-side of the Island, and shipt off at Santa Cruz.

Besides these Wines, which are yearly vended in great Plenty from the Canary Islands (chiefly from Grand Canary, Teneriffe, and Palma) here is Store of Grain, as Wheat, Barly and Maiz, which they often transport to other Places. They have also some Beans and Peas, and Coches, a Sort of Grain much like Maiz, sow'd mostly to fatten Land. They have Papah's, which I shall speak more of hereafter; Apples, Pears, Plumbs, Cherries, and excellent Peaches, Apricocks, Guava's, Pomegranates, Citrons, Oranges, Lemons, Limes, Pumpkins, Onions the best in the World, Cabbages, Turnips, Potato's, &c. They are also well stocked with Horses, Cows, Asses, Mules, Sheep, Goats, Hogs, Conies, and Plenty of Deer. The Lancerot Horses are said to be the most mettlesome, fleet, and loyal Horses that are. Lastly, here are many Fowls, as Cocks and Hens, Ducks, Pidgeons, Partridges, &c. with Plenty of Fish, as Mackril, &c. All the Canary Islands have of these Commodities and Provisions more or less: But as Lancerota is most fam'd for Horses, and Grand Canary, Teneriffe, and

Palma for Wines, Teneriffe especially for the best Malmesy, (for which Reason these 3 Islands have the chief Trade) so is Forteventura for Dunghil-Fowls, and Gomera for Deer. Fowls and other Eatables are dear on the Trading Islands; but very plentiful and cheap on the other; and therefore 'tis best for such Ships that are going out on long Voyages, and who design to take in but little Wine, to touch rather at these last; where also they may be supply'd with Wine enough, good and cheap: And for my own Part, if I had known before I came hither, I should have gone rather to one of those Islands than to Teneriffe: But enough of this.

'Tis reported they can raise 12000 armed Men on this Island. The Governor or General (as he is call'd) of all the Canary Islands lives at Laguna: His Name is Don Pedro de Ponto. He is a Native of this Island, and was not long since President of Panama in the South Seas: who bringing some very rich Pearls from thence, which he presented to the Queen of Spain, was therefore, as 'tis said, made General of the Canary Islands. The Grand Canary is an Island much superiour to Teneriffe both in Bulk and Value; but this Gentleman chuses rather to reside in this his native Island. He has the Character of a very worthy Person; and governs with Moderation and Justice, being very well beloved.

One of his Deputies was the Governor of Santa Cruz, with whom I was to have din'd; but staying so long at Laguna, I came but Time enough to sup with him. He is a civil, discreet man. He resides in the main Fort close by the Sea. There is a Centinel stands at his Door; and he has a few Servants to wait on him. I was treated in a large dark lower Room, which has but one small Window. There were about 200 Muskets hung up against the Walls, and some Pikes; no Wainscot, Hangings, nor much Furniture. There was only a small old Table, a few old Chairs, and 2 or 3 pretty long Forms to sit on. Having supp'd with him, I invited him on Board, and went off in my Boat. The next Morning he came aboard with another Gentleman in his Company, attended by 2 Servants: But he was presently Sea-sick, and so much out of order, that he could scarce eat or drink any Thing, but went quickly ashore again.

Having refresh'd my Men ashore, and taken in what we had occasion for, I sail'd away from Santa Cruz on Feb. 4. in the Afternoon; hastening out all I could, because the N. E. Winds growing stormy made so great Sea, that the Ship was scarce safe in the Road; and I was glad to get out, tho' we left behind several Goods we had bought and paid for: For a Boat could not go ashore; and the Stress was so great in weighing Anchor, that the Cable broke. I design'd next for the I. of Mayo, one of the C. Verd Islands; and ran away with a strong N.E. Wind, right afore it, all that Night and the next Day, at the Rate of 10 or 11 Miles an Hour; when it slackened to a more moderate Gale. The Canary Islands are, for their Latitude, within the usual Verge of the true or general Trade-Wind; which I have observ'd to be, on this Side the Equator, N. Easterly: But then lying not far from the African Shore, they are most subject to a N. Wind, which is the Coasting and constant Trade, sweeping that Coast down as low as to C. Verd; which spreading in Breadth, takes in mostly the Canary Islands; tho' it be there interrupted frequently with the true Trade-Wind, N. West-Winds, or other Shifts of Wind that Islands are subject to; especially where they lie many together. The Pike of Teneriffe, which had generally been clouded while we lay at Santa Cruz, appear'd now all white with Snow, hovering over the other Hills; but their Height made it seem the less considerable; for it looks most remarkable to Ships that are to the Westward of it. We had brisk N.N.E. and N.E. Winds from Teneriffe; and saw Flying-fish, and a great deal of Sea-thistle Weed floating. By the 9th of Feb. at Noon we were in the Lat. of 15 d. 4 m. so we steered away W.N.W. for the I. of Mayo, being by Judgment, not far to the E. of it, and at 8 a Clock in the Evening lay by till Day. The Wind was then at W. by South, and so it continued all Night, fair Weather, and a small easy Gale. All these were great Signs, that we were near some Land, after having had such constant brisk Winds before. In the Morning after Sun-rise, we saw the Island at about 4 Leagues distance. But it was so hazy over it, that we could see but a small Part of it; yet even by that Part I knew it to be the Isle of Mayo. See how it appear'd to us at several Views, as we were compassing the E. the S.E. and the S. of it, to get to the Road, on the S.W. of it, [Table II. N°. 1, 2, 3.] and the Road it self. [N°. 4.]

   I got not in till the next Day, Feb. 11. when I come to an Anchor in the Road, which is the Lee-ward Part of the Island; for 'tis a general Rule, never to anchor to Wind-ward of an Island between the Tropicks. We anchored at 11 a Clock in 14 Fathom clean Sand, and very smooth Water, about three quarters of a Mile from the Shore, in the same Place where I anchor'd in my Voyage round the World; and found riding here the *Newport* of London, a Merchant Man, Captain Barefoot Commander, who welcomed me with 3 Guns, and I returned one for Thanks. He came from

Table II   Cape Verd Iſlands

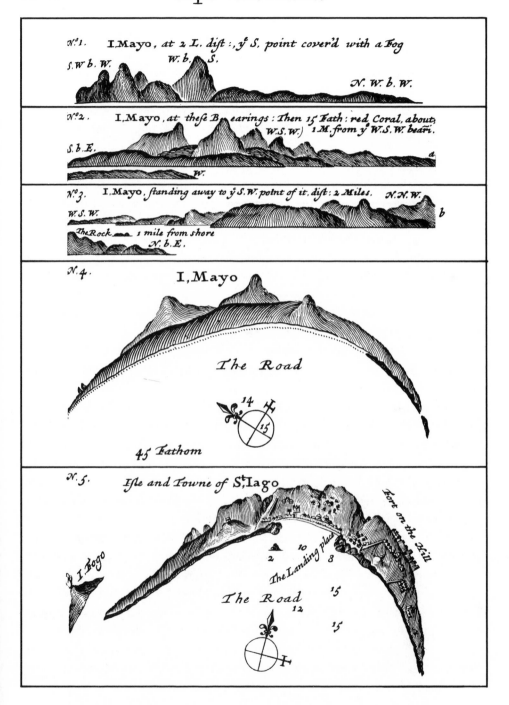

Nº 1.   I, Mayo, at 2 L. diſt:, yᵉ S. point cover'd with a Fog

S. W b. W.   W. b. S.

N. W. b. W.

Nº 2.   I, Mayo, at theſe Bearings : Then 15 Fath: red Coral, about,

W. S. W.)   1 M. from yᵉ W. S. W. beari.

S. b. E.

a.

W.

Nº 3.   I, Mayo, ſtanding away to yᵉ S. W. point of it, diſt: 2 Miles.   N. N. W.

W. S. W.

b

The Rock ⸺ 1 mile from shore

N. b. E.

N. 4.

I, Mayo

The Road

14

15

45 Fathom

N. 5.   Iſle and Towne of Sᵗ Iago

Fort on the Hill

I Fogo

10

2

The Landing place

8

The Road

12

15

15

Fayal one of the Western Islands; and had Store of Wine and Brandy aboard. He was taking in Salt to carry to New-found-land, and was very glad to see one of the King's Ships, being before our coming afraid of Pyrates; which, of late Years, had much infested this and the rest of the Cape Verd Islands.

I have given some Account of the Island of Mayo, and of other of these Islands, in my *Voyage round the World,* [Vol. I.] but I shall now add some further Observations that occurr'd to me in this Voyage. The I. of Mayo is about 7 Leagues in Circumference, of a roundish Form, with many small rocky Points shooting out into the Sea a Mile, or more. Its Lat. is 15 d. N. and as you sail about the Isle, when you come pretty nigh the Shore, you will see the Water breaking off from those Points; which you must give a Birth to, and avoid them. I sail'd at this Time two Parts in three round the Island, but saw nothing dangerous besides these Points; and they all shew'd themselves by the Breaking of the Water: Yet 'tis reported, that on the N. and N.N.W. Side there are dangerous Sholes, that lye farther off at Sea; but I was not on that side. There are 2 Hills on this Island of a considerable Heighth; one pretty bluff, the other peeked at top. The rest of the Island is pretty level, and of a good Heighth from the Sea. The Shore clear round hath sandy Bays, between the rocky Points I spake of; and the whole Island is a very dry Sort of Soil.

On the West-side of the Isle where the Road for Ships is, there is a large sandy Bay, and a Sandbank, of about 40 Paces wide within it, which runs along the Shore 2 or 3 Miles; within which there is a large Salina or Salt-pond, contained between the Sand-bank and the Hills beyond it. The whole Salina is about 2 Miles in length, and half a Mile wide; but above one half of it is commonly dry. The North End only of the Pond never wants Water, producing Salt from November till May, which is here the dry Season of the Year. The Water which yields this Salt, works in from out of the Sea through a Hole in the Sand-bank before-mentioned, like a Sluce, and that only in Spring-tides; when it fills the Pond more or less, according to the Height of the Tides. If there is any Salt in the Ponds when the Flush of Water comes in, it presently dissolves: But then in 2 or 3 Days after it begins to kern; and so continues kerning till either all, or the greatest part of the Salt-water is congeal'd or kern'd; or till a fresh Supply of it comes in again from the Sea. This Water is known to come in only at that one Passage on the N. part of the Pond; where also it is deepest. It was at a Spring of the

New Moon when I was there; and I was told that it comes in at no other
Time but at the New Moon Spring-tides: But why that should be I can't
guess. They who come hither to lade Salt rake it up as it kerns, and lay it in
Heaps on the dry Land, before the Water breaks in a-new: And this is
observable of this Salt-pond, that the Salt kerns only in the dry Season,
contrary to the Salt-ponds in the West-Indies, particularly those of the Island
Salt-Tortuga, which I have formerly mentioned [Vol. I.] for they never kern
there till the Rains come in about April; and continue to do so in May, June,
July &c. while the wet Season lasts; and not without some good Shower of
Rain first: But the Reason also of this Difference between the Salt-ponds of
Mayo, and those of the West-Indies, why these should kern in the wet
Season, and the former in the dry Season, I shall leave to Philosophers.

Our Nation drives here a great Trade for Salt, and have commonly a
Man of War here for the Guard of our Ships and Barks that come to take it
in; of which I have been inform'd that in some Years there have not been
less than 100 in a Year. It costs nothing but Men's Labour to rake it
together, and wheel it out of the Pond, except the Carriage: And that also is
very cheap; the Inhabitants having Plenty of Asses, for which they have little
to do besides carrying the Salt from the Ponds to the Sea-side at the Season
when Ships are here. The Inhabitants lade and drive their Asses themselves,
being very glad to be imploy'd; for they have scarce any other Trade but this
to get a Penny by. The Pond is not above half a Mile from the Landing-
place, so that the Asses make a great many Trips in a Day. They have a set
Number of Turns to and fro both Forenoon and Afternoon, which their
Owners will not exceed. At the Landing-place there lies a Frape-boat, as our
Seamen call it, to take in the Salt. 'Tis made purposely for this Use, with a
Deck reaching from the Stern a third Part of the Boat; where there is a kind
of Bulk-head that rises, not from the Boat's Bottom, but from the Edge of
the Deck, to about 2 Foot in Heighth; all calk'd very tight. The Use of it is
to keep the Waves from dashing into the Boat, when it lies with its head to
the Shore, to take in Salt: For here commonly runs a great Sea; and when
the Boat lies so with its Head to the Shore, the Sea breaks in over the Stern,
and would soon fill it, was it not for this Bulk-head, which stops the Waves
that come flowing upon the Deck, and makes them run off into the Sea on
each Side. To keep the Boat thus with the Head to the Shore, and the Stern
to the Sea, there are two strong Stantions set up in the Boat; the one at the
Head, the other in the Middle of it, against the Bulk-head, and a Foot

higher than the Bulk-head. There is a large Notch cut in the Top of each of
these Stantions big enough for a small Hazer or Rope to lie in; one End of
which is fasten'd to a Post ashore, and the other to a Grapling or Anchor
lying a pretty way off at Sea: This Rope serveth to hale the Boat in and out,
and the Stantions serve to keep her fast, so that she cannot swing to either
Side when the Rope is hal'd tight: For the Sea would else fill her, or toss her
ashore and stave her. The better to prevent her staving and to keep her the
tighter together, there are two Sets of Ropes more: The first going athwart
from Gunnal to Gunnal, which, when the Rowers Benches are laid, bind the
Boats Sides so hard against the Ends of the Benches that they cannot easily
fall asunder, while the Benches and Ropes mutually help each other; the
Ropes keeping the Boat's Sides from flying off, and the Benches from being
crush'd together inwards. Of these Ropes there are usually but two, dividing
the Boat's length, as they go across the Sides, into there equal Parts. The
other Set of Ropes are more in Number, and are so plac'd as to keep the
Ribs and Planks of the Boat from starting off. For this Purpose there are
Holes made at certain Distances through the Edge of the Keel that runs
along on the Inside of the Boat; through which these Ropes passing are laid
along the Ribs, so as to line them, or be themselves as Ribs upon them,
being made fast to them by Rattan's brought thither, or small Cords twisted
close about both Ropes and Ribs, up to the Gunnal: By which Means tho'
several of the Nails or Pegs of the Boat should by any Shock fall out, yet the
Ropes of these two Sets might hold her together: Especially with the Help
of a Rope going quite round about the Gunnal on the out-side, as our Long-
boats have. And such is the Care taken to strengthen the Boats; from which
girding them with Ropes, which our Seamen call Fraping, they have the
name of Frape-boats. Two Men suffice to hale her in and out, and take in
the Salt from Shore (which is brought in Bags) and put it out again. As soon
as the Boat is brought nigh enough to the Shore, he who stands by the
Bulk-head takes instantly a turn with the Hazer about the Bulk-head-
Stantion; and that stops her fast before the Sea can turn her aside: And when
the two men have got in their Lading, they hale off to Sea, till they come a
little without the Swell; where they remove the Salt into another Boat that
carries it on board the Ship. Without such a Frape-boat here is but bad
Landing at any Time: For tho' 'tis commonly very smooth in the Road, yet
there falls a great Sea on the Shore, so that every Ship that comes here
should have such a Boat, and bring, or make, or borrow one of other Ships

that happen to be here; for the Inhabitants have none. I have been thus particular in the Description of these Frape-boats, because of the Use they may be of in any Places where a great Sea falls in upon the Shore: as it doth especially in many open Roads in the East and West-Indies; where they might therefore be very serviceable; but I never saw any of them there.

The Island Mayo is generally barren, being dry, as I said; and the best of it is but a very indifferent Soil. The sandy Bank that pens in the Salt-pond hath a Sort of Silk Cotton growing upon it, and a Plant that runs along upon the Ground, branching out like a Vine, but with thick broad Leaves. The Silk-Cotton grows on tender Shrubs, 3 or 4 Foot high, in Cods as big as an Apple, but of a long Shape; which when ripe open at one End, parting leisurely into 4 Quarters; and at the first opening the Cotton breaks forth. It may be of use for stuffing of Pillows, or the like; but else is of no Value, any more than that of the great Cotton-tree. I took of these Cods before they were quite ripe, and laid them in my Chest; and in 2 or 3 Days they would open and throw out the Cotton. Others I have bound fast with Strings, so that the Cod could not open; and in a few Days after, as soon as I slackned the String never so little, the Cod would burst, and the Cotton fly out force-ably, at a very little Hole, just as the Pulp out of a roasting Apple, till all has been out of the Cod. I met with this Sort of Cotton afterwards at Timor (where it was ripe in November) and no where else in all my Travels; but I found two other Sorts of Silk-cotton at Brazil, which I shall there describe. The right Cotton-shrub grows here also, but not on the Sand-bank. I saw some Bushes of it near the Shore; but the most of it is planted in the Middle of the Isle, where the Inhabitants live, Cotton-cloth being their chief Manu-facture; but neither is there any great Store of this Cotton. There also are some Trees within the Island, but none to be seen near the Sea-side; nothing but a few Bushes scattering up and down against the Sides of the adjacent Hills; for, as I said before, the Land is pretty high from the Sea. The Soil is for the most part either a Sort of Sand, or loose crumbling Stone, without any fresh Water Ponds or Streams, to moisten it; but only Showers in the Wet-season, which run off as fast as they fall; except a small Spring in the Middle of the Isle, from which proceeds a little Stream of Water that runs through a Valley between the Hills. There the Inhabitants live in three small Towns, having a Church and Padre in each Town: And these Towns, as I was inform'd, are 6 or 7 Miles from the Road. Pinose is said to be the chief Town, and to have 2 Churches: St John's the next; and the third Lagoa. The

Houses are very mean; small, low Things. They build with Fig-tree; here being, as I was told, no other Trees fit to build with. The Rafters are a Sort of wild Cane. The Fruits of this isle are chiefly Figs, and Water-Melons. They have also Callavances (a Sort of Pulse like French Beans) and Pumpkins, for ordinary Food. The Fowls are Flamingo's, Great Curlews, and Guinea-Hens; which the Natives of those Islands call Gallena Pintata, or the Painted Hen; but in Jamaica, where I have seen also those Birds in the dry Savannah's and Woods, (for they love to run about in such Places) they are call'd Guinea-Hens. They seem to be much of the Nature of Partridges. They are bigger than our Hens, have long Legs, and will run apace. They can fly too, but not far, having large heavy Bodies, and but short Wings and short Tails: As I have generally observed that Birds have seldom long Tails unless such as fly much; in which their Tails are usually serviceable to their turning about, as a Rudder to a Ship or Boat. These Birds have thick and strong, yet sharp Bills, pretty long Claws, and short Tails. They feed on the Ground, either on Worms, which they find by tearing open the Earth; or on Grashoppers, which are plentiful here. The Feathers of these Birds are speckled with dark and light Grey; the Spots so regular and uniform, that they look more beautiful than many Birds that are deck'd with gayer Feathers. Their Necks are small and long; their Heads also but little. The Cocks have a small Rising on their Crowns, like a Sort of a Comb. 'Tis of the Colour of a dry Wallnut-shell, and very hard. They have a small red Gill on each side of their Heads, like Ears, strutting out downwards; but the Hens have none. They are so strong that one cannot hold them; and very hardy. They are very good Meat, tender, and sweet; and in some the Flesh is extraordinary white; tho' some others have black Flesh: But both Sorts are very good. The Natives take them with Dogs, running them down whenever they please; for here are Abundance of them. You shall see 2 or 300 in a Company. I had several brought aboard alive, where they throve very well; some of them 16 or 18 Months; when they began to pine. When they are taken young they will become tame like our Hens. The Flamingo's I have already describ'd at large [Vol. I.]. They have also many other Sort of Fowls, viz. Pidgeons and Turtle-doves; Miniota's, a Sort of Land-fowls as big as Crows, of a grey Colour, and good Food; Crusia's, another Sort of grey-colour'd Fowl almost as big as a Crow, which are only seen in the Night (probably a Sort of Owls) and are said to be good for consumptive People, but eaten by none else. Rabek's, a Sort of large grey eatable Fowls with long Necks and Legs, not unlike Herons; and many Kinds of small Birds.

Of Land-Animals, here are Goats, as I said formerly, and Asses good Store. When I was here before they were said to have had a great many Bulls and Cows: But the Pirates, who have since miserably infested all these Islands, have much lessen'd the Number of those; not having spar'd the Inhabitants themselves: for at my being there this Time the Governor of Mayo was but newly return'd from being a Prisoner among them, they having taken him away, and carried him about with them for a Year or two.

The Sea is plentifully stock'd with Fish of divers Sorts, *viz.* Dolphins, Boneta's, Mullets, Snappers, Silver-fish, Gar-fish, *&c.* and here is a good Bay to hale a Sain or Net in. I hal'd mine several Times, and to good Purpose; dragging ashore at one Time 6 Dozen of great Fish, most of them large Mullets of a Foot and a half or two Foot long. Here are also Porposes, and a small Sort of Whales, that commonly visit this Road every Day. I have already said, [Vol. I.] That the Months of May, June, July and August, (that is, the wet Season) are the Time when the green Turtle come hither, and go ashore to lay their Eggs. I look upon it as a Thing worth taking Notice of, that the Turtle should always, both in North and South Latitude, lay their Eggs in the wet Months. It might be thought, considering what great Rains there are then in some Places where these Creatures lay, that their Eggs should be spoiled by them. But the Rain, tho' violent, is soon soaked up by the Sand, wherein the Eggs are buried; and perhaps sinks not so deep into it as the Eggs are laid: And keeping down the Heat may make the Sand hotter below than it was before, like a Hot-bed. Whatever the Reason may be why Providence determines these Creatures to this Season of laying their Eggs, rather than the dry, in Fact it is so, as I have constantly observ'd; and that not only with the Sea-Turtle, but with all other Sorts of amphibious Animals that lay Eggs; as Crocodils, Alligators, Guano's, *&c.* The Inhabitants of this Island, even their Governour and Padre's, are all Negro's, Wool-pated like their African-Neighbours; from whom 'tis like they are descended; tho' being Subjects to the Portugeuze, they have their Religion and Language. They are stout, lusty, well-limb'd People, both Men and Women, fat and fleshy; and they and their Children as round and plump as little Porposes; tho' the Island appears so barren to a Stranger as scarce to have Food for its Inhabitants. I inquired how many People there might be on the Isle; and was told by one of the Padre's that here were 230 Souls in all. The Negro-Governour has his Patent from the Portugueze Governour of St. Jago. He is a very civil and sensible poor Man; and they are generally a good Sort of People. He expects a small Present from every Commander that lades Salt here; and is glad to be invited aboard their Ships. He spends most of his Time with the English in the Salting Season, which is his Harvest; and indeed, all the Islanders are then fully employed in getting somewhat; for they have no Vessels of their own to trade with, nor do any Portugueze-Vessels come hither: scarce any but English, on whom they depend for Trade: and tho' Subjects of Portugal, have a particular Value for us. We don't pay them for their Salt, but for the labour of themselves and their Beasts in lading it: for which we give them Victuals, some Money, and old Cloaths, *viz.* Hats, Shirts, and other Cloaths: By which Means many of them are indifferently well rigg'd; but some of them go almost naked. When the Turtle-season comes in they watch the Sandy-bays in the Night to turn them; and having small Huts at particular Places on the Bays to keep them from the Rain, and to sleep in: And this is another Harvest they have for Food; for by Report there come a great many Turtle to this and the rest of the Cape Verd Islands. When the Turtle Season is over they have little to do, but to hunt for Guinea-Hens, and manage their small Plantations. But by these means they have all the year some Employment or other; whereby they get a Subsistence, tho' but little else. When any of them are desirous to go over to St Jago they get a Licence from the Governour, and desire Passage in any English Ship that is going thither: And indeed all Ships that lade Salt here will be obliged to touch at St. Jago for Water, for here at the Bay is none, not so much as for drinking. 'Tis true there is a small Well of brackish Water not half a Mile from the Landing-place, which the Asses that carry Salt drink at; but 'tis very bad Water. Asses themselves are a Commodity in some of these Islands, several of our Ships coming hither purposely to freight with them, and carry them to Barbadoes and our other Plantations. I stay'd at Mayo 6 Days, and got 7 or 8 Ton of Salt aboard for my Voyage: In which Time there came also into this Road several Sail of Merchants Ships for Salt; all bound with it for Newfoundland.

The 19th Day of February, at about One a Clock in the Morning I weighed from Mayo-Road, in order to water at St. Jago, which was about 5 or 6 Leagues to the West-ward. We coasted along the Island St. Jago, and past by the Port on the East of it, I mention'd formerly [Vol. I.] which they call Praya; where some English outward-bound East-India Men still touch, but not so many of them as heretofore. We saw the Fort upon the Hill, the Houses and Coco-nut Trees: But I would not go in to anchor here, because I expected better Water on the S.W. of the Island, at St. Jago Town. By 8 a Clock in the Morning we saw the Ships in that Road, being within 3 Leagues of it: But were forc'd to keep Turning many Hours to get in, the Flaws of Wind coming so uncertain; as they do especially to the Leeward of Islands that are high Land. At length two Portugueze Boats came off to help tow us in; and about 3 a Clock in the Afternoon we came to an Anchor; and took the Prospect of the Town, [Table II. N.° 5.] We found here, besides two Portugueze Ships bound for Brazil, whose Boats had tow'd us in, an English Pink that had taken in Asses at one of the Cape Verd Islands, and was bound to Barbadoes with them. Next Morning I went ashore with my Officers to the Governour, who treated us with Sweet-meats: I told him, the Occasion of my coming was chiefly for Water; and that I desired also to take in some Refreshments of Fowls, &c. He said I was welcome, and that he would order the Townsmen to bring their Commodities to a certain House, where I might purchase what I had occasion for: I told him I had not Money, but would exchange some of the Salt which I brought from Mayo for their Commodities. He reply'd, that Salt was indeed an acceptable Commodity with the poor People, but that if I designed to buy any Cattle, I must give Money for them. I contented my self with taking in Dunghill Fowls: The Governour ordering a Cryer to go about the Town and give Notice to the People, that they might repair to such a Place with Fowls and Maiz for feeding them, where they might get Salt in Exchange for them: So I sent on Board for Salt, and order'd some of my Men to truck the same for the Fowls and maiz, while the rest of them were busy in filling of Water. This is the Effect of their keeping no Boats of their own on the several Islands, that they are glad to buy even their own Salt of Foreigners, for want of being able to transport it themselves from Island to Island.

St. Jago Town lies on the S.W. part of the Island, in Lat. about 15 Deg. N. and is the Seat of the General Governour, and of the Bishop of all the Cape Verd Islands. This Town stands scattering against the Sides of two Mountains, between which there is a deep Valley, which is about 200 Yards wide against the Sea; but within a quarter of a Mile it closes up so as not to be 40 Yards wide. In the Valley, by the Sea, there is a straggling Street, Houses on each Side, and a Run of Water in the Bottom, which empties it self into a fine small Cove or sandy Bay, where the Sea is commonly very smooth; so that here is good Watering and good Landing at any Time; tho' the Road be rocky and bad for Ships. Just by the Landing-place there is a small Fort, almost level with the Sea, where is always a Court of Guard kept. On the Top of the Hill, above the Town, there is another Fort; which, by the Wall that is to be seen from the Road, seems to be a large Place. They have Cannon mounted there, but how many know I not: Neither what use that Fort can be of, except it be for Salutes. The Town may consist of 2 or 300 Houses, all built of rough Stone; having also one Convent, and one Church.

The People in general are black, or at least of a mixt Colour, except only some few of the better Sort, *viz.* the Governour, the Bishop, some Gentlemen, and some of the Padres; for some of these also are black. The People about Praya are Thievish; but these of St. Jago Town, living under their Governour's Eye, are more orderly, tho' generally poor, having little Trade: Yet besides chance Ships of other Nations, there come hither a Portugueze Ship or two every Year, in their way to Brazil. These vend among them a few European Commodities, and take of their principal Manufactures, *viz.* striped Cotton-cloth, which they carry with them to Brazil. Here is also another Ship comes hither from Portugal for Sugar, their other Manufacture, and returns with it directly thither: For 'tis reported that there are several small Sugar-works on this Island, from which they send home near 100 Ton every year; and they have Plenty of Cotton growing up in the Country, wherewith they cloath themselves, and send also a great deal to Brazil. They have Vines, of which they make some Wine; but the Eoropean Ships furnish them with better; tho' they drink but little of any. Their chief Fruits are, (besides Plantains in Abundance) Oranges, Lemons, Citrons, Melons, (both Musk and Water-melons) Limes, Guava's, Pomegranates, Quinces, Custard-Apples, and Papah's, &c.

The Custard-Apple (as we call it) is a Fruit as big as a Pomegranate, and much of the same Colour. The out-side Husk, Shell or Rind, is for Substance and Thickness between the Shell of a Pomegranate, and the Peel of a Sevil-Orange; softer than this, yet more brittle than that. The Coat or Covering is also remarkable in that it is beset round with small regular Knobs or Risings; and the Inside of the Fruit is full of a white soft Pulp, sweet and very pleasant, and most resembling a Custard of any Thing, both in Colour and Taste; from whence probably it is called a Custard-Apple by our English. It has in the Middle a few small black Stones or Kernels; but no Core, for 'tis all Pulp. The Tree that bears this Fruit is about the Bigness of a Quince-tree, with long, small, and thick-set Branches spread much abroad: At the Extremity of here and there one of which the Fruit grows upon a Stalk of its own about 9 or 10 inches long, slender and tough, and hanging down with its own Weight. A large Tree of this Sort does not bear usually above 20 or 30 Apples; seldom more. This Fruit grows in most Countries within the Tropicks, I have seen of them (tho' I omitted the Description of them before) all over the West-Indies, both Continent and Islands; as also in Brazil, and in the East-Indies.

The Papah too is found in all these Countries, though I have not hitherto describ'd it. It is a Fruit about the Bigness of a Musk-Melon, hollow as that is, and much resembling it in Shape and Colour, both Outside and Inside: Only in the Middle, instead of flat Kernels, which the Melons have, these have a handful of small blackish Seeds, about the Bigness of Pepper-corns; whose Taste is also hot on the Tongue somewhat like Pepper. The Fruit it self is sweet, soft and luscious, when ripe; but while green 'tis hard and unsavory: tho' even then being boiled and eaten with Salt-pork or Beef, it serves instead of Turnips, and is as much esteemed. The Papah-Tree is about 10 or 12 Foot high. The Body near the Ground may be a Foot and an half or 2 Foot Diameter; and it grows up tapering to the Top. It has no Branches at all, but only large Leaves growing immediately upon Stalks from the Body. The Leaves are of a roundish Form and jagg'd about the Edges, having their Stalks or Stumps longer or shorter as they grow near to or further from the Top. They begin to spring from out of the Body of the Tree at about 6 or 7 Foot heighth from the Ground, the Trunk being bare below: But above that the Leaves grow thicker and larger still towards its Top, where they are close and broad. The Fruit grows only among the Leaves; and thickest among the thickest of them; insomuch that towards the Top of the Tree the Papahs spring forth from its Body as thick as they can stick one by another. But then lower down, where the Leaves are thinner, the Fruit is larger, and of the Size I have describ'd: And at the Top, where they are thick, they are but small, and no bigger than ordinary Turnips; yet tasted like the rest.

Their chief Land-Animals are their Bullocks, which are said to be many; tho' they ask us 20 Dollars apiece for them; They have also Horses, Asses, and Mules, Deer, Goats, Hogs, and black-fac'd long-tail'd Monkeys. Of

Fowls they have Cocks and Hens, Ducks, Guinea-Hens, both tame and wild, Parrakites, Parrots, Pidgeons, Turtle-Doves, Herons, Hawks, Crab-catchers, Galdens (a larger Sort of Crab-catchers), Curlews, &c. Their Fish is the same as at Mayo and the rest of these Islands, and for the most part these Islands have the same Beasts and Birds also; But some of the Isles have Pasturage and Employment for some particular Beasts more than other; and the Birds are incourag'd, by Woods for Shelter, and Maiz and Fruits for Food, to flock rather to some of the Islands (as to this of St. Jago) than to others.

St. Jago Road is one of the worst that I have been in. There is not clean Ground enough for above three Ships; and those also must lye very near each other. One even of these must lye close to the Shore, with a Land-fast there: And that is the best for a small Ship. I should not have come in here if I had not been told that it was a good secure Place; but I found it so much otherways, that I was in Pain to be gone. Captain Barefoot, who came to an Anchor while I was here, in foul Ground, lost quickly 2 Anchors; and I had lost a small one. The Island Fogo shows its self from this Road very plain, at about 7 or 8 Leagues distance; and in the Night we saw the Flames of Fire issuing from its Top.

CHAP. II

Having dispatch'd my small Affairs at the C. Verd Islands, I meditated on the Process of my Voyage. I thought it requisite to touch once more at a cultivated Place in these Seas, where my Men might be refresh'd, and might have a Market wherein to furnish themselves with Necessaries: For designing that my next Stretch should be quite to N. Holland, and knowing that after so long a Run nothing was to be expected there but fresh Water, if I could meet even with that there, I resolved upon putting in first at some Port of Brazil, and to provide my self there with whatever I might have further Occasion for. Beside the refreshing and furnishing my Men, I aim'd also at the inuring them gradually and by Intervals to the Fatigues that were to be expected in the Remainder of the Voyage, which was to be in a part of the World they were altogether Strangers to; none of them, except two young Men, having ever cross'd the Line.

With this Design I sail'd from St. Jago on the 22d of February, with the Winds at E.N.E. and N.E. fair Weather, and a brisk Gale. We steered away S.S.E. and S.S.E. half East, till in the Lat. of 7 deg. 50. min. we met with many Riplings in the Sea like a Tide or strong Current, which setting against the Wind caus'd such a Ripling. We continu'd to meet these Currents from that Lat. till we came into the Lat of 3 deg. 22 N. when they ceased. During this Time we saw some Boneta's, and Sharks; catching one of these. We had the true general Trade-Wind blowing fresh at N.E. till in the Lat. of 4 deg. 40 min. N. when the Wind varied, and we had small Gales, with some Tornadoes. We were then to the East of St. Jago 4 deg. 54 min. when we got into Lat. 3 deg. 2 min. N. (where I said the Ripling ceas'd) and Long. to the East of St. Jago 5 deg. 2 min. we had the Wind whiffling between the S. by E. and E. by N. small Gales, frequent Calms, very black Clouds, with much Rain. In the Lat. of 3 deg. 8 min. N. and Long. E. from St. Jago 5 deg. 8 min. we had the Wind from the S.S.E. to the N.N.E. faint, and often interrupted with Calms. While we had Calms we had the Opportunity of trying the Current we had met with hitherto, and found that it set N.E. by E. half a Knot, which is 12 Mile in 24 Hours: So that here it ran at the Rate of half a Mile an Hour, and had been much stronger before. The Rains held us by Intervals till the Lat. of 1 deg. 0 min. N. with small Gales of Wind between S.S.E. and S.E. by E. and sometimes calm: Afterwards we had the Wind between the S. and S.S.E. till we cross'd the Line, small Winds, Calms, and pretty fair Weather. We saw but few Fish beside Porposes; but of them a great many, and struck one of them.

It was the 10th of March, about the Time of the Equinox, when we cross'd the Equator, having had all along from the Lat. of 4 deg. 40 min. N. where the true Trade-Wind left us, a great Swell out of the S.E. and but small uncertain Gales, mostly Southerly, so that we crept to the Southward but slowly. I kept up against these as well as I could to the Southward, and when we had now and then a Flurry of Wind at E. I still went away due South, purposely to get to the Southward as fast as I could; for while near the Line I expected to have but uncertain Winds, frequent Calms, Rains, Tornadoes, &c. which would not only retard my Course, but endanger Sickness also among my Men: especially those who were ill provided with Cloaths, or were too lazy to shift themselves when they were drench'd with the Rains. The Heat of the Weather made them careless of doing this; but taking a Dram of Brandy, which I gave them when wet, with a Charge to shift themselves, they would however lye down in their Hammocks with their wet Cloaths; so that when they turn'd out they caus'd an ill Smell where-ever they came, and their Hammocks would stink sufficiently; that I think the remedying of this is worth the Care of Commanders that cross the Line; especially when they are, it may be, a Month or more e'er they get out of the Rains, at sometimes of the Year, as in June, July, or August.

What I have here said about Currents, Winds, Calms, &c. in this Passage, is chiefly for the farther Illustration .of what I have heretofore observ'd in general about these Matters and especially as to crossing the Line, in my *Discourse of the Winds, &c. in the Torrid Zone:* [Vol. II.] Which Observations I have had very much confirm'd to me in the Course of this Voyage; and I shall particularize in several of the chief of them as they come in my Way. And indeed I think I may say this of the main of the Observations in that Treatise, that the clear Satisfaction I had about them, and how much I might rely upon them, was a great Ease to my Mind during this vexatious Voyage; wherein the Ignorance, and Obstinacy withal, of some under me, occasion'd me a great deal of Trouble: Tho' they found all along, and were often forc'd to acknowledge it, that I was seldom out in my Conjectures, when I told them usually beforehand what Winds, &c. we should meet with at such or such particular Places we should come at.

Pernambuc was the Port that I designed for at my first setting out from St. Jago; it being a Place most proper for my Purpose, by Reason of its Situation, lying near the Extremity of C. St. Augustine, the Easternmost Promontory of Brazil; by which means it not only enjoys the greater Benefit of the Sea-breezes, and is consequently more healthy than other Places to the Southward, but is withal less subject to the Southerly Coasting-Trade-winds, that blow half the Year on this Shore; which were now drawing on, and might be troublesome to me: So that I might both hope to reach soonest Pernambuc, as most directly and nearest in my Run; and might thence also more easily get away to the Southward than from Bahia de Todos los Santos, or Ria Janeira.

But notwithstanding these Advantages I propos'd to my self in going to Pernambuc, I was soon put by that Design through the Refractoriness of some under me, and the Discontents and Backwardness of some of my Men. For the Calms and Shiftings of Winds which I met with, as I was to expect, in crossing the Line, made them, who were unacquainted with these Matters, almost heartless as to the Pursuit of the Voyage, as thinking we should never be able to weather Cape St. Augustine: And though I told them that by that Time we should get to about three Degrees South of the Line, we should again have a true brisk general Trade-Wind from the North-East, that would carry us to what part of Brazil we pleas'd, yet they would not believe it till they found it so. This, with some other unforeseen Accidents, not necessary to be mention'd in this Place, meeting with the Aversion of my Men to a long unknown Voyage, made me justly apprehensive of their Revolting, and was a great Trouble and Hindrance to me. So that I was obliged partly to alter my measures, and met with many Difficulties, the Particulars of which I shall not trouble the Reader with: But I mention thus much of it in general for my own necessary Vindication, in my taking such Measures sometimes for prosecuting the Voyage as the State of my Ships Crew, rather than my own Judgment and Experience, determin'd me to. The Disorders of my Ship made me think at present that Pernambuc would not be so fit a Place for me; being told that Ships ride there 2 or 3 Leagues from the Town, under the Command of no Forts; so that whenever I should have been ashore it might have been easy for my discontented Crew to have cut or slipt their Cables, and have gone away from me: Many of them discovering already an Intention to return to England, and some of them declaring openly that they would go no further onwards than Brazil. I alter'd my Course therefore, and stood away for Bahio de todos los Santos, or the Bay of all Saints, where I hop'd to have the Governour's Help, if need should require, for securing my Ship from any such mutinous Attempt; being forced to keep my self all the way upon my Guard, and to lie with my Officers, such as I could trust, and with small Arms upon the Quarter-Deck; it scarce being safe for me to lie in my Cabbin, by Reason of the Discontents among my Men.

On the 23rd of March we saw the Land of Brazil; having had thither, from the Time when we came into the true Trade-wind again after crossing the Line, very fair Weather and brisk Gales, mostly at E.N.E. The Land we saw was about 20 Leagues to the North of Bahia; so I coasted along Shore to the Southward. This Coast is rather low than high, with Sandy-Bays all along by the Sea.

A little within Land are many very white Spots of Sand, appearing like Snow; and the Coast looks very pleasant, being checker'd with Woods and Savannahs. The Trees in general are not tall; but they are green and flourishing. There are many small Houses by the Sea-side, whose Inhabitants are chiefly Fishermen. They come off to Sea on Bark-logs, made of several Logs fasten'd Side to Side, that have one or two Masts with Sails to them. There are two Men in each Bark-log, one at either End, having small low Benches, raised a little above the Logs, to sit and fish on, and two Baskets hanging up at the Mast or Masts; one to put their Provisions in, the other for their Fish. Many of these were a-fishing now, and 2 of them came aboard, of whom I bought some Fish. In the Afternoon we sailed by one very remarkable Piece of Land, where, on a small pleasant Hill, there was a Church dedicated to the Virgin Mary. See a Sight of some Parts of this Coast [Table III. N°. 1, 2, 3, 4, 5.] and of the Hill the Church stands on [Table III. N°. 1.].

I coasted along till the Evening, and then brought to, and lay by till the next Morning. About 2 Hours after we were brought to, there came a Sail out of the Offin (from Seaward) and lay by about a Mile to Windward of

Table III   **Brazil**

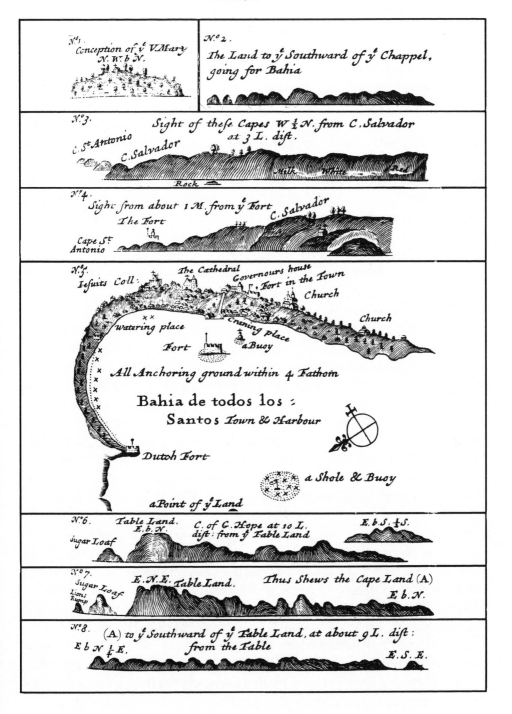

N.º 1.
Conception of ẏ V. Mary
N. W. b N.

N.º 2.
The Land to ẏ Southward of ẏ Chappel,
going for Bahia

N.º 3.
C. St Antonio
C. Salvador
Sight of these Capes W ½ N. from C. Salvador
at 3 L. dist.
Rock

N.º 4.
Sight from about 1 M. from ẏ Fort
The Fort
Cape St
Antonio
C. Salvador

N.º 5.
Iesuits Coll.
The Cathedral
Governours house
Fort in the Town
Church
Church
watering place
Craning place
Fort
a Buoy
All Anchoring ground within 4 Fathom
Bahia de todos los :
Santos Town & Harbour
Dutch Fort
a Shole & Buoy
a Point of ẏ Land

N.º 6.
Table Land.
E. b. N.
C. of G. Hope at 10 L.
dist: from ẏ Table Land
E. b. S. ¼ S.
Sugar Loaf

N.º 7.
Sugar Loaf
Lions
Rump
E. N. E. Table Land.
Thus Shews the Cape Land (A)
E. b. N.

N.º 8.
E b N ¼ E.
(A) to ẏ Southward of ẏ Table Land, at about 9 L. dist:
from the Table
E. S. E.

us, and so lay all Night. In the Morning upon speaking with her, she proved to be a Portugueze Ship bound to Bahia; therefore I sent my Boat aboard and desired to have one of his Mates to Pilot me in: He answer'd, that he had not a Mate capable of it, but that he would sail in before me, and shew me the way; and that if he went into the Harbour in the Night, he would hang out a Light for me. He said we had not far in, and might reach it before Night with a tolerable Gale; but that with so small an one as now we had we could not do it: So we jogg'd on till Night, and then he accordingly hung out his Light, which we steered after, sounding as we went in. I kept all my Men on Deck, and had an Anchor ready to let go on occasion. We had the Tide of Ebb against us, so that we went in but slowly; and it was about the Middle of the Night when we anchor'd. Immediately the Portugueze Master came aboard to see me, to whom I returned Thanks for his Civilities; and indeed I found much Respect, not only from this Gentleman, but from all of that Nation both here and in other Places, who were ready to serve me on all Occasions. The Place that we anchored in was about two Miles from the Harbour where the Ships generally ride; but the Fear I had lest my People should run away with the Ship, made me hasten to get a Licence from the Governour, to run up into the Harbour, and ride among their Ships, close by one of their Forts. So on the 25th of March about 10 a Clock in the Morning, the Tide serving, I went thither, being piloted by the Super-intendant there, whose Business it is to carry up all the King of Portugal's Ships that come hither, and to see them well moored. He brought us to an Anchor right against the Town, at the outer Part of the Harbour, which was then full of Ships, within 150 Yards of a small Fort that stands on a Rock half a Mile from the Shore. See a Prospect of the Harbour and the Town, as it appear'd to us while we lay at Anchor [Table III. No°. 5.].

Bahia de todos los Santos lies in Lat. 13. deg. S. It is the most considerable Town in Brazil, whether in Respect of the Beauty of its Buildings, its Bulk, or its Trade and Revenue. It has the Convenience of a good Harbour that is capable of receiving Ships of the greatest Burthen: The Entrance of which is guarded with a strong Fort standing without the Harbour, call'd St. Antonio: A Sight of which I have given [Table III. N°. 4.] as it appeared to us the Afternoon before we came in; and its Lights (which they hang out purposely for Ships) we saw the same Night. There are other smaller Forts that command the Harbour, one of which stands on a Rock in the Sea, about half a Mile from the Shore. Close by this Fort all Ships must pass that anchor here, and must ride also within half a Mile of it at farthest between this and another Fort (that stands on a Point at the inner part of the Harbour and is called the Dutch Fort) but must ride nearest to the former, all along against the Town: Where there is good holding Ground, and less exposed to the Southerly Winds that blow very hard here. They commonly set in about April, but blow hardest in May, June, July and August: But the place where the Ships ride is exposed to these Winds not above 3 Points of the Compass.

Beside these, there is another Fort fronting the Harbour, and standing on the Hill upon which the Town stands. The Town it self consists of about 2000 Houses; the major part of which cannot be seen from the Harbour; but so many as appear in Sight, with a great Mixture of Trees between them, and all placed on a rising Hill, make a very pleasant Prospect; as may be judg'd by the Draught, [Table III. N°. 5.].

There are in the Town 13 Churches, Chapels, Hospitals, Convents, beside one Nunnery; *viz.* the Ecclesia Major or Cathedral, the Jesuits College, which are the chief, and both in Sight from the Harbour: St. Antonio, St. Barbara, both Parish-Churches; the Franciscans Church, and the Dominicans; and 2 Convents of Carmelites; a Chapel for Seamen close by the Sea-side, where Boats commonly land, and the Seamen go immediately to Prayers; another Chapel for poor People, at the farther End of the same Street, which runs along by the Shore; and a third Chapel for Soldiers, at the Edge of the Town remote from the Sea; and an Hospital in the Middle of the Town. The Nunnery stands at the outer-edge of the Town next the Fields, wherein by Report there are 70 Nuns. Here lives an Arch-bishop, who has a fine Palace in the Town; and the Governor's Palace is a fair Stone-building, and looks handsome to the Sea, tho' but indifferently furnish'd within: Both Spaniards and Portugueze in their Plantations abroad, as I have generally observ'd, affecting to have large Houses; but are little curious about Furniture, except Pictures some of them. The Houses of the Town are 2 or 3 Stories high, the Walls thick and strong, being built with Stone, with a Covering of Pantile; and many of them have Balconies. The principal Streets are large, and all of them pav'd or pitch'd with small Stones. There are also Parades in the most eminent Places of the Town, and many Gardens, as well within the Town as in the Out-parts of it, wherein are Fruit-trees, Herbs, Salladings and Flowers in great Variety, but order'd with no great Care nor Art.

The Governour who resides here is call'd Don John de Lancastrio, being descended, as they say, from our English Lancaster Family; and he has a Respect for our Nation on that Account, calling them his Country-men. I waited on him several Times, and always found him very courteous and civil. Here are about 400 Soldiers in Garrison. They commonly draw up and exercise in a large Parade before the Governour's House; and many of them attend him when he goes abroad. The Soldiers are decently clad in brown Linnen, which in these hot Countries is far better than Woollen; but I never saw any clad in Linnen but only these. Beside the Soldiers in Pay, he can soon have some Thousands of Men up in Arms on occasion. The Magazine is on the Skirts of the Town, on a small Rising between the Nunnery and the Soldiers Church. 'Tis big enough to hold 2 or 3000 Barrels of Powder; but I was told it seldom has more than 100, sometimes but 80. There are always a Band of Soldiers to guard it, and Centinels looking out both Day and Night.

A great many Merchants always reside at Bahia; for 'tis a Place of great Trade: I found here above 30 great Ships from Europe, with 2 of the King of Portugal's Ships of War for their Convoy; beside 2 Ships that traded to Africa only, either to Angola, Gamba, or other Places on the Coast of Guinea; and Abundance of small Craft, that only run to and fro on this Coast, carrying Commodities from one Part of Brazil to another.

The Merchants that live here are said to be rich, and to have many Negro-Slaves in their Houses, both of Men and Women. Themselves are chiefly Portugueze, Foreigners having but little Commerce with them; yet here was one Mr. Cock an English Merchant, a very civil Gentleman and of good Repute. He had a Patent to be our English Consul, but did not Care to take upon him any publick Character, because English Ships seldom come hither, here having been none in 11 or 12 Years before this Time. Here was also a Dane, and a French Merchant or two; but all have their Effects transported to and from Europe in Portugueze Ships, none of any other Nation being admitted to trade hither. There is a Custom-house by the Sea-side, where all Goods imported or exported are entred. And to prevent Abuses there are 5 or 6 Boats that take their Turns to row about the Harbour, searching any Boats they suspect to be running of Goods.

The chief Commodities that the European Ships bring hither, are Linnen-cloaths, both coarse and fine; some Woollens, also, as Bays, Searges, Perpetuana's, &c. Hats, Stockings, both of Silk and Thread, Bisket-bread,

An. 1699

Wheat-flower, Wine (chiefly Port) Oil-Olive, Butter, Cheese, &c. and Salt-beef and Pork would there also be good Commodities. They bring hither also Iron, and all Sorts of Iron-Tools; Pewter-Vessels of all Sorts, as Dishes, Plates, Spoons, &c. Looking-glasses, Beads, and other Toys; and the Ships that touch at St. Jago bring thence, as I said, Cotton-cloath, which is afterwards sent to Angola.

The European Ships carry from hence Sugar, Tobacco, either in Roll or Snuff, never in Leaf, that I know of: These are the Staple Commodities. Besides which, here are Dye-woods, as Fustick, &c. with Woods for other Uses, as speckled Wood, Brazil, &c. They also carry home raw Hides, Tallow, Train-Oil of Whales, &c. Here are also kept tame Monkeys, Parrots, Parrakites, &c. which the Seamen carry home.

The Sugar of this Country is much better than that which we bring Home from our Plantations: For all the Sugar that is made here is clay'd, which makes it whiter and finer than our Muscovada, as we call our unrefin'd Sugar. Our Planters seldom refine any with Clay, unless sometimes a little to send Home as Presents for their Friends in England. Their way of doing it is by taking some of the whitest Clay and mixing it with Water, till 'tis like Cream. With this they fill up the Pans of Sugar, that are sunk 2 or 3 Inches below the Brim by the draining of the Molosses out of it: First scraping off the thin hard Crust of the Sugar that lies at the Top, and would hinder the Water of the Clay from soaking through the Sugar of the Pan. The refining is made by this Percolation. For 10 or 12 Days Time that the clayish Liquor lies soaking down the Pan, the white Water whitens the Sugar as it passes thro' it; and the gross Body of the Clay it self grows hard on the Top, and may be taken off at Pleasure; when scraping off with a Knife the very upper-part of the Sugar, which will be a little sullied, that which is underneath will be white almost to the Bottom: And such as is called Brazil Sugar is thus whiten'd. When I was here this Sugar was sold for 50s. per 100 lb. And the Bottoms of the Pots, which is very coarse Sugar, for about 20s. per 100 lb. both Sorts being then scarce; for here was not enough to lade the Ships, and therefore some of them were to lye here till the next Season.

The European Ships commonly arrive here in February or March, and they have generally quick Passages; finding at that Time of the Year brisk Gales to bring them to the Line, little Trouble, then, in crossing it, and brisk E.N.E. winds afterwards to bring them hither. They commonly

return from hence about the latter End of May, or in June. 'Twas said when
I was here that the Ships would sail hence the 20th Day of May; and
therefore they were all very busy, some in taking in their Goods, others in
careening and making themselves ready. The Ships that come hither usually
careen at their first coming; here being a Hulk belonging to the King for
that Purpose. This Hulk is under the Charge of the Superintendent I spoke
of, who has a certain Sum of Mony for every Ship that careens by her. He
also provides Firing and other Necessaries for that Purpose: And the Ships
do commonly hire of the Merchants here each 2 Cables to moor by all the
Time they lye here, and so save their own Hempen Cables; for these are
made of a Sort of Hair, that grows on a certain Kind of Trees, hanging
down from the Top of their Bodies, and is very like the black Coyre in the
East-Indies, if not the same. These Cables are strong and lasting: And so
much for the European Ships.

The Ships that use the Guinea-Trade are small Vessels in Comparison of
the former. They carry out from hence Rum, Sugar, the Cotton-cloaths of
St. Jago, Beads, &c. and bring in Return, Gold, Ivory, and Slaves; making
very good Returns.

The small Craft that belong to this Town are chiefly imployed in carrying
European Goods from Bahia, the Center of the Brasilian Trade, to the other
Places on this Coast; bringing back hither Sugar, Tobacco, &c. They are
sailed chiefly with Negro-Slaves; and about Christmas these are mostly
imployed in Whale-killing: For about that Time of the Year a Sort of
Whales, as they call them, are very thick on this Coast. They come in also
into the Harbours and inland Lakes, where the Seamen go out and kill
them. The Fat of them is boiled to Oil; the Lean is eaten by the Slaves and
poor People: And I was told by one that had frequently eaten of it, that the
Flesh was very sweet and wholsome. These are said to be but small Whales;
yet here are so many, and so easily kill'd, that they get a great deal of Money
by it. Those that strike them buy their Licence for it of the King: And I was
inform'd that he receives 30000 Dollars per Annum for this Fishery. All the
small Vessels that use this Coasting-Traffick are built here; and so are some
Men of War also for the King's Service. There was one a building when I
was here, a Ship of 40 or 50 Guns: And the Timber of this Country is very
good and proper for this Purpose. I was told it was very strong, and more
durable than any we have in Europe; and they have enough of it. As for
their Ships that use the European Trade, some of them that I saw there were

English built, taken from us by the French, during the late War, and sold by them to the Portugueze.

Besides Merchants and others that trade by Sea from this Port, here are other pretty wealthy men, and several Artificers and Trades-men of most Sorts, who by Labour and Industry maintain themselves very well; especially such as can arrive at the Purchase of a Negro-Slave or two. And indeed, excepting People of the lowest Degree of all, here are scarce any but what keep Slaves in their Houses. The richer Sort, besides the Slaves of both Sexes whom they keep for servile Uses in their Houses, have Men slaves who wait on them abroad, for State; either running by their Horse-sides when they ride out, or to carry them to and fro on their Shoulders in the Town when they make short Visits near Home. Every Gentleman or Merchant is provided with Things necessary for this Sort of Carriage. The main Thing is a pretty large Cotton Hammock of the West-India Fashion, but mostly died blue, with large Fringes of the same, hanging down on each Side. This is carried on the Negro's Shoulders by the help of a Bambo about 12 or 14 Foot long, to which the Hammock is hung; and a Covering comes over the Pole, hanging down on each Side like a Curtain: So that the Person so carry'd cannot be seen unless he pleases; but may either lye down, having Pillows for his Head; or may sit up by being a little supported with these Pillows, and by letting both his Legs hang out over one Side of the Hammock. When he hath a Mind to be seen he puts by his Curtain, and salutes every one of his Acquaintance whom he meets in the Streets; for they take a Piece of Pride in greeting one another from their Hammocks, and will hold long Conferences thus in the Street: But then their 2 Slaves who carry the Hammock have each a strong well-made Staff, with a fine Iron Fork at the upper End, and a sharp Iron below, like the Rest for a Musket, which they stick fast in the Ground, and let the Pole or Bambo of the Hammock rest upon them, till their Master's Business or the Complement is over. There is scarce a Man of any Fashion, especially a Woman, will pass the Streets but so carried in a Hammock. The chief Mechanick Traders here, are Smiths, Hatters, Shoemakers, Tanners, Sawyers, Carpenters, Coopers, &c. Here are also Taylors, Butchers, &c. which last kill the Bullocks very dexterously, sticking them at one Blow with a sharp-pointed Knife in the Nape of the Neck, having first drawn them close to a Rail; but they dress them very slovenly. It being Lent when I came hither, there was no buying any Flesh till Easter-Eve, when a great Number of Bullocks were kill'd at once in the Slaughter-houses within the Town, Men, Women and Children flocking thither with great Joy to buy, and a Multitude of Dogs, almost starv'd, following them; for whom the Meat seem'd fittest, it was so lean. All these Trades-men buy Negroes, and train them up to their several Employments, which is a great Help to them; and they having so frequent Trade to Angola, and other Parts of Guinea, they have a constant Supply of Blacks both for their Plantations and Town. These Slaves are very useful in this Place for Carriage, as Porters; for as here is a great Trade by Sea, and the Landing-place is at the Foot of a Hill, too steep for drawing with Carts, so there is great need of Slaves to carry Goods up into the Town, especially for the inferiour Sort: But the Merchants have also the Convenience of a great Crane that goes with Ropes or Pullies, one End of which goes up while the other goes down. The House in which this Crane is, stands on the Brow of the Hill towards the Sea, hanging over the Precipice; and there are Planks set shelving against the Bank from thence to the Bottom, against which the Goods lean or slide as they are hoisted up or let down. The Negro-Slaves in this Town are so numerous, that they make up the greatest Part or Bulk of the Inhabitants: Every House, as I said, having some, both Men and Women, of them. Many of the Portugueze, who are Batchelors, keep of these black Women for Misses, tho' they know the Danger they are in of being poyson'd by them, if ever they give them any Occasion of Jealousy. A Gentleman of my Acquaintance, who had been familiar with his Cook-maid, lay under some such Apprehensions from her when I was there. These Slaves also of either Sex will easily be engaged to do any Sort of Mischief; even to Murder, if they are hired to do it, especially in the Night; for which Reason, I kept my Men on board as much as I could; for one of the French King's Ships being here, had several Men murther'd by them in the Night, as I was credibly inform'd.

Having given this Account of the Town of Bahia, I shall next say somewhat of the Country. There is a Salt-water Lake runs 40 Leagues, as I was told, up the Country, N.W. from the Sea, leaving the Town and Dutch Fort on the Starboard Side. The Country all around about is for the most part a pretty flat even Ground, not high, nor yet very low: It is well water'd with Rivers, Brooks and Springs; neither wants it for good Harbours, navigable Creeks, and good Bays for Ships to ride in. The Soil in general is good, naturally producing very large Trees of divers Sorts, and fit for any Uses. The Savannahs also are loaden with Grass, Herbs, and many Sorts of smaller Vegetables; and being cultivated, produce any Thing that is proper for those hot Countries, as Sugar-Canes, Cotton, Indico, Tobacco, Maiz, Fruit-Trees of several Kinds, and eatable Roots of all Sorts. Of the several Kinds of Trees that are here, I shall give an Account of some, as I had it partly from an Inhabitant of Bahia, and partly from my Knowledge of them otherwise, *viz.* Sapiera, Vermiatico, Comesserie, Guitteba, Serrie, as they were pronounc'd to me, three Sorts of Mangrove, speckled Wood, Fustick, Cotton-Trees of 3 Sorts, *&c.* together with Fruit-Trees of divers Sorts that grow wild, beside such as are planted

Of Timber-Trees, the Sapiera is said to be large and tall; it is very good Timber, and is made use of in building of Houses; so is the Vermiatico, a tall streight-bodied Tree, of which they make Plank 2 Foot broad; and they also make Canoa's with it. Comesserie and Guitteba are chiefly used in building Ships; these are as much esteem'd here as Oaks are in England, and they say either Sort is harder and more durable than Oak. The Serrie is a Sort of Tree much like Elm, very durable in Water. Here are also all the three Sorts of Mangrove Trees, *viz.* the Red, the White, and the Black, which I have described [Vol. I.]. The Bark of the red Mangrove, is here us'd for tanning of Leather, and they have great Tan-pits for it. The black Mangrove grows larger here than in the West-Indies, and of it they make good Plank. The white Mangrove is larger and tougher than in the West-Indies; of these they make Masts and Yards for Barks.

There grow here wild or bastard Coco-Nut Trees, neither so large nor so tall as the common ones in the East or West-Indies. They bear Nuts as the others, but not a quarter so big as the right Coco-Nuts. The Shell is full of Kernel, without any hollow Place or Water in it; and the Kernel is sweet and wholsome, but very hard both for the Teeth and for Digestion. These Nuts are in much Esteem for making Beads for Pater noster's, Boles of Tobacco-Pipes, and other Toys: and every small Shop here has a great many of them to sell. At the Top of these Bastard Coco-trees, among the Branches, there grows a Sort of long black Thread like Horsehair, but much longer, which by the Portugueze is called Tresabo. Of this they make Cables which are very serviceable, strong and lasting; for they will not rot as Cables made of Hemp, tho' they lye exposed both to Wet and Heat. These are the Cables which I said they keep in their Harbours here, to let to hire to European Ships, and resemble the Coyre-Cables.

Here are 3 Sorts of Cotton-Trees that bear Silk-Cotton. One Sort is such

An. 1699 as I have formerly describ'd, [Vol. I.] by the Name of the Cotton-tree. The other 2 Sorts I never saw any where but here. The Trees of these latter Sorts are but small in Comparison of the former, which are reckon'd the biggest in all the West-India Woods; yet are however of a good Bigness and Heighth. One of these last Sorts is not so full of Branches as the other of them; neither do they produce their Fruit the same Time of the Year: For one Sort had its Fruit just ripe, and was shedding its Leaves while the other Sort was yet green, and its Fruit small and growing, having but newly done blossoming; the Tree being as full of young Fruit as an Apple-Tree ordinarily in England. These last yield very large Pods, about 6 Inches long, and as big as a Man's Arm. It is ripe in September and October; then the Pod opens, and the Cotton bursts out in a great Lump as big as a Man's Head. They gather these Pods before they open; otherways it would fly all away. It opens as well after 'tis gathered; and then they take out the Cotton, and preserve it to fill Pillows and Bolsters, for which use 'tis very much esteemed: But 'tis fit for nothing else, being so short that it cannot be spun. 'Tis of a tawney Colour; and the Seeds are black, very round, and as big as a white Pea. The other Sort is ripe in March or April. The Fruit or Pod is like a large Apple, and very round. The out-side Shell is as thick as the Top of one's Finger. Within this there is a very thin whitish Bag or Skin which incloseth the Cotton. When the Cotton-Apple is ripe, the outer thick green Shell splits it self into 5 equal Parts from Stemb to Tail, and drops off, leaving the Cotton hanging upon the Stemb, only pent up in its fine Bag. A Day or two afterwards the Cotton swells by the Heat of the Sun, breaks the Bag and bursts out, as big as a Man's Head: And then as the Wind blows 'tis by Degrees driven away, a little at a Time, out of the Bag that still hangs upon the Stemb, and is scatter'd about the Fields; the Bag soon following the Cotton, and the Stemb the Bag. Here is also a little of the right West-India Cotton Shrub: but none of the Cotton is exported, nor do they make much Cloth of it.

This Country produces great Variety of fine Fruits, as very good Oranges of 3 or 4 Sorts; (especially one Sort of China Oranges;) Limes in Abundance, Pomegranates, Pomecitrons, Plantains, Bonano's, right Coconuts, Guava's, Coco-plumbs, (call'd here Munsheroo's) Wild-Grapes, such as I have describ'd [Vol. II.] beside such Grapes as grow in Europe. Here are also Hog-plumbs, Custard-Apples, Sour-sops, Cashews, Papah's (called here Mamoons) Jennipah's (called here Jennipapah's) Manchineel-

Apples and Mango's. Mango's are yet but rare here: I saw none of them but in the Jesuit's Garden, which has a great many fine Fruits, and some Cinnamon-trees. These, both of them, were first brought from the East-Indies, and they thrive here very well: So do Pumplemusses, brought also from thence; and both China and Sevil Oranges are here very plentiful as well as good.

The Sour-sop (as we call it) is a large Fruit as big as a Man's Head, of a long or oval Shape, and of a green Colour; but one Side is yellowish when ripe. The outside Rind or Coat is pretty thick, and very rough, with small sharp Knobs; the Inside is full of spungy Pulp, within which also are many black Seeds or Kernels, in Shape and Bigness like a Pumpkin-seed. The Pulp is very juicy, of a pleasant Taste, and wholesome. You suck the Juice out of the Pulp, and so spit it out. The Tree or Shrub that bears this Fruit grows about 10 or 12 Foot high, with a small short Body; the Branches growing pretty strait up; for I did never see any of them spread abroad. The Twigs are slender and tough; and so is the Stemb of the Fruit. This Fruit grows also both in the East and West-Indies.

The Cashew is a Fruit as big as a Pippin, pretty long, and bigger near the Stemb than at the other End, growing tapering. The Rind is smooth and thin, of a red and yellow Colour. The Seed of this Fruit grows at the End of it; 'tis of an Olive Colour shaped like a Bean, and about the same Bigness, but not altogether so flat. The Tree is as big as an Apple-Tree, with Branches not thick, yet spreading off. The Boughs are gross, the Leaves broad and round, and in Substance pretty thick. This Fruit is soft and spongy when ripe, and so full of Juice that in biting it the Juice will run out on both Sides of one's Mouth. It is very pleasant, and gratefully rough on the Tongue; and is accounted a very wholesome Fruit. This grows both in the East and West-Indies, where I have seen and eaten of it.

The Jennipah or Jennipapah is a Sort of Fruit of the Calabash or Gourd-kind. It is about the Bigness of a Duck-Egg, and somewhat of an Oval Shape; and is of a grey Colour. The Shell is not altogether so thick nor hard as a Calabash: 'Tis full of whitish Pulp mixt with small flat Seeds; and both Pulp and Seeds must be taken into the Mouth, where sucking out the Pulp, you spit out Seeds. It is of a sharp and pleasing Taste, and is very innocent. The Tree that bears it is much like an Ash, streight-bodied, and of a good Height; clean from Limbs till near the Top, where there Branches forth a small Head. The Rind is of a pale grey, and so is the Fruit. We us'd of this

Tree to make Helves or Handles for Axes (for which it is very proper) in
the Bay of Campeachy; where I have seen of them, and no where else but
here.

Besides these, here are many Sorts of Fruits which I have not met with
any where but here; as Arisah's, Mericasah's, Petango's, &c. Arisah's are an
excellent Fruit, not much bigger than a large Cherry; shaped like a Cath-
erine-Pear, being small at the Stemb, and swelling bigger towards the End.
They are of a greenish Colour, and have small Seeds as big as Mustard
Seeds; they are somewhat tart, yet pleasant, and very wholsome, and may be
eaten by sick People.

Mericasah's, are an excellent Fruit, of which there are 2 Sorts; one
growing on a small Tree or Shrub, which is counted the best; the other
growing on a Kind of Shrub like a Vine, which they plant about Arbours to
make a Shade, having many broad Leaves. The Fruit is as big as a small
Orange, round and green. When they are ripe they are soft and fit to eat;
full of white Pulp mixt thick with little black Seeds, and there is no
separating one from the other, till they are in your Mouth; when you suck in
the white Pulp and spit out the Stones. They are tart, pleasant, and very
wholsome.

Petango's, are a small red Fruit, that grow also on small Trees, and are as
big as Cherries, but not so globular, having one flat Side, and also 5 or 6
small protuberant Ridges. 'Tis a very pleasant tart Fruit, and has a pretty
large flattish Stone in the Middle.

Petumbo's, are a yellow Fruit (growing on a Shrub like a Vine) bigger
than Cherries, with a pretty large Stone. These are sweet, but rough in the
Mouth.

Mungaroo's, are a Fruit as big as Cherries, red on one Side and white on
the other Side: They are said to be full of small Seeds, which are commonly
swallowed in eating them.

Muckishaw's, are said to be a Fruit as big as Crab-Apples, growing on
large Trees. They have also small Seeds in the Middle, and are well tasted.

Ingwa's, are a Fruit like the Locust-Fruit, 4 Inches long, and one broad.
They grow on high Trees.

Otee, is a Fruit as big as a large Coco-Nut. It hath a Husk on the outside,
and a large Stone within, and is accounted a very fine Fruit.

Musteran-de-ova's are a round Fruit as big as large Hazel-Nuts, cover'd
with thin brittle Shells of a blackish Colour: They have a small Stone in the

middle, inclosed within a black pulpy Substance, which is of a pleasant Taste. The outside Shell is chewed with the Fruit, and spit out with the Stone, when the Pulp is suck'd from them. The Tree that bears this Fruit is tall, large, and very hard Wood. I have not seen any of these five last named Fruits, but had them thus described to me by an Irish Inhabitant of Bahia; tho' as to this last, I am apt to believe, I may have both seen and eaten of them in Achin in Sumatra.

Palm-berries (called here Dendees) grow plentifully about Bahia; the largest are as big as Wall-nuts; they grow in Bunches on the top of the Body of the Tree, among the Roots of the Branches or Leaves, as all Fruits of the Palm-kind do. These are the same kind of Berries or Nuts as those they make the Palm-Oyl with on the Coast of Guinea, where they abound: And I was told that they make Oyl with them here also. They sometimes roast and eat them; but when I had one roasted to prove it, I did not like it.

Physick-Nuts, as our Seamen called them, are called here Pineon; and Agnus Castus is called here Carrepat: These both grow here: So do Mendibees, a Fruit like Physick-Nuts. They scorch them in a Pan over the Fire before they eat them.

Here are also great plenty of Cabbage-Trees, and other Fruits, which I did not get information about, and which I had not the Opportunity of seeing; because this was not the Season, it being our Spring, and consequently their Autumn, when their best Fruits were gone, tho' some were left. However I saw abundance of wild Berries in the Woods and Fields, but I could not learn their Names or Nature.

They have withal good plenty of ground Fruit, as Callavances, Pine-Apples, Pumkins, Water-Melons, Musk-Melons, Cucumbers, and Roots; as Yams, Potato's, Cassava's, &c. Garden-Herbs also good store; as Cabbages, Turnips, Onions, Leeks, and abundance of other Sallading, and for the Pot. Drugs of several sorts. *viz.* Sassafras, Snake-Root, &c. Beside the Woods I mentioned for Dying, and other Uses, as Fustick, Speckled-wood, &c.

I brought home with me from hence a good Number of Plants, dried between the leaves of Books; of some of the choicest of which, that are not spoil'd, I may give a Specimen at the End of the Book.

Here are said to be great plenty and variety of Wild-Fowl, *viz.* Yemma's, Maccaw's (which are called here Jackoo's, and are a larger sort of Parrots, and scarcer), Parrots, Parakites, Flamingo's, Carrion-Crows, Chattering-

Crows, Cockrecoes, Bill-Birds finely painted, Corresoes, Doves, Pidgeons, Jenetees, Clocking-Hens, Crab-Catchers, Galdens, Currecoo's, Muscovy Ducks, common Ducks, Widgeons, Teal, Curlews, Men of War Birds, Booby's, Noddy's, Pelicans, &c.

The Yemma is bigger than a Swan, grey-feathered, with a long thick sharp-pointed Bill.

The Carrion-Crow and Chattering-Crows, are called here Mackeraw's, and are like those I described in the West-Indies. [Vol. II.] The Bill of the Chattering-Crow is black, and the Upper-Bill is round, bending downwards like a Hawks-Bill, rising up in a Ridge almost Semi-circular, and very sharp, both at the Ridge or Convexity, and at the Point or Extremity: The Lower-Bill is flat and shuts even with it. I was told by a Portugueze here, that their Negro-Wenches make Love-Potions with these Birds. And the Portugueze care not to let them have any of these Birds, to keep them from that Superstition: As I found one Afternoon when I was in the Fields with a Padre and another, who shot two of them, and hid them, as they said, for that Reason. They are not good Food, but their Bills are reckoned a good Antidote against Poison.

The Bill-Birds are so called by the English, from their monstrous Bills, which are as big as their Bodies. I saw none of these Birds here, but saw several of the Breasts flea'd off and dried, for the Beauty of them; the Feathers were curiously colour'd with Red, Yellow, and Orange-colour.

The Curreso's (called here Mackeraw's) are such as are in the Bay of Campeachy. [Vol. II.]

Turtle-Doves are in great plenty here; and two sorts of Wild Pidgeons; the one sort Blackish, the other a light Grey: The Blackish or dark Grey are the Bigger, being as large as our Wood-Quests, or Wood-Pidgeons in England. Both sorts are very good Meat; and are in such plenty from May till September, that a Man may shoot 8 or 10 Dozen in several Shots at one standing, in a close misty Morning, when they come to feed on Berries that grow in the Woods.

The Jenetee is a Bird as big as a Lark, with blackish Feathers, and yellow Legs and Feet. 'Tis accounted very wholsome Food.

Clocking-Hens, are much like the Crab-catchers, which I have described [Vol. II.] but the Legs are not altogether so long. They keep always in swampy wet Places, tho' their Claws are like Land-Fowls Claws. They make a Noise or Cluck like our Brood-Hens, or Dunghil-Hens, when they have

Chickens, and for that Reason they are called by the English, Clocking-
Hens. There are many of them in the Bay of Campeachy (tho' I omitted to
speak of them there) and elsewhere in the West-Indies. There are both here
and there four sorts of these long-legg'd Fowls, near a-kin to each other, as
so many Sub-Species of the same Kind; *viz.* Crab-catchers, Clocking-Hens,
Galdens (which three are in shape and Colour like Herons in England, but
less; the Galden, the biggest of the three, the Crab-catcher the smallest;) and
a fourth sort which are Black, but shaped like the other, having long Legs
and short Tails; these are about the bigness of Crab-catchers, and feed as
they do.

Currecoos, are Water Fowls, as big as pretty large Chickens, of a bluish
Colour, with short Legs and Tail; they feed also in swampy Ground, and are
very good Meat. I have not seen of them elsewhere.

The Wild-Ducks here are said to be of two sorts, the Muscovy, and the
common-Ducks. In the wet Season here are abundance of them, but in the
dry Time but few. Wigeon and Teal also are said to be in great plenty here
in the wet Season.

To the Southward of Bahia there are also Ostridges in great plenty, tho'
'tis said, they are not so large as those of Africa: They are found chiefly in
the Southern Parts of Brazil, especially among the large Savannahs near the
River of Plate; and from thence further South towards the Streights of
Magellan.

As for Tame Fowl at Bahia, the chief beside their Ducks, are Dunghil-
Fowls, of which they have two sorts; one sort much of the size of our Cocks
and Hens; the other very large: And the Feathers of these last are a long
time coming forth: so that you see them very naked when half grown; but
when they are full grown and well feathered, they appear very large Fowls,
as indeed they are; neither do they want for Price; for they are sold at Bahia
for half a Crown or three Shillings apiece, just as they are brought first to
Market out of the Country, when they are so lean as to be scarce fit to eat.

The Land Animals here are Horses, black Cattle, Sheep, Goats, Rabbits,
Hogs, Leopards, Tygers, Foxes, Monkeys, Pecary (a sort of wild Hogs,
called here Pica) Armadillo, Alligators, Guano's (call'd Quittee) Lizards,
Serpents, Toads, Frogs, and a sort of amphibious Creatures called by the
Portugueze *Cachora's de agua,* in English Water-Dogs.

The Leopards and Tygers of this Country are said to be large and very
fierce: But here on the Coast they are either destroyed, or driven back

towards the Heart of the Country; and therefore are seldom found but in the Borders and Out-plantations, where they oftentimes do Mischief. Here are three or four sorts of Monkeys, of different Sizes and Colours. One sort is very large; and another sort is very small: These last are ugly in Shape and Feature, and have a strong Scent of Musk.

Here are several sorts of Serpents, many of them vastly great, and most of them very venomous: As the Rattle-snake for one: And for Venom, a small Green Snake is bad enough, no bigger than the Stemb of a Tobacco-pipe, and about 18 Inches long, very common here.

They have here also the Amphisbæna, or Two-headed Snake, of a grey Colour, mixt with blackish Stripes, whose Bite is reckon'd to be incurable. 'Tis said to be blind, tho' it has two small Specks in each Head like Eyes: But whether it sees or not I cannot tell. They say it lives like a Mole, mostly under Ground; and that when it is found above Ground it is easily kill'd, because it moves but slowly: Neither is its Sight (if it hath any) so good as to discern any one that comes near to kill it: as few of these Creatures fly at a Man, or hurt him but when he comes in their way. 'Tis about 14 Inches long, and about the bigness of the inner Joint of a Man's middle Finger; being of one and the same bigness from one End to the other, with a Head at each End, (as they said; for I cannot vouch it, for one I had was cut short at one End) and both alike in shape and bigness; and 'tis said to move with either Head foremost, indifferently; whence 'tis called by the Portugueze, *Cobra de dos Cabesas*, the Snake with two Heads.

The small black Snake is a very venomous Creature.

There is also a grey Snake, with red and brown Spots all over its back. 'Tis as big as a Man's Arm, and about 3 Foot long, and is said to be venomous. I saw one of these.

Here are two sorts of very large Snakes or Serpents: One of 'em a Land-snake, the other a Water-snake. The Land-snake is of a grey Colour, and about 18 or 20 Foot long: Not very venomous, but ravenous. I was promised the sight of one of their Skins, but wanted Opportunity.

The Water-snake is said to be near 30 Foot long. These live wholly in the Water, either in large Rivers, or great Lakes, and prey upon any Creature that comes within their Reach, be it Man or Beast. They draw their Prey to them with their Tails: for when they see any thing on the Banks of the River or Lake where they lurk, they swing about their Tails 10 or 12 Foot over the Bank; and whatever stands within their Sweep is snatch'd with great

Violence into the River, and drowned by them. Nay 'tis reported very
credibly that if they see only a shade of any Animal at all on the Water, they
will flourish their Tails to bring in the Man or Beast whose Shade they see,
and are oftentimes too successful in it. Wherefore Men that have Business
near any Place where these Water-Monsters are suspected to lurk, are always
provided with a Gun, which they often fire, and that scares them away, or
keeps them quiet. They are said to have great Heads, and strong Teeth
about 6 Inches long. I was told by an Irish Man who lived here, that his
Wife's Father was very near being taken by one of them about this Time of
my first Arrival here, when his Father was with him up in the Country: For
the Beast flourish'd his Tail for him, but came not nigh enough by a Yard or
two; however it scared him sufficiently.

The amphibious Creatures here which I said are called by the Portugueze
Cuchora's de Agua, or Water-dogs, are said to be as big as small Mastiffs,
and are all hairy and shaggy from Head to Tail. They have 4 short Legs, a
pretty long Head and short Tail; and are of a blackish Colour. They live in
fresh Water-ponds, and oftentimes come ashore and Sun themselves; but
retire to the Water if assaulted. They are eaten, and said to be good Food.
Several of these Creatures which I have now spoken of I have not seen, but
inform'd my self about them while I was here at Bahia, from sober and
sensible Persons among the Inhabitants, among whom I met with some that
could speak English.

In the Sea upon this Coast there is great Store and Diversity of Fish, *viz.*
Jew-fish, for which there is a great Market at Bahia in Lent: Tarpoon's,
Mullets, Groopers, Snooks, Gar-fish (called here Goolion's,) Gorasses, Bar-
rama's, Coquinda's, Cavallie's, Cuchora's (or Dog-fish) Conger-Eels,
Herrings (as I was told) the Serrew, the Olio de Boy, (I write and spell
them just as they were named to me) Whales, *&c.*

Here is also Shell-fish (tho' in less Plenty about Bahia than on other Parts
of the Coast,) *viz.* Lobsters, Crawfish, Shrimps, Crabs, Oysters of the
common Sort, Conchs, Wilks, Cockles, Muscles, Perriwinkles, *&c.* Here
are three Sorts of Sea-Turtle, *viz.* Hawksbill, Loggerhead, and Green: But
none of them are in any esteem, neither Spaniards nor Portugueze loving
them: Nay they have a great Antipathy against them, and would much rather
eat a Porpoise, tho' our English count the green Turtle very extraordinary
Food. The Reason that is commonly given in the West-Indies for the
Spaniards not caring to eat of them, is the Fear they have lest, being usually

foul-bodied, and many of them pox'd (lying, as they do, so promiscuously with their Negrines and other She-slaves) they should break out loathsomely like Lepers; which this Sort of Food, 'tis said, does much encline Men to do, searching the Body, and driving out any such gross Humours: For which Cause many of our English Valetudinarians have gone from Jamaica (tho' there they have also Turtle) to the I. Caimanes, at the Laying-time, to live wholly upon Turtle that then abound there; purposely to have their Bodies scoured by this Food, and their Distempers driven out; and have been said to have found many of them good Success in it. But this by the way. The Hawks-bill-Turtle on this Coast of Brazil is most sought after of any, for its Shell; which by Report of those I have convers'd with at Bahia, is the clearest and best clouded Tortoise-shell in the World. I had some of it shewn me, which was indeed as good as I ever saw. They get a pretty deal of it in some Parts on this Coast; but 'tis very dear.

Beside this Port of Bahia de todos los Santos, there are 2 more principal Ports on Brazil, where European Ships Trade, *viz.* Pernambuc and Ria Janeira; and I was told that there go as many Ships to each of these Places as to Bahia, and 2 Men of War to each Place for their Convoys. Of the other Ports in this Country none is of greater Note than that of St. Paul's, where they gather much Gold; but the Inhabitants are said to be a Sort of Banditti, or loose People that live under no Government: But their Gold brings them all Sorts of Commodities that they need, as Clothes, Arms, Ammunition, &c. The Town is said to be large and strong.

CHAP. III

My Stay here at Bahia was about a Month; during which Time the Vice-Roy of Goa came hither from thence in a great Ship, said to be richly laden with all Sorts of India Goods; but she did not break Bulk here, being bound Home for Lisbon; only the Vice-Roy intended to refresh his Men (of whom he had lost many, and most of the rest were very sickly, having been 4 Months in their Voyage hither) and so to take in Water, and depart for Europe, in Company with the other Portugueze Ships thither bound; who had Orders to be ready to sail by the twentieth of May. He desir'd me to carry a Letter for him, directed to his Successor the new Vice-Roy of Goa; which I did, sending it thither afterwards by Captain Hammond, whom I found near the Cape of Good Hope. The refreshing my Men, and taking in Water, was the main also of my Business here; beside the having the better Opportunity to compose the Disorders among my Crew: Which, as I have before related, were grown to so great a Heighth, that they could not without great Difficulty be appeased: However, finding Opportunity, during my Stay in this Place, to allay in some Measure the Ferment that had been raised among my Men, I now set my self to provide for the carrying on of my Voyage with more Heart than before, and put all Hands to work, in order to it, as fast as the Backwardness of my Men would permit; who shew'd continually their Unwillingness to proceed farther. Besides, their Heads were generally fill'd with strange Notions of Southerly Winds that were now setting in (and there had been already some Flurries of them) which, as they surmis'd, would hinder any farther Attempts of going on to the Southward, so long as they should last.

The Winds begin to shift here in April and September, and the Seasons of the Year (the Dry and the Wet) alter with them. In April the Southerly Winds make their Entrance on this Coast, bringing in the wet Season, with violent Tornado's, Thunder and Lightening, and much Rain. In September the other Coasting Trade, at East North-East comes in, and clears the Sky, bringing fair Weather. This, as to the Change of Wind, is what I have observ'd [Vol. II.] but as to the Change of Weather accompanying it so exactly here at Bahia, this is a particular Exception to what I have experienc'd in all other Places of South Latitudes that I have been in between the Tropicks, or those I have heard of; for there the dry Seasons sets in, in April, and the Wet about October or November, sooner or later (as I have said that they are, in South Latitudes, the Reverse of the Seasons, or Weather, in the same Months in N. Latitudes, [Vol. II.]) whereas on this Coast of Brazil, the wet Season comes in in April, at the same Time that it doth in N. Latitudes, and the dry (as I have said here) in September; the Rains here not lasting so far in the Year as in other Places; For in September the Weather is usually so fair, that in the latter part of that Month they begin to cut their Sugar-Canes here, as I was told; for I enquired particularly about the Seasons: Though this, as to the Season of cutting of Canes, which I was now assur'd to be in September, agrees not very well with that I was formerly told [Vol. II.] that in Brazil they cut the Canes in July. And so, as to what is said a little lower in the same Page, that in managing their Canes they are not confin'd to the Seasons, this ought to have been express'd only of planting them; for they never cut them but in the dry Season.

But to return to the Southerly Winds, which came in (as I expected they would) while I was here: These daunted my Ship's Company very much, tho' I had told them they were to look for them: But they being ignorant as to what I told them farther, that these were only Coasting-Winds, sweeping the Shore to about 40 or 50 Leagues in Breadth from it, and imagining that they had blown so all the Sea over, between America and Africa; and being confirm'd in this their Opinion by the Portugueze Pilots of the European Ships, with whom several of my Officers conversed much, and who were themselves as ignorant that these were only Coasting Trade-Winds (themselves going away before them, in their Return homewards, till they cross the Line, and so having no Experience of the Breadth of them) being thus possess'd with a Conceit that we could not sail from hence till September; this made them still the more remiss in their Duties, and very listless to the getting Things in a Readiness for our Departure. However I was the more diligent my self to have the Ship scrubb'd, and to send my Water-Casks ashore to get them trimm'd, my Beer being now out. I went also to the Governour to get my Water fill'd; for here being but one Watering-place (and the Water running low, now at the End of the dry Season) it was always so crouded with the European Ships Boats, who were preparing to be gone, that my men could seldom come nigh it, till the Governour very kindly sent an Officer to clear the Water-place for my Men, and to stay there till my Water-Casks were all full, whom I satisfied for his Pains. Here I also got aboard 9 or 10 Ton of Ballast, and made my Boatswain fit the Rigging that was amiss: and I enquired also of my particular Officers whose Business it was, whether they wanted any Stores, especially Pitch and Tar; for that here I would supply my self before I proceeded any farther; but they said they had enough, tho' it did not afterwards prove so.

I commonly went ashore every Day, either upon Business, or to recreate my self in the Fields, which were very pleasant, and the more for a Shower of Rain now and then, that ushers in the wet Season. Several Sorts of good Fruits were also still remaining, especially Oranges, which were in such Plenty, that I and all my Company stocked our selves for our Voyage with them, and they did us a great Kindness; and we took in also a good Quantity of Rum and Sugar: But for Fowls they being here lean and dear, I was glad I had stock'd my self at St. Jago. But by the little Care my Officers took for fresh Provisions, one might conclude, they did not think of going much farther. Besides, I had like to have been imbroiled with the Clergy here (of the Inquisition, as I suppose) and so my Voyage might have been hindred. What was said to them of me, by some of my Company that went ashore, I know not; but I was assured by a Merchant there, that if they got me into their Clutches (and it seems, when I was last ashore they had narrowly watch'd me) the Governour himself could not release me. Besides I might either be murther'd in the Streets, as he sent me Word, or poisoned, if I came ashore any more; and therefore he advised me to stay aboard. Indeed I had now no further Business ashore but to take leave of the Governour, and therefore took his Advice.

Our Stay here was till the 23d of April. I would have gone before if I could sooner have fitted my self; but was now earnest to be gone, because this Harbour lies open to the S. and S.S.W. which are raging Winds here, and now was the Season for them. We had 2 or 3 Touches of them; and one pretty severe, and the Ships ride there so near each other, that if a Cable should fail, or an Anchor start, you are instantly aboard of one Ship or other: And I was more afraid of being disabled here in Harbour by these

blustring Winds, than discouraged by them, as my People were, from prosecuting the Voyage; for at present I even wish'd for a brisk Southerly Wind
as soon as I should be once well out of the Harbour, to set me the sooner
into the true General Trade-Wind.

The Tide of Flood being spent, and having a fine Land-Breeze on the 23d
in the Morning. I went away from the Anchoring place before 'twas light;
and then lay by till Day-light that we might see the better how to go out of
the Harbour. I had a Pilot belonging to Mr. Cock, who went out with me,
to whom I gave 3 Dollars; but I found I could as well have gone out my
self, by the Soundings I made at coming in. The Wind was E. by N. and
fair Weather. By 10 a Clock I was got past all Danger, and then sent away
my Pilot. At 12 Cape Salvadore bore N. distant 6 Leagues, and we had the
Winds between the E. by N. and S.E. a considerable Time, so that we kept
along near the Shore, commonly in Sight of it. The Southerly Blasts had
now left us again; for they come at first in short Flurries, and shift to other
Points (for 10 or 12 Days sometimes) before they are quite set in: And we
had uncertain Winds, between Sea and Land-Breezes, and the Coasting-
Trade, which was its self unsettled.

The Easterly Winds at present made me doubt I should not weather a
great Shoal which lies in Lat. between 18 deg. and 19 deg. S. and runs a
great way into the Sea, directly from the Land, Easterly. Indeed the
Weather was fair (and continued so a good while) so that I might the better
avoid any Danger from it: And if the Wind came to the Southward I knew I
could stretch off to Sea; so that I jogg'd on couragiously. The 27th of April
we saw a small Brigantine under the Shore plying to the Southward. We also
saw many Men of War-birds and Boobies, and Abundance of Albicore-Fish.
Having still fair Weather, small Gales, and some Calms, I had the
Opportunity of trying the Current, which I found to set sometimes
Northerly and sometimes Southerly: And therefore knew I was still within
the Verge of the Tides. Being now in the Lat. of the Abrohlo Shoals, which
I expected to meet with, I sounded, and had Water lessening from 40 to 33,
and so to 25 Fathom: But then it rose again to 33, 35, 37, &c. all Coral
Rocks. Whilst we were on this Shoal (which we cross'd towards the further
part of it from Land, where it lay deep, and so was not dangerous) we
caught a great many Fish with Hook and Line: and by evening Amplitude
we had 6 deg. 38 min. East Variation. This was the 27th of April; we were
then in Lat. 18 deg. 13 min. S. and East Longitude from Cape Salvadore

31 min. On the 29th, being then in Lat. 18 deg. 39 min. S. we had small Gales from the W.N.W. to the W.S.W. often shifting. The 30th we had the Winds from W. to S.S.E. Squalls and Rain: And we saw some Dolphins and other Fish about us. We were now out of Sight of Land, and had been so 4 or 5 Days: But the Winds now hanging in the South was an apparent Sign that we were still too nigh the Shore to receive the true General East-Trade; as the Easterly Winds we had before shew'd that we were too far off the Land to have the Benefit of the Coasting South-Trade: and the Faintness of both these Winds, and their often shifting from the S.S.W. to the S.E. with Squalls, Rain and small Gales, were a Confirmation of our being between the Verge of the S. Coasting-Trade, and that of the true Trade; which is here, regularly, S.E.

The 3d of May being in Lat 20 deg. 00 min. and Merid. distance West from Cape Salvadore 234 Miles, the Variation was 7 deg. 00 min. We saw no Fowl but Shear-waters, as our Sea-men call them, being a small black Fowl that sweep the Water as they fly, and are much in the Seas that lie without either of the Tropicks: they are not eaten. We caught 3 small Sharks, each 6 Foot 4 Inches long; and they were very good Food for us. The next Day we caught 3 more Sharks of the same Size, and we eat them also, esteeming them as good Fish boil'd and press'd, and then stew'd with Vinegar and Pepper.

We had nothing of Remark from the 3d of May to the 10th, only now and then seeing a small Whale spouting up the Water. We had the Wind Easterly, and we ran with it to the Southward, running in this Time from the Lat. of 20 deg. 00 m. to 29 deg. 5 min. S. and having then 7 d. 3 m. E. Long. from C. Salvadore; the Variation increasing upon us, at present notwithstanding we went East. We had all along a great Difference between the Morning and Evening Amplitudes; usually a Degree or two, and sometimes more. We were now in the true Trade, and therefore made good Way to the Southward, to get without the Verge of the General Trade-Wind into a Westerly Wind's way, that might carry us towards the Cape of Good Hope. By the 12th of May, being in Lat. 31 Deg. 10 min. we began to meet with Westerly Winds, which freshned on us, and did not leave us till a little before we made the Cape. Sometimes it blew so hard that it put us under a Fore-course; especially in the Night; but in the Day-time we had commonly our Main Top-sail rift. We met with nothing of Moment; only we past by a dead Whale, and saw Millions (as I may say) of Sea-Fowls

An. 1699 about the Carcass (and as far round about it as we could see) some feeding, and the rest flying about, or sitting on the Water, waiting to take their Turns. We first discovered the Whale by the Fowls; for indeed I did never see so many Fowls at once in my Life before, their Numbers being inconceivably great: They were of divers Sorts, in Bigness, Shape and Colour. Some were almost as big as Geese, of a grey Colour, with white Breasts, and with such Bills, Wings, and Tails. Some were Pintado-Birds, as big as Ducks, and speckled black and white. Some were Shear-waters; some Petrels; and there were several Sorts of large Fowls. We saw of these Birds, especially the Pintado-birds, all the Sea over from about 200 Leagues distant from the Coast of Brazil, to within much the same Distance of New-Holland. The Pintado is a Southern Bird, and of that temperate Zone; for I never saw of them much to the Norward of 30 deg. S. The Pintado-Bird is as big as a Duck; but appears, as it flies, about the Bigness of a tame Pidgeon, having a short Tail, but the Wings very long, as most Sea-Fowls have; especially such as these that fly far from the Shore, and seldom come nigh it; for their Resting is sitting afloat upon the Water; but they lay, I suppose, ashore. There are three Sorts of these Birds, all of the same Make and Bigness, and are only different in Colour. The first is black all over: The second Sort are grey, with white Bellies and Breasts. The third Sort, which is the true Pintado, or Painted-Bird, is curiously spotted white and black. Their Heads, and the Tips of their Wings and Tails, are black for about an Inch; and their Wings are also edg'd quite round with such a small black List; only within the black on the Tip of their Wings there is a white Spot seeming as they fly (for then their Spots are best seen) as big as a Half-crown. All this is on the Outside of the Tails and Wings; and as there is a white Spot in the black Tip of the Wings, so there is in the Middle of the Wings which is white, a black Spot; but this, towards the Back of the Bird, turns gradually to a dark grey. The Back its self, from the Head to the Tip of the Tail, and the Edge of the Wings next to the Back, are all over-spotted with fine small, round, white and black Spots, as big as a Silver Two-pence, and as close as they can stick one by another: The Belly, Thighs, Sides, and inner-part of the Wings, are of a light grey. These Birds, of all these Sorts, fly many together, never high, but almost sweeping the Water. We shot one a while after on the Water in a Calm, and a Water-Spaniel we had with us brought it in: I have given a Picture of it [See Birds, Fig. 1.] but it was so damaged, that the Picture doth not shew it to Advantage; and

F.2.

*This very much resembles
the Guarauna, described,
and figured by Piso.*

F.1.

The Pintado Bird.

its Spots are best seen when the Feathers are spread as it flies.

The Petrel is a Bird not much unlike a Swallow, but smaller, and with a shorter Tail. 'Tis all over black, except a white Spot on the Rump. They fly sweeping like Swallows, and very near the Water. They are not so often seen in fair Weather; being Foul-weather Birds, as our Seamen call them, and presaging a Storm when they come about a Ship; who for that Reason don't love to see them. In a Storm they will hover close under the Ship's Stern, in the Wake of the Ship (as 'tis call'd) or the Smoothness which the Ship's passing has made on the Sea; And there as they fly (gently then) they pat the Water alternately with their Feet, as if they walk'd upon it; tho' still upon the Wing. And from hence the Seamen give them the Name of Petrels, in Allusion to St. Peter's walking upon the Lake of Gennesareth.

We also saw many Bunches of Sea-weeds in the Lat. of 39. 32. and by Judgment, near the Meridian of the Island Tristian d' Aconha: And then we had about 2 d. 20 min. East Variation: which was now again decreasing as we ran to the Eastward, till near the Meridian of Ascension; where we found little or no Variation: But from thence, as we ran farther to the East, our Variation increased Westerly.

Two Days before I made the Cape of G. Hope, my Variation was 7 deg. 58 min. West. I was then in 43 deg. 27 min. East Longit. from C. Salvador, being in Lat. 35 deg. 30 min. this was the first of June. The second of June I saw a large black Fowl, with a whitish flat Bill, fly by us; and took great Notice of it, because in the East-India Waggoner, Pilot-book, there is mention made of large Fowls, as big as Ravens, with white flat Bills and black Feathers, that fly not above 30 Leagues from the Cape, and are look'd on as a Sign of ones being near it. My Reckoning made me then think my self above 90 Leagues from the Cape, according to the Longitude which the Cape hath in the common Sea-Charts: So that I was in some doubt, whether these were the right Fowls spoken of in the Waggoner; or whether those Fowls might not fly farther off Shore than is there mentioned; or whether, as it prov'd, I might not be nearer the Cape than I reckoned myself to be; for I found, soon after, that I was not then above 25 or 30 Leagues at most from the Cape. Whether the Fault were in the Charts laying down the Cape too much to the East from Brazil, or were rather in our Reckoning, I could not tell: But our Reckonings are liable to such Uncertainties from Steerage, Log, Currents, Half-Minute-Glasses; and sometimes want of Care, as in so long a Run cause often a Difference of many Leagues in the whole Account.

Most of my Men that kept Journals imputed it to the Half-Minute-Glasses: and indeed we had not a good Glass in the Ship beside the Half-watch or Two-Hour-Glasses. As for our Half-Minute-Glasses we tried them all at several Times, and we found those that we had used from Brazil as much too short, as others we had used before were too long; which might well make great Errors in those several Reckonings. A Ship ought therefore to have its Glasses very exact; and besides, an extra-ordinary Care ought to be used in heaving the Log, for Fear of giving too much Stray-Line in a moderate Gale; and also to stop quickly in a brisk Gale, for when a Ship runs 8, 9 or 10 Knots, half a Knot or a Knot is soon run out, and not heeded: But to prevent Danger, when a Man thinks himself near Land, the best way is to look out betimes, and lye by in the Night, for a Commander may err easily himself; beside the Errors of those under him, tho' never so carefully eyed.

Another Thing that stumbled me here was the Variation, which, at this Time, by the last Amplitude I had I found to be but 7 deg. 58 min. W. whereas the Variation at the Cape (from which I found my self not 30 Leagues distant) was then computed, and truly, about 11 deg. or more: And yet a while after this, when I was got 10 Leagues to the Eastward of the Cape, I found the Variation but 10 deg. 40 min. W. whereas it should have been rather more than at the Cape. These Things, I confess, did puzzle me: Neither was I fully satisfied as to the Exactness of the taking the Variation at Sea: For in a great Sea, which we often meet with, the Compass will traverse with the Motion of the Ship; besides the Ship may and will deviate somewhat in steering, even by the best Helmsmen: And then when you come to take an Azimuth, there is often some Difference between him that looks at the Compass, and the Man that takes the Altitude heighth of the Sun; and a small Error in each, if the Error of both should be one way, will make it wide of any great Exactness. But what was most shocking to me, I found that the Variation did not always increase or decrease in Proportion to the Degrees of Longitude East or West; as I had a Notion they might do to a certain Number of Degrees of Variation East or West, at such or such particular Meridians. But finding in this Voyage that the Difference of Variation did not bear a regular Proportion to the Difference of Longitude, I was much pleas'd to see it thus observ'd in a Scheme shewn me after my Return home, wherein are represented the several Variations in the Atlantick Sea, on both Sides the Equator; and there, the Line of no Variation in that Sea is not a Meridian Line, but goes very oblique, as do those also which shew the Increase of Variation on each Side of it. In that Draught there is so large an Advance made as well towards the accounting for those seemingly irregular Increases and Decreases of Variation towards the S.E. Coast of America, as towards the fixing a general Scheme or System of the Variation every where, which would be of such great Use in Navigation, that I cannot but hope that the ingenious Author, Capt. Hally, who to his profound Skill in all Theories of these kinds, hath added and is adding continually Personal Experiments, will e'er long oblige the World with a fuller Discovery of the Course of the Variation, which hath hitherto been a Secret. For my Part I profess my self unqualified for offering at any thing of a General Scheme; but since Matter of Fact, and whatever increases the History of the Variation, may be of use towards the settling or confirming the Theory of it, I shall here once for all insert a Table of all the Variations I observed beyond the Equator in this Voyage, both in going out, and returning back; and what Errors there may be in it, I shall leave to be corrected by the Observations of others.

A Table of Variations

	1699.	D. S.Lat.	M.	D. Longit.	M.	D. Variat.	M.
Mar.	14	6	15	1	47a	3	27E
	21	12	45	12	9	3	27
Apr.	25	14	49	00	10b	7	0
	28	18	13	00	31	6	38
	30	19	00	2	20	6	30
May.	2	19	22	3	51	8	15
	3	20	1	3	40	7	0
	5	22	47	3	48	9	40
	6	24	23	3	53	7	36
	7	25	44	3	53	10	15
	8	26	47	4	35	7	14
	9	28	9	5	50	9	45
	10	29	5	7	3	11	41
	11	29	23	7	38	12	47
	17	34	58	18	43	5	40

a   W. from St. Jago.
b   E. from C. Salvador in Brazil.

1699.	D. M. S.Lat.		D. M. Longit.		D. M. Variat.	
May. 18	34	54	19	06	6	19E
19	35	48	19	45	5	6
23	39	42	27	1	2	55
25	39	11	31	35	2	0
June. 1	35	30	43	27	7	58W
5	35	8	00	23c	10	40
6	36	7	3	6	11	10
8	36	17	10	3	15	00
9	35	59	12	0	19	38
12	35	20	20	18	21	35
14	35	5	26	13	23	50
15	34	51	29	24	25	56
17	34	27	36	8	24	54
19	34	17	39	24	25	29
20	34	15	42	25	24	22
22	33	34	45	41	22	15
25	35	8	45	28	24	30
28	36	40	49	33	22	50
29	36	40	53	12	22	44
30	36	15	56	22	21	40
July. 1	35	35	58	44	19	45
4	33	32	66	22	16	40
6	31	30	68	34	12	20
7	31	45	69	00	12	2
10	32	39	70	21	13	36
11	33	4	72	00	12	29
13	21	17	74	43	10	0
15	29	20	75	25	10	28
18	28	16	78	29	9	51
23	26	43	84	19	9	11
24	26	28	85	20	8	9
25	26	14	85	52	8	40
26	25	36	86	21	8	20
27	26	43	86	16	7	0
29	27	38	87	25	8	20
31	26	54	88	1	9	0
Aug. 5	25	30	86	3	7	24
15	24	41	86	2d	6	6

c   E. from C. G. Hope.
d   E. from Sharks-Bay in N. Holland.

1699.	D. S.Lat.	M.	D. Longit.	M.	D. Variat.	M.
Aug. 17	23	2	00	22	7	6W
20	19	37	3	00	7	00
24	19	52	4	41	7	7
25	19	45	5	10	6	40
27	19	24	6	11	5	18
28	18	38	6	57	6	12
Sept. 6	17	16	9	18	4	3
7	16	9	8	57	2	7
8	15	37	9	34	2	20
10	13	55	10	55	1	47
11	13	12	11	42	1	47
Dec. 29	5	1	6	34e	1	2E
1700. Jan. 3	1	32	6	53	4	8
Feb. 13	0	9	2	48f	4	0
16	0	12	7	31	6	26
21	0	12	15	23	8	45
23	0	43	18	00	8	45
27	2	43	19	41	9	50
Mar. 10	5	10	00	5g	1	0
13	5	35	00	44h	9	0
30	5	15	6	4	8	25W
Apr. 6	3	32	8	25	7	16
22	1	32	00	37i	3	00
May. 1	3	00		k	2	15E
24	9	59	00	25l	0	15W
27	14	33	3	30	1	25
June. 2	19	44	8	7	5	38
3	19	51	9	58	6	10
4	19	46	11	6	6	20
5	20	00	12	22	4	58
6	20	00	14	17	7	20
9	19	59	16	01	6	32

e E. from Babao-Bay in J. Timor.
f E. from C. Mabo in N. Guinea.
g E. from C. St. George on I.N. Britannia.
h W. from ditto.
i W. from C. Mabo.
k At Anchor off I. Ceram.
l W. from Babao-Bay.

1700.	D. M. S.Lat.		D. M. Longit.		D. M. Variat.	
June. 11	9	57	17	42	8	1W
12	19	48	19	0	6	0
Nov. 7	21	26		*m*	9	0
14	27	1	35	35	16	50
15	27	10	36	34	18	57
16	27	11	37	54	17	24
19	28	14	41	40	19	39
21	29	24	44	47	20	50
23	29	42	47	34	21	38
24	30	16	49	26	26	00
25	30	40	51	24	22	38
27	31	51	55	5	22	40
29	32	55	56	28	27	10
30	31	55	57	25	27	10
Dec. 1	31	57	58	17	24	30
2	31	57	59	33	27	57
4	32	3	61	45	24	50
6	32	15	66	00	23	30
7	37	28	68	36	24	48
8	33	49	64	38	21	53
9	32	49	70	09	24	00
11	32	50	71	45	21	15
Dec. 13	31	55	72	32	20	16
14	31	35	73	39	20	00
15	32	21	75	22	20	00
17	33	5	79	39	18	42
18	33	0	80	39	17	15
21	34	39	82	46	16	41
22	34	36	83	19	14	36
23	34	21	83	42	14	00
25	34	38	84	21	14	00
1701. Jan. 15	31	25	2	32*n*	10	20
16	30	5	4	42	9	36
17	28	46	6	8	8	25
18	27	26	7	32	7	40
19	26	11	9	9	7	30
20	25	00	10	49	7	9
21	23	42	12	34	6	55

m W. from Princes Isle by Java-Head.
n W. from the Table Land at C.G. Hope.

1701	D.	M. S.Lat.	D.	M. Longit.	D.	M. Variat.
Jan.	22	22	51	14	10	5	56W
	23	21	48	15	17	5	32
	24	21	24	15	51	4	56
	26	19	57	16	48	4	20
	27	19	10	17	22	3	24
	28	18	13	18	23	4	00
	29	17	22	19	29	2	00
Feb.	16	12	52	3	8o	1	50
	17	11	55	4	42	1	10
	18	11	17	5	30	0	20
	19	10	22	6	32	1	10
	21	We made the I. Ascention.					

o W. Santa Helena.

An. 1699 But to return from this Digression: Having fair Weather, and the Winds hanging Southerly, I jog'd on to the Eastward, to make the Cape. On the third of June we saw a Sail to Leeward of us, shewing English Colours. I bore away to speak with her, and found her to be the *Antelope* of London, commanded by Captain Hammond, and bound for the Bay of Bengal in the Service of the New-East-India Company. There were many Passengers aboard, going to settle there under Sir Edward Littleton, who was going Chief thither: I went aboard, and was known by Sir Edward and Mr. Hedges, and kindly received and treated by them and the Commander; who had been afraid of us before, tho' I had sent one of my Officers aboard. They had been in at the Cape, and came from thence the Day before, having stocked themselves with Refreshments. They told me that they were by Reckoning, 60 Miles to the West of the Cape. While I was aboard them, a fine small Westerly Wind sprang up; therefore I shortned my stay with them, because I did not design to go into the Cape. When I took leave I was presented with half a Mutton, 12 Cabbages, 12 Pumkins, 6 Pound of Butter, 6 Couple of Stock-fish, and a quantity of Parsnips; sending them some Oatmeal, which they wanted.

From my first setting out from England, I did not design to touch at the Cape; and that was one Reason why I touch'd at Brazil, that there I might refresh my Men, and prepare them for a long Run to New Holland. We had not yet seen the Land; but about 2 in the Afternoon we saw the Cape-Land bearing East, at about 16 Leagues distance: And Captain Hammond being also bound to double the Cape, we jog'd on together this Afternoon and the next Day, and had several fair Sights of it; which may be seen [Table III. N°. 6, 7, 8.].

To proceed: Having still a Westerly Wind, I jog'd on in company with the *Antelope*, till Sunday June the 4th at 4 in the Afternoon, when we parted; they steering away for the East-Indies, and I keeping an E.S.E. Course, the better to make my way for New Holland: For tho' New Holland lies North-Easterly from the Cape, yet all Ships bound towards the Coast, or the Streights of Sundy, ought to keep for a while in the same Parallel, or in a Lat. between 35 and 40. at least a little to the S. of the East. that they may continue in a variable Winds way; and not venture too soon to stand so far to the North, as to be within the Verge of the Trade-Wind, which will put them by their Easterly Course. The Wind increased upon us; but we had yet sight of the *Antelope*, and of the Land too, till Tuesday the 6th June: And then we saw also by us an innumerable Company of Fowls of divers sorts; so that we look'd about to see if there were not another dead Whale, but saw none.

The Night before, the Sun set in a black Cloud, which appeared just like Land; and the Clouds above it were gilded of a dark red Colour. And on the Tuesday, as the Sun drew near the Horizon, the Clouds were gilded very prettily to the Eye, tho' at the same time my Mind dreaded the Consequences of it. When the Sun was now not above 2 deg. high, it entered into a dark Smoaky-coloured Cloud that lay parallel with the Horizon, from whence presently seem'd to issue many dusky blackish Beams. The Sky was at this time covered with small hard Clouds (as we call such a lye scattering about, not likely to Rain) very thick one by another; and such of them as lay next to the Bank of Clouds at the Horizon, were of a pure Gold Colour to 3 or 4 deg. high above the Bank. From these to about 10 deg. high they were redder, and very bright; above them they were of a darker Colour still, to about 60 or 70 deg. high; where the Clouds began to be of their common Colour. I took the more particular Notice of all this, because I have generally observed such colour'd Clouds to appear before an approaching Storm: And this being Winter here, and the time for bad Weather, I expected and provided for a violent blast of Wind, by riffing our Topsails, and giving a strict charge to my Officers to hand them or take

them in, if the Wind should grow stronger. The Wind was now at
W.N.W. a very brisk Gale. About 12 a Clock at Night we had a pale
whitish Glare in the N.W. which was another Sign, and intimated the
Storm to be near at hand; and the Wind increasing upon it, we presently
handed our Top-sails, furled the Main-sail, and went away only with our
Fore-sail. Before 2 in the Morning it came on very fierce, and we kept right
before Wind and Sea, the Wind still encreasing: But the Ship was very
governable, and steered incomparably well. At 8 in the Morning we settled
our Fore-yard, lowering it 4 or 5 Foot, and we ran very swiftly; especially
when the Squalls of Rain or Hail, from a black Cloud, came over Head, for
then it blew excessive hard. These, tho' they did not last long, yet came very
thick and fast one after another. The Sea also ran very high; But we running
so violently before Wind and Sea, we ship'd little or no Water; tho' a little
wash'd into our upper Deck-Ports; and with it a Scuttle or Cuttle-Fish was
cast upon the Carriage of a Gun.

The Wind blew extraordinary hard all Wednesday the 7th of June, but
abated of its fierceness before Night: Yet it continued a brisk Gale till about
the 16th, and still a moderate one till the 19th Day; by which time we had
run about 600 Leagues: For the most part of which time the Wind was in
some point of the West, *viz.* from the W.N.W. to the S. by W. It blew
hardest when at W. or between the W. and S.W. but after it veered more
Southerly the foul Weather broke up: This I observed at other times also in
these Seas, that when the Storms at West veered to the Southward they grew
less; and that when the Wind came to the E. of the S. we had still smaller
Gales, Calms, and fair Weather. As for the Westerly Winds on that side the
Cape, we like them never the worse for being violent, for they drive us the
faster to the Eastward; and are therefore the only Winds coveted by those
who Sail towards such parts of the East-Indies, as lye South of the Equator;
as Timor, Java, and Sumatra; and by the Ships bound for China, or any
other that are to pass through the Streights of Sundy. Those Ships having
once past the Cape, keep commonly pretty far Southerly, on purpose to meet
with these West-winds, which in the Winter Season of these Climates they
soon meet with; for then the Winds are generally Westerly at the Cape, and
especially to the Southward of it: But in their Summer Months they get to
the Southward of 40 deg. usually e're they meet with the Westerly Winds.
I was not at this time in a higher Lat. than 36 deg. 40 min. and oftentimes
was more Northerly, altering my Latitude often as Winds and Weather

required; for in such long Runs 'tis best to shape one's Course acording to the Winds. And if in steering to the East, we should be obliged to bear a little to the N. or S. of it, 'tis no great Matter; for 'tis but sailing 2 or 3 Points from the Wind, when 'tis either Northerly or Southerly; and this not only easeth the Ship from straining, but shortens the way more than if a Ship was kept close on a Wind, as some Men are fond of doing.

The 19th of June, we were in Lat. 34 deg. 17 min. S. and Long. from the Cape 39 deg. 24 min. E. and had small Gales and Calms. The Winds were at N.E. by E. and continued in some Part of the E. till the 27th Day. When it having been some Time at N.N.E. it came about at N. and then to the W. of the N. and continued in the West-board (between the N.N.W. and S.S.W.) till the 4th of July; in which Time we ran 782 Miles; then the Winds came about again to the East, we reckoning our selves to be in a Meridian 1100 L. East of the Cape; and having fair Weather, sounded, but had no Ground.

We met with little of Remark in this Voyage, besides being accompanied with Fowls all the way, especially Pintado-Birds, and seeing now and then a Whale: But as we drew nigher the Coast of New-Holland, we saw frequently 3 or 4 Whales together. When we were about 90 Leagues from the Land we began to see Sea-weeds, all of one Sort; and as we drew nigher the Shore we saw them more frequently. At about 30 Leagues distance we began to see some Scuttle-bones floating on the Water; and drawing still nigher the Land we saw greater Quantities of them.

July 25. being in Lat. 26. deg. 14 min. S. and Longitude E. from the C. of Good Hope 85 deg. 52 min. we saw a large Gar-fish leap 4 Times by us, which seemed to be as big as a Porpose. It was now very fair Weather, and the Sea was full of a Sort of very small Grass or Moss, which as it floated in the Water seem'd to have been some Spawn of Fish; and there was among it some small Fry. The next Day the Sea was full of small round Things like Pearl, some as big as white Peas; they were very clear and transparent, and upon crushing any of them a Drop of Water would come forth: The Skin that contain'd the Water was so thin that it was but just discernable. Some Weeds swam by us, so that we did not doubt but we should quickly see Land. On the 27th also, some Weeds swam by us, and the Birds that had flown along with us all the way almost from Brazil, now left us, except only 2 or 3 Shear-waters. On the 28th we saw many Weeds swim by us, and some Whales, blowing. On the 29th we had dark cloudy

Weather, with much Thunder, Lightning, and violent Rains in the Morning; but in the Evening it grew fair. We saw this Day a Scuttle-bone swim by us, and some of our young Men a Seal, as it should seem by their Description of its Head. I saw also some Boneta's, and some Skipjacks, a Fish about 8 Inches long, broad, and sizeable, not much unlike a Roach; which our Seamen call so from their leaping about.

The 30th of July, being still nearer the Land, we saw Abundance of Scuttle-bones and Sea-weed, more Tokens that we were not far from it; and saw also a Sort of Fowls, the like of which we had not seen in the whole Voyage, all the other Fowls having now left us. These were as big as Lapwings; of a grey Colour, black about their Eyes, with red sharp Bills, long Wings, their Tails long and forked like Swallows; and they flew flapping their Wings like Lapwings. In the Afternoon we met with a Ripling like a Tide or Current, or the Water of some Shoal or Over-fall; but were past it before we could sound. The Birds last mention'd and this were further Signs of Land. In the Evening we had fair Weather, and a small Gale at West. At 8 a Clock we sounded again; but had no Ground.

We kept on still to the Eastward, with an easy Sail, looking out sharp: For by the many Signs we had, I did expect that we were near the Land. At 12 a Clock in the Night I sounded, and had 45 Fathom, coarse Sand and small white Shells. I presently clapt on a Wind and stood to the South, with the Wind at W. because I thought we were to the South of a Shoal call'd the Abrohles (an Appellative Name for Shoals, as it seems to me) which in a Draught I had of that Coast is laid down in 27 deg. 28 min. Lat. stretching about 7 Leagues into the Sea. I was the Day before in 27 deg. 38 min. by Reckoning. And afterwards steering E. by S. purposely to avoid it, I thought I must have been to the South of it: But sounding again, at 1 a Clock in the Morning, Aug. the first, we had but 25 Fathom, Coral Rocks; and so found the Shoal was to the South of us. We presently tack'd again, and stood to the North, and then soon deepned our Water; for at 2 in the Morning we had 26 Fathom Coral still: At 3 we had 28 Coral-ground: At 4 we had 30 Fathom, coarse Sand, with some Coral: At 5 we had 45 Fathom, coarse Sand and Shells; being now off the Shoal, as appear'd by the Sand and Shells, and by having left the Coral. By all this I knew we had fallen into the North of the Shoal, and that it was laid down wrong in my Sea-Chart: For I found it lye in about 27 deg. Lat. and by our Run in the next Day, I found that the Outward-edge of it, which I sounded on, lies 16 Leagues off

Shore. When it was Day we steered in E.N.E. with a fine brisk Gale; but did not see the Land till 9 in the Morning, when we saw it from our Topmast-head, and were distant from it about 10 Leagues; having then 40 Fathom-water, and clean Sand. About 3 Hours after we saw it on our Quarter-Deck, being by Judgment about 6 Leagues off, and we had then 40 Fathom, clean Sand. As we ran in, this Day and the next, we took several Sights of it, at different Bearings and Distances; from which it appear'd as you see in [Table IV. N°. 1, 2, 3, 4, 5.] And here I would note once for all, that the Latitudes mark'd in the Draughts, or Sights here given, are not the Latitude of the Land, but of the Ship when the Sight was taken. This Morning, August the first, as we were standing in we saw several large Sea-fowls, like our Gannets on the Coast of England, flying 3 or 4 together; and a Sort of white Sea-Mews, but black about the Eyes, and with forked Tails. We strove to run in near the Shore to seek for a Harbour to refresh us after our tedious Voyage; having made one continued Stretch from Brazil hither of about 114 deg. designing from hence also to begin the Discovery I had a Mind to make on N. Holland and N. Guinea. The Land was low, and appear'd even, and as we drew nearer to it, it made (as you see in Table IV. N°. 3, 4, 5.) with some red and some white Clifts; these last in Lat. 26. 10 S. where you will find 54 Fathom, within 4 Miles of the Shore.

About the Lat. of 26 deg. S. we saw an Opening, and ran in, hoping to find a Harbour there: But when we came to its Mouth, which was about 2 Leagues wide, we saw Rocks and foul Ground within, and therefore stood out again: There we had 20 Fathom-water within 2 Mile of the Shore. The Land every where appear'd pretty low, flat and even; but with steep Cliffs to the Sea; and when we came near it there were no Trees, Shrubs or Grass to be seen. The Soundings in the Lat. of 26 deg. S. from about 8 or 9 Leagues off till you come within a League of the Shore, are generally about 40 Fathom; differing but little, seldom above 3 or 4 Fathom. But the Lead brings up very different Sorts of Sand, some coarse, some fine; and of several Colours, as Yellow, White, Grey, Brown, Blueish and Reddish.

When I saw there was no Harbour here, nor good anchoring, I stood off to Sea again, in the Evening of the second of August, fearing a Storm on a Leeshore, in a Place where there was no Shelter, and desiring at least to have Sea-room: For the Clouds began to grow thick in the Western-board, and the Wind was already there, and began to blow fresh almost upon the Shore; which at this Place lies along N.N.W. and S.S.E. By 9 a Clock at Night we

Table IV **New Holland**

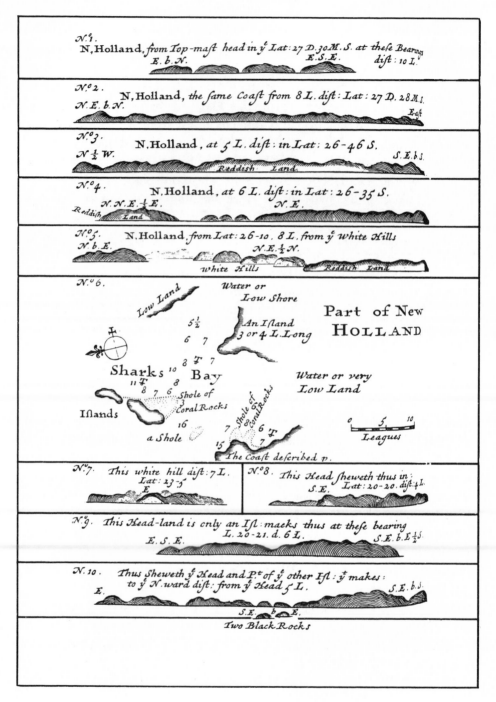

N.ȝ.
N, Holland, *from Top-maſt head in yᵉ Lat: 27 D. 30 M. S. at theſe Bearings*
E. b. N.   E. S. E.   *diſt :* 10 L.

Nᵒ 2.   N, Holland, *the ſame Coaſt from* 8 L. *diſt : Lat : 27 D. 28 M s.*
N. E. b. N.
East

Nᵒ 3.   N. Holland, *at* 5 L. *diſt : in Lat : 26 - 46 S.*
N. ½ W.   S. E. b. s.
Reddish   Land

Nᵒ 4.   N. Holland, *at* 6 L. *diſt : in Lat : 26 - 35 S.*
N. N. E. ½ E.   N. E.
Reddiſh   Land

Nᵒ 5.   N, Holland, *from Lat : 26 - 10.* 8 L. *from yᵉ White Hills*
N. b. E.   N. E. ½ N.
White Hills   Reddish Land

Nᵒ 6.
Low Land   *Water or*
Low Shore
5½   *An Iſland*   Part of New
6   7   *3 or 4 L. Long*   HOLLAND
8 T 7
Sharks 10   Bay   *Water or very*
11 T 8   *Low Land*
8 7 6
Shole of
Coral Rocks
Iſlands   *Shole of*
Coral Rocks
16   7   6 T   0   5   10
a Shole   15   7   *Leagues*
The Coaſt deſcribed p.

Nᵒ 7. *This white hill diſt :* 7 L.   Nᵒ 8. *This Head ſheweth thus in :*
Lat : 23 - 5   S. E.   *Lat : 20 - 20. diſt: 4 L.*
E.

Nᵒ 9. *This Head-land is only an Iſl : maeks thus at theſe bearing*
L. 20 - 21. d. 6 L.
E. S. E.   S. E. b. E ½ S.

N. 10. *Thus Sheweth yᵉ Head and Pᵗ of yᵉ other Iſl : yᵗ makes :*
to yᵉ N. ward diſt : from yᵉ Head 5 L.
E.   S. E. b. s.
S. E. b E.
Two Black Rocks

had got a pretty good Offin; but the Wind still increasing, I took in my Main Top-sail, being able to carry no more Sail than two Courses and the Mizen. At 2 in the Morning, Aug. 3. it blew very hard, and the Sea was much raised; so that I furled all my Sails but my Main-sail. Tho' the Wind blew so hard, we had pretty clear Weather till Noon: But then the whole Sky was blackned with thick Clouds, and we had some Rain, which would last a Quarter of an Hour at a Time, and then it would blow very fierce while the Squalls of Rain were over our Heads; but as soon as they were gone the Wind was by much abated, the Stress of the Storm being over. We sounded several Times, but had no Ground till 8 a Clock Aug. the 4th in the Evening; and then had 60 Fathom-water, Coral-ground. At 10 we had 56 Fathom fine Sand. At 12 we had 55 Fathom, fine Sand, of a pale blueish Colour. It was now pretty moderate Weather; yet I made no Sail till Morning; but then, the Wind veering about to the S.W. I made Sail and stood to the North: And at 11 a Clock the next Day, Aug. 5. we saw Land again, at about 10 Leagues distance. This Noon we were in Lat. 25 deg. 30 min. and in the Afternoon our Cook died, an old Man, who had been sick a great while, being infirm before we came out of England.

The 6th of August in the Morning we saw an Opening in the Land, and we ran into it, and anchored in 7 and a half Fathom-water, 2 Miles from the Shore, clean Sand. It was somewhat difficult getting in here, by Reason of many Shoals we met with: But I sent my Boat sounding before me. The Mouth of this Sound, which I call'd Shark's Bay, lies in about 25 deg. S. Lat. and our Reckoning made its Longitude from the C. of Good Hope to be about 87 Degrees; which is less by 195 Leagues than is usually laid down in our common Draughts, if our Reckoning was right, and our Glasses did not deceive us. As soon as I came to anchor in this Bay (of which I have given a Plan, Table IV. N°. 6.) I sent my Boat ashore to seek for fresh Water: But in the Evening my Men returned, having found none. The next Morning I went ashore, my self, carrying Pick-axes and Shovels with me, to dig for Water: and Axes to cut Wood. We tried in several Places for Water, but finding none after several Trials, nor in several Miles Compass, we left any farther Search for it, and spending the rest of the Day in cutting Wood, we went abroad at Night.

The Land is of an indifferent Height, so that it may be seen 9 or 10 Leagues off. It appears at a Distance very even; but as you come nigher you find there are many gentle Risings, tho' none steep nor high. 'Tis all a steep

Shore against the open Sea: But in this Bay or Sound we were now in, the Land is low by the Sea-side, rising gradually in within the Land. The Mould is Sand by the Sea-side, producing a large Sort of Sampier, which bears a white Flower. Farther in, the Mould is reddish, a Sort of Sand producing some Grass, Plants, and Shrubs. The Grass grows in great Tufts, as big as a Bushel, here and there a Tuft: Being intermix'd with much Heath, much of the kind we have growing on our Commons in England. Of Trees or Shrubs here are divers Sorts; but none above 10 Foot high: There Bodies about 3 Foot about, and 5 or 6 Foot high before you come to the Branches, which are bushy and compos'd of small Twigs there spreading abroad, tho' thick set, and full of Leaves; which were mostly long and narrow. The Colour of the Leaves was on one Side whitish, and on the other green; and the Bark of the Trees was generally of the same Colour with the Leaves, of a pale green. Some of these Trees were sweet-scented, and reddish within the Bark, like the Sassafras, but redder. Most of the Trees and Shrubs had at this Time either Blossoms or Berries on them. The Blossoms of the different Sort of Trees were of several Colours, as red, white, yellow, &c. but mostly blue: And these generally smelt very sweet and fragrant, as did some also of the rest. There were also beside some Plants, Herbs, and tall Flowers, some very small Flowers, growing on the Ground, that were sweet and beautiful, and for the most part unlike any I had seen elsewhere.

There were but few Land-Fowls; we saw none but Eagles, of the larger Sorts of Birds; but 5 or 6 Sorts of Small Birds. The biggest Sort of these were not bigger than Larks; some no bigger than Wrens, all singing with great Variety of fine shrill Notes; and we saw some of their Nests with young Ones in them. The Water-Fowls are Ducks, (which had young Ones now, this being the Beginning of the Spring in these Parts;) Curlews, Galdens, Crab-catchers, Cormorants, Gulls, Pelicans; and some Water-Fowl, such as I have not seen any where besides. I have given the Pictures of 4 several Birds on this Coast. [See Birds: Fig. 3, 4, 5, 6.]

The Land-Animals that we saw here were only a Sort of Raccoons, different from those of the West-Indies, chiefly as to their Legs; for these have very short Fore-Legs; but go jumping upon them as the others do, (and like them are very good Meat:) And a Sort of Guano's, of the same Shape and Size with other Guano's, describ'd [Vol. I.] but differing from them in 3 remarkable Particulars: For these had a larger and uglier Head,

F. 3.

A Noddy. of N. Holland.

F. 5.

The head & greatest part
of ẏ neck of this bird is
red. & therein differs from
the Avosetta of Italy.

A Comon Noddy

F. 6.

F. 4.

The Bill & Leggs of this Bird are of a Bright Red

and had no Tail: And at the Rump, instead of the Tail there, they had a Stump of a Tail, which appear'd like another Head; but not really such, being without Mouth or Eyes: Yet this Creature seem'd by this Means to have a Head at each End; and, which may be reckon'd a fourth Difference, the Legs also seem'd all 4 of them to be Fore-legs, being all alike in Shape and Length, and seeming by the Joints and Bending to be made as if they were to go indifferently either Head or Tail foremost. They were speckled black and yellow like Toads, and had Scales or Knobs on their Backs like those of Crocodiles, plated on to the Skin, or stuck into it, as part of the Skin. They are very slow in Motion; and when a Man comes nigh them they will stand still and hiss, not endeavouring to get away. Their Livers are also spotted black and yellow: And the Body when opened hath a very unsavory Smell. I did never see such ugly Creatures any where but here. The Guano's I have observ'd to be very good Meat: And I have often eaten of them with Pleasure; but tho' I have eaten of Snakes, Crocodiles and Allegators and many Creatures that look frightfully enough, and there are but few I should have been afraid to eat of, if prest by Hunger, yet I think my Stomach would scarce have serv'd to venture upon these N. Holland Guano's, both the Looks and the Smell of them being so offensive.

The Sea-fish that we saw here (for here was no River, Land or Pond of fresh Water to be seen) are chiefly Sharks. There are Abundance of them in this particular Sound, and I therefore give it the Name of Shark's Bay. Here are also Skates, Thornbacks, and other Fish of the Ray-kind; (one Sort especially like the Sea-Devil) and Gar-fish, Boneta's, &c. Of Shell-fish we got here Muscles, Periwinkles, Limpits, Oysters, both of the Pearl-kind and also Eating-Oysters, as well the common Sort as long Oysters; beside Cockes, &c. The Shore was lined thick with many other sorts of very strange and beautiful Shells, for variety of Colour and Shape, most finely spotted with Red, Black, or Yellow, &c. such as I have not seen any where but at this place. I brought away a great many of them; but lost all, except a very few, and those not of the best.

There are also some green Turtle weighing about 200 lb. Of these we caught 2 which the Water Ebbing had left behind a Ledge of Rock, which they could not creep over. These served all my Company 2 Days; and they were indifferent sweet Meat. Of the Sharks we caught a great many, which our Men eat very savourily. Among them we caught one which was 11 Foot long. The space between its two Eyes was 20 Inches, and 18 Inches from one Corner of his Mouth to the other. Its Maw was like a Leather Sack, very thick, and so tough that a sharp Knife could scarce cut it: In which we found the Head and Boans of a Hippopotamus; the hairy Lips of which were still sound and not putrified, and the Jaw was also firm, out of which we pluckt a great many Teeth, 2 of them 8 Inches long, and as big as a Man's Thumb, small at one end, and a little crooked; the rest not above half so long. The Maw was full of Jelly which stank extreamly: However I saved for a while the Teeth and the Sharks Jaw: The Flesh of it was divided among my Men; and they took care that no waste should be made of it.

'Twas the 7th of August when we came into Shark's Bay; in which we Anchor'd at three several Places, and stay'd at the first of them (on the W. side of the Bay) till the 11th. During which time we searched about, as I said, for fresh Water, digging Wells, but to no purpose. However, we cut good store of Fire-wood at this first Anchoring place; and my Company were all here very well refreshed with Raccoons, Turtle, Shark, and other Fish, and some Fowls; so that we were now all much brisker than when we came in hither. Yet still I was for standing farther into the Bay, partly because I had a Mind to increase my Stock of fresh Water, which was began to be low; and partly for the sake of discovering this Part of the Coast. I was invited to go further, by seeing from this Anchoring-place all open before me; which therefore I designed to search before I left the Bay. So on the 11th about Noon, I steer'd farther in, with an easy Sail, because we had but shallow Water: We kept therefore good looking out for Fear of Shoals; sometimes shortning, sometimes deepning the Water. About 2 in the Afternoon we saw the Land a-Head that makes the S. of the Bay, and before Night we had again Sholdings from that Shore: And therefore shortned Sail and stood off and on all Night, under 2 Topsails, continually sounding, having never more than 10 Fathom, and seldom less than 7. The Water deepned and sholdned so very gently, that in heaving the Lead 5 or 6 Times we should scarce have a Foot difference. When we came into 7 Fathom either way, we presently went about. From this S. part of the Bay, we could not see the Land from whence we came in the Afternoon: And this Land we found to be an Island of 3 or 4 Leagues long, as is seen in the Plan, [Table IV. N°. 6.] but it appearing barren, I did not strive to go nearer it; and the rather because the Winds would not permit us to do it without much Trouble, and at the Openings the Water was generally shoal. I therefore made no farther Attempts in this S.W. and S. part of the Bay, but steered away to the Eastward, to see if there was any Land that Way, for as yet we had seen none there. On the 12th in the Morning we pass'd by the N. Point of that Land and were confirm'd in the Persuasion of its being an Island, by seeing an Opening to the East of it, as we had done on the W. Having fair Weather, a small Gale and smooth Water, we stood further on in the Bay, to see what Land was on the E. of it. Our Soundings at first were 7 Fathom, which held so a great while, but at length it decreas'd to 6. Then we saw the Land right a-head, that in the Plan makes the E. of the Bay. We could not come near it with the Ship, having but Shoal-water; and it being dangerous lying there, and the Land extraordinary low, very unlikely to have fresh Water (though it had a few Trees on it, seemingly Mangroves) and much of it probably covered at High-water, I stood out again that Afternoon, deepning the Water, and before Night anchored in 8 Fathom, clean white Sand, about the Middle of the Bay. The next Day we got up our Anchor; and that Afternoon came to an Anchor once more near 2 Islands, and a Shoal of Coral Rocks that face the Bay. Here I scrubb'd my Ship; and finding it very improbable I should get any thing further here, I made the best of my way out to Sea again, sounding all the way: but finding by the Shallowness of the Water that there was no going out to Sea to the East of the two Islands that face the Bay, nor between them, I return'd to the West Entrance, going out by the same way I came in at, only on the East instead of the West-side of the small Shoal to be seen in the Plan; In which Channel we had 10, 12, and 13 Fathom-water, still deepning upon us till we were out at Sea. The Day before we came out I sent a Boat ashore to the most Northerly of the 2 Islands, which is the least of them, catching many small Fish in the mean while with Hook and Line. The Boat's Crew returning, told me, that the Isle produces nothing but a Sort of green, short, hard, prickly Grass, affording neither Wood nor fresh Water; and that a Sea broke between the 2 Islands, a Sign that the Water was shallow. They saw a large Turtle, and many Skates and Thornbacks, but caught none.

It was August the 14th when I sail'd out of this Bay or Sound, the Mouth of which lies, as I said, in 25 deg. 5. min. designing to coast along to the N.E. 'till I might commodiously put in at some other part of N. Holland. In passing out we saw 3 Water-Serpents swimming about in the Sea, of a yellow Colour, spotted with dark brown Spots. They were each about 4 Foot long, and about the Bigness of a Man's Wrist, and were the first I saw on this Coast, which abounds with several Sorts of them. We had the Winds at

our first coming out at N. and the Land lying North-Easterly. We plied off
and on, getting forward but little till the next Day: when the Wind coming
at S.S.W. and S. we began to coast it along the Shore to the Northward,
keeping at 6 or 7 Leagues off Shore; and sounding often, we had between 40
and 46 Fathom-water, brown Sand, with some white Shells. This 15th of
August we were in Lat. 24 deg. 41 min. On the 16th Day at Noon we were
in 23 deg. 22. min. The Wind coming at E. by N. we could not keep the
Shore aboard, but were forc'd to go farther off, and lost Sight of the Land.
Then sounding we had no Ground with 80 Fathom-line; however the Wind
shortly after came about again to the Southward, and then we jogg'd on
again to the Northward, and saw many small Dolphins and Whales, and
Abundance of Scuttle-shells swimming on the Sea; and some Water-snakes
every Day. The 17th we saw the Land again, and took a Sight of it. [See
Table. IV. N°. 7.]

The 18th in the Afternoon, being 3 or 4 Leagues off Shore, I saw a
Shoal-point, stretching from the Land into the Sea, a League or more. The
Sea broke high on it; by which I saw plainly there was a Shoal there. I stood
farther off, and coasted along Shore, to about 7 or 8 Leagues distance: And
at 12 a Clock at Night we sounded, and had but 20 Fathom, hard Sand. By
this I found I was upon another Shoal, and so presently steered off W. half
an Hour, and had then 40 Fathom. At One in the Morning of the 18th Day
we had 85 Fathom: By two we could find no Ground; and then I ventur'd to
steer along Shore again, due N. which is two Points wide of the Coast (that
lies N.N.E.) for fear of another Shoal. I would not be too far off from the
Land, being desirous to search into it where-ever I should find an Opening
or any Convenience of searching about for Water, &c. When we were off
the Shoal-point I mention'd where we had but 20 Fathom-water, we had in
the Night Abundance of Whales about the Ship, some a-head, others a-stern,
and some on each side blowing and making a very dismal Noise; but when
we came out again into deeper Water they left us. Indeed the Noise that they
made by blowing and dashing of the Sea with their Tails, making it all of a
Breach and Foam, was very dreadful to us, like the Breach of the Waves in
very Shoal-water, or among Rocks. The Shoal these Whales were upon had
Depth of Water sufficient, no less than 20 Fathom, as I said; and it lies in
Lat. 22 deg. 22 min. The Shore was generally bold all along; we had met
with no Shoal at Sea since the Abrohlo-shoal, when we first fell on the N.
Holland Coast in the Lat. of 28, till Yesterday in the Afternoon, and this

Night. This Morning also when we expected by the Draught we had with us to have been 11 Leagues off Shore, we were but 4; so that either our Draughts were faulty, which yet hitherto and afterwards we found true enough as to the lying of the Coast, or else here was a Tide unknown to us that deceived us; tho' we had found very little of any Tide on this Coast hitherto. As to our Winds in the Coasting thus far, as we had been within the Verge of the general Trade (tho' interrupted by the Storm I mention'd) from the Lat. of 28, when we first fell in with the Coast: And by that Time we were in the Lat. of 25. we had usually the regular Trade-wind (which is here S.S.E.) when we were at any Distance from Shore: But we had often Sea and Land-Breezes, especially when near Shore, and when in Shark's-bay; and had a particular N. West Wind, or Storm, that set us in thither. On this 18th of August we coasted with a brisk Gale of the true Trade-wind at S.S.E. very fair and clear Weather; but haling off in the Evening to Sea, were next Morning out of Sight of Land; and the Land now trending away N. Easterly, and we being to the Norward of it, and the Wind also shrinking from the S.S.E. to the E.S.E. (that is, from the true Trade-Wind to the Sea-breeze, as the Land now lay) we could not get in with the Land again yet a-while, so as to see it, tho' we trim'd sharp and kept close on a Wind. We were this 19th day in Lat. 21 deg. 42 min. The 20th we were in Lat. 19 deg. 37 min. and kept close on a Wind to get Sight of the Land again, but could not yet see it. We had very fair Weather; and tho' we were so far from the Land as to be out of Sight of it, yet we had the Sea and Land-Breezes. In the Night we had the Land-Breeze at S.S.E. a small gentle Gale; which in the Morning about Sun-rising would shift about gradually (and withal increasing in Strength) till about Noon we should have it at E.S.E. which is the true Sea-breeze here. Then it would blow a brisk Gale, so that we could scarce carry our Top-sails double rift: And it would continue thus till 3 in the Afternoon, when it would decrease again. The Weather was fair all the while, not a Cloud to be seen; but very hazy, especially nigh the Horizon. We sounded several Times this 20th Day, and at first had no Ground; but had afterwards from 52 to 45 Fathom, coarse brown Sand, mixt with small brown and white Stones, with Dints besides in the *Tallow.

The 21st Day also we had small Land-breezes in the Night, and Sea-

---

* Part of the lead sounding weight.

breezes in the Day: And as we saw some Sea-snakes every Day, so this Day we saw a great many, of two different Sorts or Shapes. One Sort was yellow, and about the Bigness of a Man's Wrist, about 4 Foot long, having a flat Tail about 4 Fingers broad. The other Sort was much smaller and shorter, round and spotted black and yellow. This Day we sounded several Times, and had 45 Fathom Sand. We did not make the Land till Noon, and then saw it first from our Topmast-head. It bore S.E. by E. about 9 Leagues distance; and it appeared like a Cape or Head of Land. The Sea-breeze this Day was not so strong as the Day before, and it veered out more; so that we had a fair Wind to run in with to the Shore, and at Sunset anchored in 20 Fathom, clean Sand, about 5 Leagues from the bluff Point; which was not a Cape (as it appear'd at a great Distance) but the Eastermost End of an Island, about 5 or 6 Leagues in length, and 1 in breadth. There were 3 or 4 Rocky Islands about a League from us between us and the bluff Point; and we saw many other Islands both to the East and West of it, as far as we could see either way from our Topmast-head: And all within them to the S. there was nothing but Islands of a pretty Heighth, that may be seen 8 or 9 Leagues off. By what we saw of them they must have been a Range of Islands of about 20 Leagues in length, stretching from E.N.E. to W.S.W. and for ought I know, as far as to those of Shark's-Bay; and to a considerable Breadth also, (for we could see 9 or 10 Leagues in among them) towards the Continent or main Land of N. Holland, if there be any such Thing hereabouts: And by the great Tides I met with a while afterwards, more to the N. East, I had a strong Suspicion that here might be a kind of Archipelago of Islands, and a Passage possibly to the S. of N. Holland and N. Guinea into the great S. Sea Eastward; which I had Thoughts also of attempting in my Return from N. Guinea (had Circumstances permitted) and told my Officers so: But I would not attempt it at this Time, because we wanted Water, and could not depend upon finding it there. This Place is in the Lat. of 20 deg. 21 min. but in the Draught that I had of this Coast, which was Tasman's, it was laid down in 19 deg. 50 min. and the Shore is laid down as all along joining in one Body or Continent, with some Openings appearing like Rivers; and not like Islands, as really they are. See several Sights of it, Table IV. N°. 8, 9, 10. This Place lies more Northerly by 40 min. than is laid down in Mr. Tasman's Draught: And beside its being made a firm, continued Land, only with some Openings like the Mouths of Rivers, I found the Soundings also different from what the prick'd Line of his Course

shews them, and generally shallower than he makes them; which inclines me
to think that he came not so near the Shore as his Line shews, and so had
deeper Soundings, and could not so well distinguish the Islands. His
Meridian or Difference of Longitude from Shark's-Bay agrees well enough
with my Account, which is 232 Leagues, tho' we differ in Lat. And to
confirm my Conjecture that the Line of his Course is made too near the
Shore, at least not far to the East of this Place, the Water is there so shallow
that he could not come there so nigh.

But to proceed; in the Night we had a small Land-breeze, and in the
Morning I weighed Anchor, designing to run in among the Islands, for
they had large Channels between them, of a League wide at least, and some
2 or 3 Leagues wide. I sent in my Boat before to sound, and if they found
Shoal-water to return again; but if they found Water enough, to go ashore
on one of the Islands, and stay till the Ship came in: where they might in the
mean Time search for Water. So we followed after with the Ship, sounding
as we went in, and had 20 Fathom, till within 2 Leagues of the Bluff-head,
and then we had shoal Water, and very uncertain Soundings: Yet we ran in
still with an easy Sail, sounding and looking out well, for this was dangerous
Work. When we came abreast of the Bluff-head, and about 2 Mile from it,
we had but 7 Fathom: Then we edg'd away from it, but had no more Water;
and running in a little farther, we had but 4 Fathoms; so we anchored
immediately; and yet when we had veered out a third of a Cable we had 7
Fathom Water again; so uncertain was the Water. My Boat came
immediately aboard, and told me that the Island was very rocky and dry,
and they had little Hopes of finding Water there. I sent them to sound, and
bad them, if they found a Channel of 8 or 10 Fathom Water, to keep on,
and we would follow with the Ship. We were now about 4 Leagues within
the outer small rocky Islands, but still could see nothing but Islands within
us; some 5 or 6 Leagues long, others not above a Mile round. The large
Islands were pretty high; but all appeared dry, and mostly rocky and barren.
The Rocks look'd of a rusty yellow Colour, and therefore I despair'd of
getting Water on any of them; but was in some Hopes of finding a Channel
to run in beyond all these Islands, could I have spent Time here, and either
get to the Main of New Holland, or find out some other Islands that might
afford us Water and other Refreshments; Besides, that among so many
Islands, we might have found some Sort of rich Mineral, or Ambergreece,
it being a good Latitude for both these. But we had not sailed above a

League farther before our Water grew shoaler again, and then we anchored in 6 Fathom hard Sand.

We were now on the inner Side of the Island, on whose out-side is the Bluff-point. We rode a League from the Island, and I presently went ashore, and carried Shovels to dig for Water, but found none. There grow here 2 or 3 Sorts of Shrubs, one just like Rosemary; and therefore I called this Rosemary Island. It grew in great Plenty here, but had no Smell. Some of the other Shrubs had blue and yellow Flowers; and we found 2 Sorts of Grain like Beans: The one grew on Bushes; the other on a Sort of a creeping Vine that runs along on the Ground, having very thick broad Leaves, and the Blossom like a Bean Blossom, but much larger, and of a deep red Colour, looking very beautiful. We saw here some Cormorants, Gulls, Crabcatchers, &c. a few small Land-Birds, and a Sort of white Parrots, which flew a great many together. We found some Shell-fish, *viz.* Limpits, Perriwinkles, and Abundance of small Oysters growing on the Rocks, which were very sweet. In the Sea we saw some green Turtle, a pretty many Sharks, and Abundance of Water-Snakes of several Sorts and Sizes. The Stones were all of rusty Colour, and ponderous.

We saw a Smoak on an Island 3 or 4 Leagues off; and here also the Bushes had been burned, but we found no other Sign of Inhabitants: 'Twas probable that on the Island where the Smoak was there were Inhabitants, and fresh Water for them. In the Evening I went aboard, and consulted with my Officers whether it was best to send thither, or to search among any other of these Islands with my Boat; or else go from hence, and coast along Shore with the Ship, till we could find some better Place than this was to ride in, where we had shoal Water, and lay expos'd to Winds and Tides. They all agreed to go from hence; so I gave Orders to weigh in the Morning as soon as it should be light, and to get out with the Land-breeze.

According, August the 23rd, at 5 in the Morning we ran out, having a pretty fresh Land-breeze at S.S.E. By 8 a Clock we were got out, and very seasonably; for before 9 the Sea-breeze came on us very strong, and increasing, we took in our Top-sails and stood off under 2 Courses and a Mizen, this being as much Sail as we could carry. The Sky was clear, there being not one Cloud to be seen; but the Horizon appeared very hazy, and the Sun at setting the Night before, and this Morning at rising, appeared very red. The Wind continued very strong till 12, then it began to abate: I have seldom met with a stronger Breeze. These strong Sea-breezes lasted

A Fish taken on the Coast of New Holland.

F.3.

A Cuttle taken near N. Holland.

F.8.

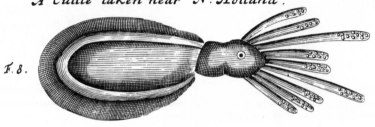

The Monk Fish.

F.1.

A Flying Fish taken
in ye open Sea

F.9.

F.6.

A Remora taken sticking to Sharks backs.

thus in their Turns 3 or 4 Days. They sprung up with the Sun-rise; by 9 a Clock they were very strong, and so continued till Noon, when they began to abate; and by Sunset there was little Wind, or a Calm till the Land-breezes came; which we should certainly have in the Morning about 1 or 2 a Clock. The Land-breezes were between the S.S.W. and S.S.E. The Sea-breezes between the E.N.E. and N.N.E. In the Night while Calm, we fish'd with Hook and Line, and caught good Store of Fish, *viz.* Snappers, Breams, Old-Wives and Dog-fish. When these last came we seldom caught any others; for if they did not drive away the other Fish, yet they would be sure to keep them from taking our Hooks, for they would first have them themselves, biting very greedily. We caught also a Monk-fish, of which I brought Home the Picture. See Fish, Fig. I.

On the 25th of August, we still coasted along Shore, that we might the better see any Opening; kept sounding, and had about 20 Fathom clean Sand. The 26th Day, being about 4 Leagues off Shore, the Water began gradually to sholden from 20 to 14 Fathom. I was edging in a little towards the Land, thinking to have anchored; but presently after the Water decreas'd almost at once, till we had but 5 Fathom. I durst therefore adventure no farther, but steer'd out the same way that we came in; and in a short Time had 10 Fathom (being then about 4 Leagues and a half from the Shore) and even Soundings. I steer'd away E.N.E. coasting along as the Land lies. This Day the Sea-breezes began to be very moderate again, and we made the best of our way along Shore, only in the Night edging off a little for Fear of Sholes. Ever since we left Shark's-Bay we had fair clear Weather, and so for a great while still.

The 27th Day, we had 20 Fathom Water all Night, yet we could not see Land till 1 in the Afternoon from our Topmast-head. By 3 we could just discern Land from our Quarter-deck; we had then 16 Fathom. The Wind was at N. and we steer'd E. by N. which is but one Point in on the Land; yet we decreas'd our Water very fast; for at 4 we had but 9 Fathom; the next Cast but 7, which frighted us; and we then tackt instantly and stood off: But in a short Time the Wind coming at N.W. and W.N.W. we tackt again, and steer'd N.N.E. and then deepned our Water again, and had all Night from 15 to 20 Fathom.

The 28th Day we had between 20 and 40 Fathom. We saw no Land this Day, but saw a great many Snakes and some Whales. We saw also some Boobies, and Noddy-birds; and in the Night caught one of these last. It was of another Shape and Colour than any I had seen before. It had a small long Bill, as all of them have, flat Feet like Ducks Feet; its Tail forked like a Swallow, but longer and broader, and the Fork deeper than that of the Swallow, with very long Wings; the Top or Crown of the Head of this Noddy was Coal-black, having also small black Streaks round about and close to the Eyes; and round these Streaks on each Side, a pretty broad white Circle. The Breast, Belly, and underpart of the Wings of this Noddy were white; and the Back and upper-part of its Wings of a faint black or smoak Colour. See a Picture of this, and of the common one, Birds, Fig. 5, 6. Noddies are seen in most Places between the Tropicks, as well in the East-Indies, and on the Coast of Brazil, as in the West-Indies. They rest ashore a Nights, and therefore we never see them far at Sea, not above 20 or 30 Leagues, unless driven off in a Storm. When they come about a Ship they commonly perch in the Night, and will sit still till they are taken by the Seamen. They build on Cliffs against the Sea, or Rocks, as I have said [Vol. I.].

The 30th day, being in Lat. 18 deg. 21 min. we made the Land again, and saw many great Smokes near the Shore; and having fair Weather and moderate Breezes, I steer'd in towards it. At 4 in the Afternoon I anchor'd in 8 Fathom Water, clear Sand, about 3 Leagues and a half from the Shore. I presently sent my Boat to sound nearer in, and they found 10 Fathom about a Mile farther in; and from thence still farther in the Water decreased gradually to 9, 8, 7, and at 2 Mile distance to 6 Fathom. This Evening we saw an Eclipse of the Moon, but it was abating before the Moon appear'd to us; for the Horizon was very hazy, so that we could not see the Moon till she had been half an Hour above the Horizon: And at 2 hours, 22 min. after Sun-set, by the Reckoning of our Glasses, the Eclipse was quite gone, which was not of many Digits. The Moon's Center was then 33 deg. 40 min. high.

The 31st of August betimes in the Morning I went ashore with 10 or 11 Men to search for Water. We went armed with Muskets and Cutlasses for our defence, expecting to see people there; and carried also Shovels and Pickaxes to dig Wells. When we came near the Shore we saw 3 tall black naked Men on the sandy Bay a-head of us: But as we row'd in, they went away. When we were landed, I sent the Boat with two Men in her to lie a little from the Shore at an Anchor, to prevent being seiz'd; while the rest of us went after the 3 black Men, who were now got on the top of a small Hill about a quarter of a Mile from us, with 8 or 9 Men more in their Company. They seeing us coming, ran away. When we came on the top of the Hill where they first stood, we saw a plain Savannah, about half a Mile from us, farther in from the Sea. There were several Things like Haycocks, standing in the Savannah; which at a distance we thought were Houses, looking just like the Hottentot's Houses at the Cape of G. Hope: but we found them to be so many Rocks. We searched about these for Water, but could find none, nor any Houses; nor People, for they were all gone. Then we turned again to the Place where we landed, and there we dug for Water.

While we were at work there came 9 or 10 of the Natives to a small Hill a little way from us, and stood there menacing and threatning of us, and making a great Noise. At last one of them came towards us, and the rest followed at a distance. I went out to meet him, and came within 50 Yards of him, making to him all the Signs of Peace and Friendship I could; but then he ran away, neither would they any of them stay for us to come nigh them; for we tried two or three Times. At last I took two Men with me, and went in the Afternoon along by the Sea-side, purposely to catch one of them, if I could, of whom I might learn where they got their fresh Water. There were 10 or 12 of the Natives a little way off, who seeing us three going away from the rest of our Men, followed us at a distance. I thought they would follow us: But there being for a while a Sand-bank between us and them, that they could not then see us, we made a halt, and hid our selves in a bending of the Sand-bank. They knew we must be thereabouts, and being 3 or 4 times our Number, thought to seize us. So they dispers'd themselves, some going to the Seashore, and others beating about the Sand-hills. We knew by what Rencounter we had had with them in the Morning that we could easily out-run them; So a nimble young Man that was with me, seeing some of them near, ran towards them; and they for some time, ran away before him. But he soon over-taking them, they faced about and fought him. He had a Cutlass, and they had wooden Lances; with which, being many of them, they were too hard for him. When he first ran towards them I chas'd two more that were by the Shore; But fearing how it might be with my young Man, I turn'd back quickly, and went up to the top of a Sandhill, whence I saw him near me, closely engag'd with them. Upon their seeing me, one of them threw a Lance at me, that narrowly miss'd me. I discharg'd my Gun to scare them, but avoided shooting any of them; till finding the

young Man in great danger from them, and my self in some; and that tho'
the Gun had a little frighted them at first, yet they had soon learnt to despise
it, tossing up their Hands, and crying *Pooh, Pooh, Pooh*; and coming on
afresh with a great Noise, I thought it high time to charge again, and shoot
one of them, which I did. The rest, seeing him fall, made a stand again; and
my young Man took the Opportunity to disengage himself, and come off to
me; my other Man also was with me, who had done nothing all this while,
having come out unarm'd; and I return'd back with my Men, designing to
attempt the Natives no farther, being very sorry for what had happened
already. They took up their wounded Companion; and my young Man, who
had been struck though the Cheek by one of their Lances, was afraid it had
been poison'd: But I did not think that likely. His Wound was very painful
to him, being made with a blunt Weapon: But he soon recover'd of it.

Among the N. Hollanders, whom we were thus engag'd with, there was
one who by his Appearance and Carriage, as well in the Morning as this
Afternoon, seem'd to be the Chief of them, and a kind of Prince or Captain
among them. He was a young brisk Man, not very tall, nor so personable as
some of the rest, tho' more active and couragious: He was painted (which
none of the rest were at all) with a Circle of white Paste or Pigment (a sort
of Lime, as we thought) about his Eyes, and a white streak down his Nose
from his Forehead to the tip of it. And his Breast and some part of his Arms
were also made white with the same Paint; not for Beauty or Ornament, one
would think, but as some wild Indian Warriors are said to do, he seem'd
thereby to design the looking more Terrible; this his Painting adding very
much to his natural Deformity; for they all of them have the most unpleasant
Looks and the worst Features of any People that ever I saw, tho' I have seen
great variety of Savages. These New-Hollanders were probably the same
sort of People as those I met with on this Coast in my *Voyage round the
World*; [See Vol. I.] for the Place I then touched at was not above 40 or 50
Leagues to the N.E. of this: And these were much the same blinking
Creatures (here being also abundance of the same kind of Flesh-flies teizing
them) and with the same black Skins, and Hair frizled, tall and thin, &c. as
those were: But we had not the Opportunity to see whether these, as the
former, wanted two of their Fore-Teeth.

We saw a great many places where they had made Fires; and where there
were commonly 3 or 4 Boughs stuck up to Windward of them; for the
Wind (which is the Sea-breeze) in the day-time blows always one way with

them; and the Land-breeze is but small. By their Fire-places we should always find great heaps of Fish-shells, of several sorts; and 'tis probable that these poor Creatures here lived chiefly on the Shell-fish, as those I before describ'd did on small Fish, which they caught in Wires or Holes in the Sand at Low-water. These gather'd their Shell-fish on the Rocks at Low-water; but had no Wires (that we saw) whereby to get any other sorts of Fish: As among the former I saw not any heaps of Shells as here, though I know they also gather'd some Shell-fish. The Lances also of those were such as these had; however they being upon an Island, with their Women and Children, and all in our Power, they did not there use them against us, as here on the Continent, where we saw none but some of the Men under Head, who come out purposely to observe us. We saw no Houses at either Place; and I believe they have none, since the former People on the Island had none, tho' they had all their Families with them.

Upon returning to my Men I saw that tho' they had dug 8 or 9 Foot deep, yet found no Water. So I returned aboard that Evening, and the next day being September 1st, I sent my Boatswain ashore to dig deeper, and sent the Sain with him to catch Fish. While I staid aboard I observed the flowing of the Tide, which runs very swift here, so that our Nun-buoy would not bear above the Water to be seen. It flows here (as on that part of N. Holland I described formerly) about 5 Fathom: And here the Flood runs S.E. by S. till the last Quarter; then it sets right in towards the Shore (which lies here S.S.W. and N.N.E.) and the Ebb runs N.W. by N. When the Tides slackned we fish'd with Hook and Line, as we had already done in several Places on this Coast; on which in this Voyage hitherto, we had found but little Tides: But by the Heighth, and Strength, and Course of them here-abouts, it should seem that if there be such a Passage or Streight going through Eastward to the Great South-Sea, as I said one might suspect, one would expect to find the Mouth of it somewhere between this Place and Rosemary Island, which was the part of New Holland I came last from.

Next Morning my Men came aboard and brought a Rundlet of brackish Water which they got out of another Well that they dug in a Place a mile off, and about half as far from the Shore; but this Water was not fit to drink. However we all concluded that it would serve to boil our Oatmeal, for Burgoo, whereby we might save the Remains of our other Water for drinking, till we should get more; and accordingly the next Day we brought aboard 4 Hogsheads of it: But while we were at work about the Well we were sadly pester'd with the Flies, which were more troublesome to us than the Sun, tho' it shone clear and strong upon us all the while, very hot. All this while we saw no more of the Natives, but saw some of the Smoaks of some of their Fires at 2 or 3 miles distance.

The Land hereabouts was much like the part of New Holland that I formerly described [Vol. I.], 'tis low, but seemingly barricado'd with a long Chain of Sand-hills to the Sea, that let's nothing be seen of what is farther within Land. At high Water the Tides rising so high as they do, the Coast shews very low; but when 'tis low Water it seems to be of an indifferent heighth. At low Water-mark the Shore is all Rocky, so that then there is no Landing with a Boat: but at high Water a Boat may come in over those Rocks to the Sandy Bay, which runs all along on this Coast. The Land by the Sea for about 5 or 600 yards is a dry Sandy Soil, bearing only Shrubs and Bushes of divers sorts. Some of these had them at this time of the Year, yellow Flowers or Blossoms, some blue, and some white; most of them of a very fragrant Smell. Some had Fruit like Peascods; in each of which there were just ten small Peas; I opened many of them, and found no more nor less. There are also here some of that sort of Bean which I saw at Rosemary-Island: And another sort of small, red, hard Pulse, growing in Cods also, with little black Eyes like Beans. I know not their Names, but have seen them used often in the East-Indies for weighing Gold; and they make the same use of them at Guinea, as I have heard, where the Women also make Bracelets with them to wear about their Arms. These grow on Bushes; but here are also a Fruit like Beans growing on a creeping sort of Shrub-like Vine. There was great plenty of all these sorts of Cod-fruit growing on the Sand-hills by the Sea-side, some of them green, some ripe, and some fallen on the Ground: But I could not perceive that any of them had been gathered by the Natives; and might not probably be wholesome Food.

The Land farther in, that is lower than what borders on the Sea, was so much as we saw of it, very plain and even; partly Savannahs, and partly Woodland. The Savannahs bear a sort of thin coarse Grass. The Mould is also a coarser Sand than that by the Sea-side, and in some places 'tis Clay. Here are a great many Rocks in the large Savannah we were in, which are 5 or 6 Foot high, and round at top like a Hay-cock, very remarkable; some red, and some white. The Woodland lies farther in still; where there were divers sorts of small Trees, scarce any three Foot in circumference; their Bodies 12 or 14 Foot high, with a Head of small Knibs or Boughs. By the sides of the Creeks, especially nigh the Sea, there grow a few small black Mangrove-Trees.

There are but few Land-Animals. I saw some Lizards; and my Men saw two or three Beasts like hungry Wolves, lean like so many Skeletons, being nothing but Skin and Bones: 'Tis probable that it was the Foot of one of those Beasts that I mention'd as seen by us in N. Holland, [Vol. I.]. We saw a Rackoon or two, and one small speckled Snake.

The Land-fowls that we saw here were Crows (just such as ours in England) small Hawks, and Kites; a few of each sort: But here are plenty of small Turtle-Doves, that are plump, fat and very good Meat. Here are 2 or 3 sorts of smaller Birds, some as big as Larks, some less; but not many of either sort. The Sea-Fowl are Pelicans, Boobies, Noddies, Curlews, Sea-pies, &c. and but few of these neither.

The Sea is plentifully stock'd with the largest Whales that I ever saw; but not to compare with the vast ones of the Northern Seas. We saw also a great many Green Turle, but caught none; here being no place to set a Turtle-Net in; here being no Channel for them, and the Tides running so strong. We saw some Sharks, and Parracoots; and with Hooks and Lines we caught some Rock-fish and Old-Wives. Of Shell-fish, here were Oysters both of the common kind for Eating, and of the Pearl kind: And also Wilks, Conchs, Muscles, Limpits, Perriwinkles, &c. and I gather'd a few strange Shells; chiefly a sort not large, and thick-set all about with Rays or Spikes growing in Rows.

And thus having ranged about, a considerable time, upon this Coast, without finding any good fresh Water, or any convenient Place to clean the Ship, as I had hop'd for: And it being moreover the heighth of the dry Season, and my Men growing Scorbutick for want of Refreshments, so that I had little incouragement to search further; I resolved to leave this Coast, and accordingly in the beginning of September set sail towards Timor.

AN ACCOUNT OF SEVERAL PLANTS

Collected in

Brazil, New Holland, Timor, and New Guinea, referring to the Figures Engraven on the Copper Plates.

Tab 1. Fig. 1. Cotton-flower from *Baya in Brazil. The Flower consists of a great many Filaments, almost as small as Hairs, betwixt three and four Inches long, of a Murrey-colour; on the Top of them stand small ash-colour'd Apices. The Pedicule of the Flower is inclos'd at the Bottom with 5 narrow stiff Leaves, about 6 Inches long. There is one of this Genus in Mr. Ray's Supplement, which agrees exactly with this in every Respect, only that is twice larger at the least. It was sent from Surinam by the Name of Momoo.

Tab. 1. Fig. 2. *Jasminum Brasilanum luteum, mali limoniae folio nervoso, petalis crassis.*

Tab. 1. Fig. 3. *Crista Pavonis Brasiliana Bardanae foliis.* The Leaves are very tender and like the top Leaves of *Bardana major*, both as to Shape and Texture: In the Figure they are represented too stiff and too much serrated.

Tab. 1. Fig. 4. *Filix Brasiliana Osmundae minori serrato folio.* This fern is of that Kind, which bears its Seed-Vessels in Lines on the Edge of the Leaves.

Tab. 2. Fig. 1. *Rapuntium Novae Hollandiae, flore magno coccineo.* The Perianthium compos'd of five long-pointed Parts, the Form of the Seed-Vessel and the Smallness of the Seeds, together with the irregular Shape of the Flower and Thinness of the Leaves, argue this Plant to be a Rapuntium.

Tab. 2. Fig. 2. *Fucus foliis capillaceis brevissimis, vesiculis minimis donatis.* This elegant Fucus is of the *Erica Marina* or *Sargazo* kind, but has much

* Bahia

Table 1   Plants

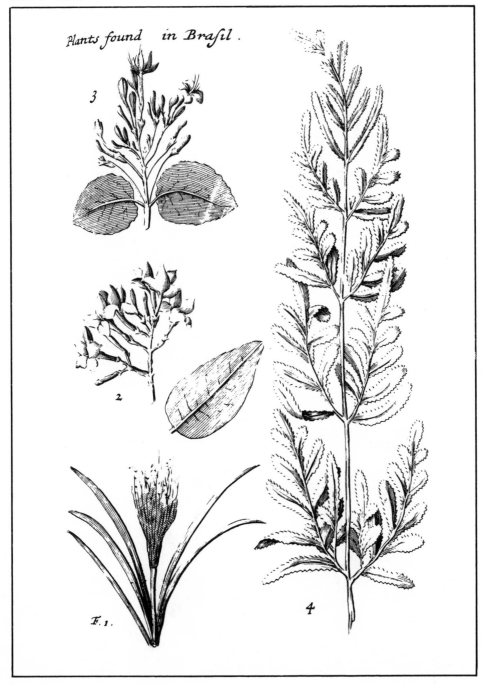

Plants found in Brasil.

Table 2   Plants

Plants found in New Holland.

F. 1.

2.

4

3

finer Parts than that. It was collected on this Coast of New Holland.

Tab. 2. Fig. 3. *Ricinoides Novæ Hollandiæ anguloso crasso folio.* This Plant is shrubby, has thick woolly Leaves, especially on the under side. Its Fruit is tricoccous, hoary on the out-side with a Calix divided into 5 Parts. It comes near *Ricini fructu parvo frucosa Curassavica, folio Phylli, P.B. pr.*

Tab. 2. Fig. 4. *Solanum spinosum Novæ Hollandiæ Phylli foliis subrotundis.* This new Solanum bears a blueish Flower like the others of the same Tribe; the Leaves are of a whitish Colour, thick and woolly on both Sides, scarce an Inch long and near as broad. The Thorns are very sharp and thick set, of a deep Orange colour, especially towards the Points.

Tab. 3. Fig. 1. *Scabiosa (forte) Novæ Hollandiæ, statices foliis subtus argenteis.* The Flower stands on a Foot-stalk 4 Inches long, incuded in a rough Calix of a yellowish Colour. The Leaves are not above an Inch long, very narrow like Thrift, green on the upper and hoary on the under side, growing in Tufts. Whether this Plant be a Scabious, Thrift or Helichrysum is hard to judge from the imperfect Flower of the dry'd Specimen.

Tab. 3. Fig. 2. *Alcea Novæ Hollandiæ foliis augustis utrinque villosis.* The Leaves, Stalk, and under side of the Perianthium of this Plant are all woolly. The Petala are very tender, 5 in Number, scarce so large as the Calix: In the middle stands a Columella thick set with thrummy apiculæ, which argue this Plant to belong to the Malvaceous Kind.

Tab. 3. Fig. 3. Of what Genus this Shrub or Tree is, is uncertain, agreeing with none yet described, as far as can be judg'd by the State it is in. It has a very beautiful Flower, of a red Colour, as far as can be guess'd by the dry Specimen, consisting of 10 large Petala, hoary on both Sides, especially underneath; the Middle of the Flower is thick set with Stamina, which are woolly at the Bottom, the Length of the Petala, each of them crown'd with its Apex. The Calix is divided into 5 Round pointed Parts. The Leaves are like those of *Amelanchier Lob.* green at Top and very woolly underneath, not running to a Point, as is common in others, but with an Indenture at the upper-end.

Tab. 3. Fig. 4. *Dammara ax Nova-Hollandia, Sanamundæ secundæ Chysii foliis.* This new Genus was first sent from Amboyna by Mr. Rumphius, by the Name of Dammara, of which he transmitted 2 Kinds; one with narrow and long stiff Leaves, the other with shorter and broader. The first of them is mention'd in Mr. Petiver's *Centuria,* p. 350. by the Name of *Arbor Hortensis Javanorum foliis visce augustioribus aromaticis floribus, spicatis*

Table 3   Plants

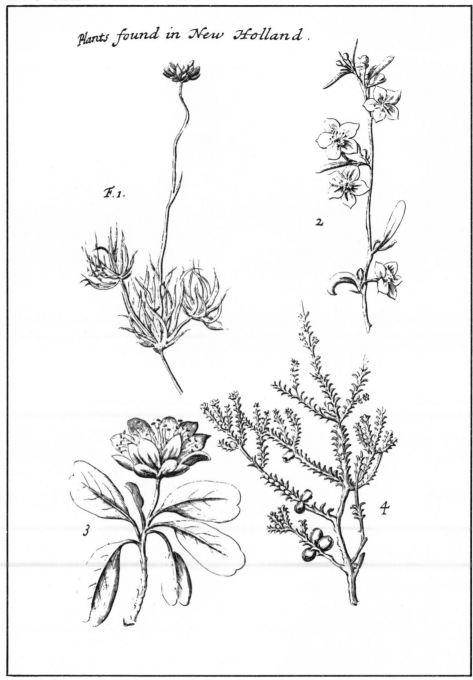

Plants found in New Holland.

F.1.

2

3

4

Table 4   Plants

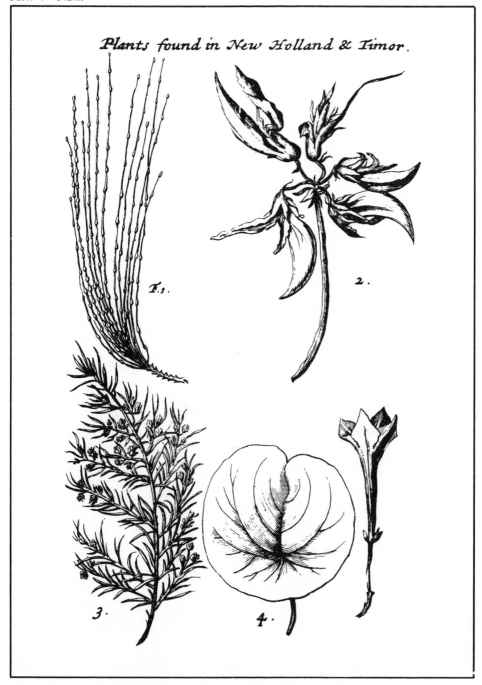

Plants found in New Holland & Timor.

1.
2.
3.
4.

Table 5   Plants

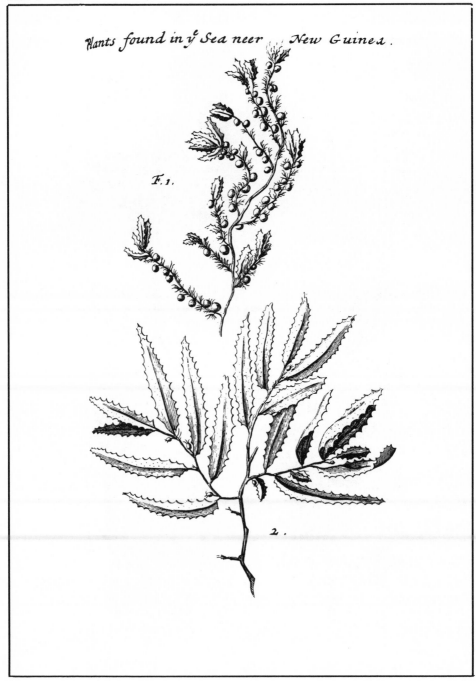

Plants found in y.e Sea neer   New Guinea.

F. 1.

2.

flamineis lutescentibus; Mus. Pet. As also in Mr. Ray's Supplement to his History of Plants now in the Press. This is of the same Genus with them, agreeing both in Flower and Fruit, tho' very much differing in Leaves. The Flowers are stamineous and seem to be of an herbaceous Colour, growing among the Leaves, which are short and almost round, very stiff and ribb'd on the under side, of a dark Green above, and a Pale Colour underneath, thick set on by Pairs, answering one another crossways, so that they cover the Stalk. The Fruit is as big as a Pepper-corn, almost round, of a whitish Colour, dry and tough, with a Hole on the Top, containing small Seeds. Any one that sees this Plant without its Seed-Vessels, would take it for an Erica or Sanamunda. The Leaves of this Plant are of a very aromatick Taste.

Tab. 4. Fig. 1. *Equisetum Novæ Hollandiæ frutesceus foliis longissimis.* 'Tis doubtful whether this be an Equisetum or not; the Textures of the Leaves agrees best with that Genus of any, being articulated one within another at each Joint, which is only proper to this Tribe. The longest of them are about 9 Inches.

Tab. 4. Fig. 2. *Colutea Novæ Hollandiæ floribus amplis coccineis, umbellatim dispositis macula purpurea notatis.* There being no Leaves to this Plant, 'tis hard to say what Genus it properly belongs to. The Flowers are very like to the *Colutea Barbæ Jovis folio flore coccineo Breynii*; of the same Scarlet Colour, with a large deep Purple Spot in the Vexillum, but much bigger, coming all from the same Point after the Manner of an Umbel. The Rudiment of the Pod is very woolly, and terminates in a Filament near 2 Inches long.

Tab. 4. Fig. 3. *Conyza Novæ Hollandiæ angustis Rorismarini foliis.* This Plant is very much branch'd and seems to be woody. The Flowers stand on very short Pedicules, arising from the Sinus of the Leaves, which are exactly like Rosemary, only less. It tastes very bitter now dry.

Tab. 4. Fig. 4. *Mohoh Insulæ Timor.* This is a very odd Plant, agreeing with no describ'd Genus. The Leaf is almost round, green on the upper side and whitish underneath, with several Fibres running from the Insertion of the Pedicule towards the Circumference 'tis umbilicated as *Cotyledon aquatica* and *Faba Ægyptia*. The Flowers are white, standing on single Foot-stalks, of the Shape of a Stramonium, but divided into 4 Points only, as is the Perianthium.

Tab. 5. Fig. 1. *Fucus ex Nova Guinea uva marina dictus, foliis variis.*

This beautiful Fucus is thick set with very small short Tufts of Leaves, which by the Help of a magnifying Glass, seem to be round and articulated, as if they were Seed-Vessels; besides these, there are other broad Leaves, chiefly at the Extremity of the Branches, serrated on the Edges. The Vesiculæ are round, of the Bigness express'd in the Figure.

Tab. 5. Fig. 2. *Fucus ex Nova Guinea Fluviatilis Pisanæ J.B. foliis.* These Plants are so apt to vary in their Leaves, according to their different States, that 'tis hard to say this is distinct from the last. It has in several Places (not all express'd in the Figure) some of the small short Leaves, or Seed-Vessels mention'd in the former; which makes me apt to believe it the same, gather'd in a different State; besides the broad Leaves of that and this agree as to their Shape and Indentures.

AN ACCOUNT OF SOME FISHES

That are figured in Plate 2 and 3

Plate 3. Fig. 5.

This is a Fish of the Tunny-kind, and agrees well enough with the Figure in Tab. 3. of the Appendix to Mr. Willughby's History of Fishes under the Name of Gurabuca; it differs something, in the Fins especially, from Piso's Figure of the Guarapuca.

Plate 3. Fig. 4.

This resembles the Figure of the *Guaperva maxima candata* in Willughby's *Ichthyol.* Tab. 9. 23. and the Guaparva of Piso, but does not answer their Figures in every particular.

Plate 2. Fig. 2.

There are 2 Sorts of Porpusses: The one the long-snouted Porpuss, as the Seamen call it; and this is the Dolphin of the Greeks. The other is the Bottle-nose Porpuss, which is generally thought to be the Phæcena of Aristotle.

Plate 2. Fig. 7.

This is the Guaracapema of Piso and Marcgrave, by others called the Dorado. 'Tis figured in Willughby's *Ichthyol.* Tab. 0. 2. under the Name of *Delphin Belgis*.

Plate 3 Fishes

A Fish of the Tunny kind taken on ỹ Coast of N. Hol

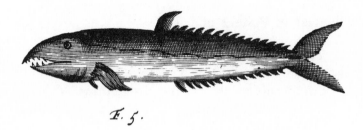

F. 5.

A Fish called by the seamen the Old Wife

F. 4.

Plate 2 Fishes

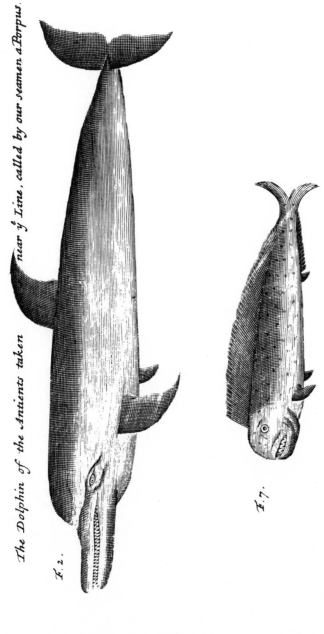

The Dolphin of the Antients taken near y.e Line, called by our seamen a Porpus.

F. 2.

F. 7.

A Dolphin as it is usually called by our seamen taken in the open Sea

A

CONTINUATION

OF A

VOYAGE

TO

NEW-HOLLAND, &c.

In the YEAR 1699.

Wherein are defcribed,

The Iflands *Timor, Rotee* and *Anabao.* A Paffage between the Iflands *Timor* and *Anabao.* *Copang* and *Laphao* Bays. The Iflands *Omba, Fetter, Bande* and *Bird.* A Defcription of the Coaft of *New-Guinea.* The Iflands *Pulo Sabuda, Cockle,* King *William's, Providence, Garret Dennis, Ant. Cave's* and St. *John's.* Alfo a new Paffage between *N. Guinea* and *Nova Britannia.* The Iflands *Ceram, Bonao, Bouro,* and feveral Iflands before unknown. The Coaft of *Java,* and Streights of *Sunda.* Author's Arrival at *Batavia, Cape of Good Hope,* St. *Helens, I. Afcenfion,* &c. Their Inhabitants, Cuftoms, Trade, *&c.* Harbours, Soil, Birds, Fifh, *&c.* Trees, Plants, Fruits, *&c.*

Illuftrated with MAP s and D R AUGH T s: Alfo divers Birds, Fifhes, *&c.* not found in this Part of the World, Ingraven on Eighteen Copper-Plates.

By Captain WILLIAM DAMPIER.

L O N D O N,
Printed for J AMES *and* J OHN KNAPTON, at the *Crown* in St. *Paul's* Church-Yard. MDCCXXIX.

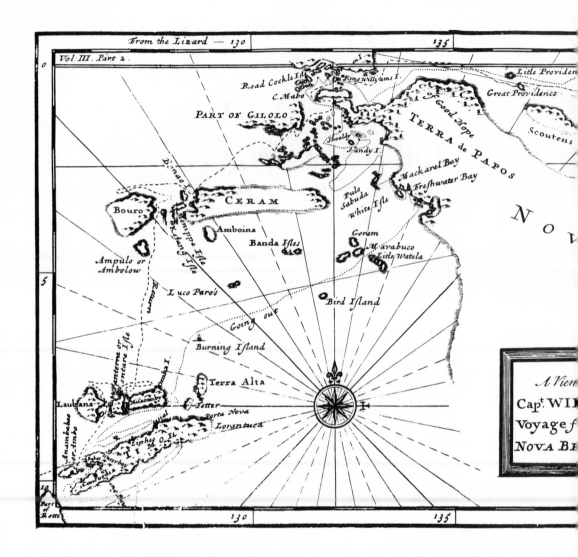

Vol. III. Part 2.

Read Cockle Isle
C. Mabo
King Williams I.
Litle Providen
Great Providence
PART OF GILOLO
Good Hope
Scoutens
TERRA de PAPOS
Shoaldy
Sandy I.
Mackarel Bay
Freshwater Bay
CERAM
Pulo
Sabuda
White Isle
N O V
Bouro
Amboina
Goram
Banda Isles
M. avabuco
Litle Watela
Ampulo or
Ambolow
Luco Paro's
Bird Island
Going out
Burning Island
Terra Alta
Laubana
Fetter
Porta Nova
Lorantuca
Part of
Rotte

130   135

A View
Capt. WIL
Voyage f
NOVA BR

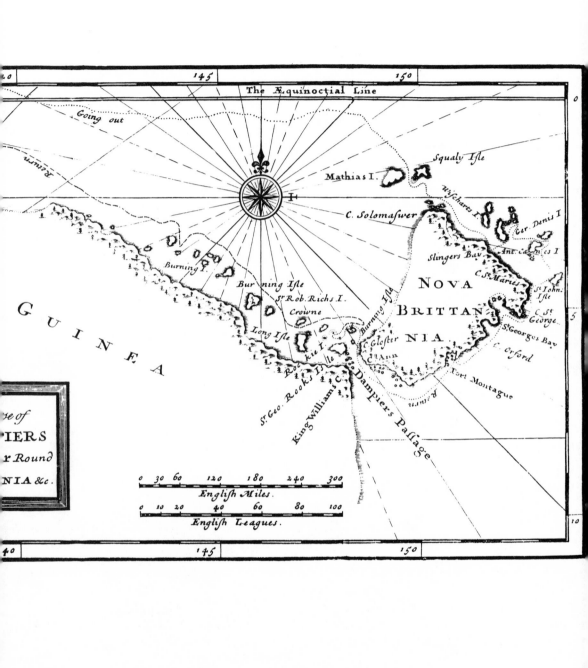

The Æquinoctial Line

145   150   0

Going out

Return

Squaly Isle

Mathias I.

W.fcharts I.

C. Solomaswer

Ser. Denis I.

Ant. Ca.nes I.

Slingers Bay

C. St. Maries

St John. Isle

NOVA

C. St. George

St Georges Bay

BRITTAN

Burning I.

C. Orford

Burning Isle

NIA.

Sr Rob. Richs. I.

Crowne

Long Isle

Glester

Burning Isle

GUINEA

Roo. kie I.

C. Ann

Port Montague

Return

St. Geo. Rooks Isle

King William's C.

Dampiers Passage

5

10

re of
IERS
r Round
NIA &c.

0   30   60   120   180   240   300
English Miles.

0   10   20   40   60   80   100
English Leagues.

40   145   150

PART II

THE CONTENTS

CHAP. I

The A.'s Departure from the Coast of New Holland, with the Reasons of it.
Water-Snakes. The A.'s Arrival at the Island Timor. Search for fresh Water
on the South-side of the Island, in vain. Fault of the Charts. The Island
Rotee. A Passage between the Islands Timor and Anabao. Fault of the
Charts. A Dutch Fort, called Concordia. Their Suspicion of the A. The
Island Anabao described. The A.'s Parly with the Governour of the Dutch
Fort. They, with great Difficulty, obtain leave to water. Copang Bay.
Coasting along the North-side of Timor. They find Water and an Anchor-
ing-place. A Description of a small Island, seven Leagues East from the
Watering Bay. Laphao Bay. How the A. was treated by the Portugueze
there. Designs of making further Searches upon and about the Island. Port
Sesial. Return to Babao in Copang Bay. The A.'s Entertainment at the Fort
of Concordia. His stay seven Weeks at Babao.

CHAP. II

A particular Description of the Island Timor. Its Coast. The Island Anabao.
Fault of the Draughts. The Channel between Timor and Anabao. Copang-
bay. Fort Concordia. A particular Description of the Bay. The Anchoring-
place, called Babao. The Malayans here kill all the Europeans they can.
Laphao, a Portugueze Settlement, described. Port Ciccale. The Hills,
Water, Low-lands, Soil, Woods, Metals, in the Island Timor. Its Trees.
Cana-fistula-tree described. Wild Fig-trees described. Two new Sorts of
Palm-trees described. The Fruits of the Island. The Herbs. Its Land
Animals. Fowls. The Ringing Bird. Its Fish. Cockle-merchants and
Oysters. Cockles as big as a Man's Head. Its original Natives described.

The Portugueze and Dutch Settlements. The Malayan Language generally spoken here. L' Orantuca on the Island Ende. The Seasons, Winds, and Weather at Timor.

CHAP. III

Departure from Timor. The Islands Omba and Fetter. A burning Island. Their missing the Turtle-Isles. Bande-Isles. Bird-Island. They descry the Coast of New-Guinea. They anchor on the Coast of New-Guinea. A Description of the Place, and of a strange Fowl found there. Great Quantities of Mackerel. A white Island. They anchor at an Island called by the Inhabitants Pulo Sabuda. A Description of it and its Inhabitants and Product. The Indians manner of Fishing there. Arrival at Mabo, the North West Cape of New-Guinea. A Description of it. Cockle-Island. Cockles of seventy-eight Pound Weight. Pidgeon-Island. The Wind hereabouts. An empty Cockle-shell weighing two hundred fifty-eight Pound. King William's Island. A Description of it. Plying on the Coast of New-Guinea. Fault of the Draughts. Providence Island. They cross the Line. A Snake pursued by Fish. Squally Island. The Main of New-Guinea.

CHAP. IV

The main Land of New-Guinea. Its Inhabitants. Slingers Bay. Small Islands. Garret Dennis Isle described. Its Inhabitants. Their Proes. Anthony Cave's Island. Its Inhabitants. Trees full of Worms found in the Sea. St. John's Island. The main Land of New-Guinea. Its Inhabitants. The Coast described. Cape and Bay St. George. Cape Orford. Another Bay. The Inhabitants there. A large Account of the Author's Attempts to trade with them. He names the Place Port Mountague. The Country thereabouts described, and its Produce. A Burning Island described. A new Passage found. Nova Britannia. Sir George Rook's Island. Long Island and Crown Island, discovered and described. Sir R. Rich's Island. A Burning Island. A strange Spout. A Conjecture concerning a new Passage Southward. King William's Island. Strange Whirlpools. Distance between Cape Mabo and Cape St. George computed.

CHAP. V

The A.'s Return from the Coast of New-Guinea. A deep Channel. Strange Tides. The Island Ceram described. Strange Fowls. The Islands Bonao, Bouro, Misacombi, Pentare, Laubana, and Potoro. The Passage between Pentare and Laubana. The Island Timor. Babao Bay. The Island Rotee. More Islands than are commonly laid down in the Draughts. Great Currents. Whales. Coast of New-Holland. The Tryal-Rocks. The Coast of Java. Princes Isle. Streights of Sunda. Thwart-the-way Island. Indian Proes, and their Traffick. Passage through the Streight. Arrival at Batavia.

CHAP. VI

The A. continues in Batavia-Road to refit, and to get Provisions. English Ships then in the Road. Departure from Batavia. Touch at the Cape of Good Hope. And at St. Helena. Arrival at the Island of Ascension. A Leak Sprung. Which being impossible to be stopped, the Ship is lost, but the Men saved. They find Water upon the Island: And are brought back to England.

CHAP. I

I had spent about 5 Weeks in ranging off and on the Coast of New-Holland, a Length of about 300 Leagues: and had put in at 3 several Places, to see what there might be thereabouts worth discovering; and at the same Time to recruit my Stock of fresh Water and Provisions for the further Discoveries I purposed to attempt on the Terra Australis. This large and hitherto almost unknown Tract of Land is situated so very advantageously in the richest Climates of the World, the Torrid and Temperate Zones; having in it especially all the Advantages of the Torrid Zone, as being known to reach from the Equator it self (within a Degree) to the Tropick of Capricorn, and beyond it; that in coasting round it, which I design'd by this Voyage, if possible: I could not but hope to meet with some fruitful Lands, Continent or Islands, or both, productive of any of the rich Fruits, Drugs, or Spices, (perhaps Minerals also, &c.) that are in the other Parts of the Torrid Zone, under equal Parallels of Latitude; at least a Soil and Air capable of such, upon transplanting them hither, and Cultivation. I meant also to make as diligent a Survey as I could, of the several smaller Islands, Shores, Capes, Bays, Creeks, and Harbours, fit as well for Shelter as Defence, upon fortifying them; and of the Rocks and Shoals, the Soundings, Tides, and Currents, Winds and Weather, Variation, &c. Whatever might be beneficial for Navigation, Trade or Settlement; or be of use to any who should prosecute the same Designs hereafter; to whom it might be serviceable to have so much of their Work done to their Hands; which they might advance and perfect by their own repeated Experiences. As there is no Work of this Kind brought to Perfection at once, I intended especially to observe what Inhabitants I should meet with, and to try to win them over to somewhat of Traffick and useful Intercourse, as there might be Commodities among any of them that might be fit for Trade or Manufacture, or any found in which they might be employed. Though as to the New Hollanders hereabouts, by the Experience

I had had of their Neighbours formerly, I expected no great Matters from them.

With such Views as these, I set out at first from England; and would, according to the Method I proposed formerly [Vol. I.] have gone Westward, through the Magellanick Streight, or round Terra del Fuego rather, that I might have begun my Discoveries upon the Eastern and least known Side of the Terra Australis. But that way 'twas not possible for me to go, by Reason of the Time of Year in which I came out; for I must have been compassing the South of America in a very high Latitude, in the Depth of the Winter there. I was therefore necessitated to go Eastward by the Cape of Good Hope; and when I should be past it, 'twas requisite I should keep in a pretty high Latitude, to avoid the general Trade-winds that would be against me, and to have the Benefit of the variable Winds: By all which I was in a Manner unavoidably determin'd to fall in first with those Parts of New Holland I have hitherto been describing. For should it be ask'd why at my first making that Shore, I did not coast it to the Southward, and that way try to get round to the East of New Holland and New Guinea; I confess I was not for spending my Time more than was necessary in the higher Latitudes; as knowing that the Land there could not be so well worth the discovering, as the Parts that lay nearer the Line, and more directly under the Sun. Besides, at the Time when I should come first on New Holland, which was early in the Spring, I must, had I stood Southward, have had for some Time a great deal of Winter-weather, increasing in Severity, though not in Time, and in a Place altogether unknown; which my Men, who were heartless enough to the Voyage at best, would never have born, after so long a Run as from Brazil hither.

For these Reasons therefore I chose to coast along to the Northward, and so to the East, and so thought to come round by the South of Terra Australis in my Return back, which should be in the Summer-season there: And this Passage back also I now thought I might possibly be able to shorten, should it appear, at my getting to the East Coast of New Guinea, that there is a Channel there coming out into these Seas, as I now suspected near Rosemary Island: Unless the high Tides and great Indraught thereabout should be occasion'd by the Mouth of some large River; which hath often low Lands on each Side of its Outlet, and many Islands and Sholes lying at its Entrance. But I rather thought it a Channel or Streight, than a River: And I was afterwards confirmed in this Opinion, when by coasting New Guinea, I

found that other Parts of this great Tract of Terra Australis, which had
hitherto been represented as the Shore of a Continent, were certainly Islands;
and 'tis probably the same with New Holland: Though for Reasons I shall
afterwards shew, I could not return by the way I propos'd to my self, to fix
the Discovery. All that I had now seen from the Latitude of 27 d. South to
25, which is Shark's Bay; and again from thence to Rosemary Islands, and
about the Latitude of 20; seems to be nothing but Ranges of pretty large
Islands against the Sea, whatever might be behind them to the Eastward,
whether Sea or Land, Continent or Islands.

But to proceed with my Voyage. Though the Land I had seen as yet, was
not very inviting, being but barren towards the Sea, and affording me
neither fresh Water, nor any great Store of other Refreshments, nor so
much as a fit Place for careening; yet I stood out to Sea again, with Thoughts
of coasting still along Shore (as near as I could) to the North Eastward, for
the further Discovery of it: Perswading my self, that at least the Place I
anchor'd at in my Voyage round the World, in the Latitude of 16 deg. 15
min. from which I was not now far distant, would not fail to afford me
sweet Water upon digging, as it did then; for the brackish Water I had
taken in here, though it serv'd tolerably well for boiling, was yet not very
wholsome.

With these Intentions I put to Sea on the 5th of September 1699, with a
gentle Gale, sounding all the way; but was quickly induc'd to alter my
Design. For I had not been out above a Day, but I found that the Sholes
among which I was engaged all the while on the Coast, and was like to be
engag'd in, would make it a very tedious Thing to sail along by the Shore,
or to put in where I might have occasion. I therefore edged farther off to
Sea, and so deepned the Water from 11 to 32 Fathom. The next Day, being
September the 6th, we could but just discern the Land, though we had then
no more than about 30 Fathom, uncertain Soundings; For even while we
were out of Sight of land, we had once but 7 Fathom, and had also great and
uncertain Tides whirling about, that made me afraid to go near a Coast so
shallow, where we might be soon a-ground, and yet have but little Wind to
bring us off: For should a Ship be near a Shoal, she might be hurl'd upon it
unavoidably by a strong Tide, unless there should be a good Wind to work
her and keep her off. Thus also on the 7th Day we saw no Land, though our
Water decreas'd again to 26 Fathom; for we had deepned it, as I said, to 30.

This Day we saw two Water-snakes, different in Shape from such as we had formerly seen. The one was very small, though long; the other long and as big as a Man's Leg, having a red Head; which I never saw any have, before or since. We had this Day, Lat. 16 d. 9 m. by Observation.

I was by this Time got to the North of the Place I had thought to have put in at, where I dug Wells in my former Voyage; and though I knew by the Experience I had of it then, that there was a deep Entrance in thither from the Eastward; yet by the Shoals I had hitherto found so far stretcht on this Coast, I was afraid I should have the same Trouble to coast all along afterwards beyond that Place: And besides the Danger of running almost continually amongst Shoals on a strange Shore, and where the Tides were strong and high; I began to bethink my self, that a great Part of my Time must have been spent in being about a Shore I was already almost weary of, which I might employ with greater Satisfaction to my Mind, and better Hopes of Success in going forward to New Guinea. Add to this the particular Danger I should have been in upon a Leeshore, such as is here describ'd, when the North-West Monsoon should once come in; the ordinary Season of which was not now far off, though this Year it staid beyond the common Season; and it comes on storming at first, with Tornadoes, violent Gusts, &c. Wherefore quitting the Thoughts of putting in again at New Holland, I resolv'd to steer away for the Island Timor; where, besides getting fresh Water, I might probably expect to be furnished with Fruits, and other Refreshments to recruit my Men, who began to droop; some of them being already to my great Grief, afflicted with the Scurvy, which was likely to increase upon them and disable them, and was promoted by the brackish Water they took in last for boiling their Oatmeal. 'Twas now also towards the latter End of the dry Season; when I might not probably have found Water so plentifully upon digging at that Part of New Holland, as when I was there before in the wet Season. And then, considering the Time also that I must necessarily spend in getting in to the Shore, through such Sholes as I expected to meet with; or in going about to avoid them; and in digging of Wells when I should come thither: I might very well hope to get to Timor, and find fresh Water there, as soon as I could expect to get it at New Holland; and with less Trouble and Danger.

On the 8th of September therefore, shaping our Course for Timor, we were in Lat. 15 d. 37 m. We had 26 Fathom, coarse Sand; and we saw one Whale. We found them lying most commonly near the Shore, or in Shoal Water. This Day we also saw some small white Clouds; the first that we had seen since we came out of Shark's Bay. This was one Sign of the Approach of the North-North-West Monsoon. Another Sign was the shifting of the Winds; for from the Time of our coming to our last Anchoring place, the Sea-Breezes which before were Easterly and very strong, had been whiffling about and changing gradually from the East to the North, and thence to the West, blowing but faintly, and now hanging mostly in some Point of the West. This Day the Winds were at South-West by West, blowing very faint; and the 9th Day we had the Wind at North-West by North, but then pretty fresh; and we saw the Clouds rising more and thicker in the North-West. This Night at 12 we lay by for a small low sandy Island, which I reckoned my self not far from. The next Morning at Sun-rising we saw it from the Top-mast-head, right a-head of us; and at Noon were up within a Mile of it: When, by a good Observation, I found it to lye in 13 d. 55 m. I have mentioned it in my first Vol, but my Account then made it to lye in 13 d. 50 m. We had Abundance of Boobies and Man of War Birds flying about us all the Day; especially when we came near the Island; which had also Abundance of them upon it; though it was but a little Spot of Sand, scarce a Mile round.

I did not anchor here, nor send my Boat ashore; there being no appearance of getting any Thing on that Spot of Sand, besides Birds that were good for little: Though had I not been in haste, I would have taken some of them. So I made the best of my way to Timor; and on the 11th in the Afternoon we saw 10 small Land-birds, about the Bigness of Larks, that flew away North West. The 13th we saw a great many Sea-snakes. One of these, of which I saw great Numbers and Variety in this Voyage, was large, and all black: I never saw such another for his Colour.

We had now had for some Days small Gales, from the South-South-West to the North-North-West, and the Sky still more cloudy especially in the Mornings and Evenings. The 14th it look'd very black in the North-West all the Day; and a little before Sun-set we saw, to our great Joy, the Tops of the high Mountains of Timor, peeping out of the Clouds, which had before covered them, as they did still the lower Parts.

We were now running directly towards the Middle of the Island, on the South-side: But I was in some doubt whether I should run down along Shore on this Southside towards the East-end; or pass about the West-end, and so range along on the North-side, and go that way towards the East-end: But as the Winds were now Westerly, I thought it best to keep on the South-side, till I should see how the Weather would prove; For, as the Island lies, if the Westerly Winds continued and grew tempestuous, I should be under the Lee of it, and have smooth Water, and so could go along Shore more safely and easily on this South-side: I could sooner also run to the East-end, where there is the best Shelter, as being still more under the Lee of the Island when those Winds blow. Or if, on the other Side, the Winds should come about again to the Eastward, I could but turn back again, (as I did afterwards;) and passing about the West-end, could there prosecute my Search on the North-side of the Island for Water, or Inhabitants, or a good Harbour, or whatever might be useful to me. For both Sides of the Island were hitherto alike to me, being wholly unacquainted here; only as I had seen it at a Distance in my former Voyage. [Vol. I.]

I had heard also, that there were both Dutch and Portugueze Settlements on this Island; but whereabouts, I knew not: However, I was resolved to search about till I found, either one of these Settlements, or Water in some other place.

It was now almost Night, and I did not care to run near the Land in the dark, but clapt on a Wind, and stood off and on till the next Morning, being September 15th, when I steered in for the Island, which now appear'd very plain, being high, double and treble Land, very remarkable, on whatever Side you view it. See a Sight of it in 2 Parts, Table V. N°. 1. At 3 in the Afternoon we anchored in 14 Fathom, soft black oasy Ground, about a Mile from the Shore. See 2 Sights more of the Coast, in Table V. N°. 2, 3. and the Island it self in the Particular Map; which I have here inserted, to shew the Course of the Voyage from hence to the Eastward; as the General Map, set before the Title of this Volume, shews the Course of the whole Voyage. But in making the Particular Map, I chose to begin only with Timor, that I might not, by extending it too far, be forced to contract the Scale too much among the Islands, &c. of the New Guinea Coast, which I chiefly designed it for.

The Land by the Sea, on this South-side, is low and sandy, and full of tall Streight-bodied Trees like Pines, for about 200 Yards inwards from the Shore. Beyond that, further in towards the Mountains, for a Breadth of about 3 Miles more or less, there is a Tract of swampy Mangrovy Land, which runs all along between the sandy Land of the Shore on one Side of it, and the Feet of the Mountains on the other. And this low Mangrovy Land is overflown every Tide of Flood, by the Water that flows into it through

Table V　　　　　Timor

N.º 1

S. W. b. W.

Thus Shews Part of the Isl. of Timor Lat: 9.44 Dist. 5 L

N.º 2.

Thus Shews the Land in Lat: 9. 26. Dist: 1 L.

N.º 3.　Thus Shews the Land in Lat: 9. 26 Dist: 1 L.

N. ½ W.　　　　　　　　　N. E. b. N.

N.ª 4.

Thus Shews the Isl: Rote to the S. W. ward

S. W.

of Timor at the S. W. end Dist: 9 L.

a　　　　　　　　　w

N.º 5.　Thus Shews Timor and the Isl: Anamabao apering in one
Dist: 10 L. the letter T Shews the goeing in between y.ᵉ two Isl.

W. N. W.　　　　　T

several Mouths or Openings in the outer sandy Skirt against the Sea. We came to an Anchor right against one of these Openings; and presently I went in my Boat to search for fresh Water, or get Speech of the Natives; for we saw Smoaks, Houses, and Plantations against the Sides of the Mountains, not far from us. It was ebbing Water before we got ashore, though the Water was still high enough to float us in without any great Trouble. After we were within the Mouth, we found a large Salt-Water Lake, which we hoped might bring us up through the Mangroves to the fast Land: But before we went further, I went ashore on the sandy Land by the Sea-side, and look'd about me; but saw there no Sign of fresh Water. Within the sandy Bank, the Water forms a large Lake: Going therefore into the Boat again, we rowed up the Lake towards the firm Land, where no doubt there was fresh Water, could we come at it. We found many Branches of the Lake entring within the Mangrove Land, but not beyond it. Of these we left some on the Right-hand, and some on the Left, still keeping in the biggest Channel; which still grew smaller, and at last so narrow, that we could go no farther, ending among the Swamps and Mangroves. We were then within a Mile of some Houses of the Indian Inhabitants and the firm Land by the Sides of the Hills: But the Mangroves thus stopping our way, we return'd as we came: But it was almost dark before we reach'd the Mouth of the Creek. 'Twas with much ado that we got out of it again; for it was now low Water, and there went a rough short Sea on the Bar; which, however, we past over without any Damage, and went aboard.

The next Morning at five we weighed, and stood along Shore to the Eastward, making use of the Sea and Land-Breezes. We found the Sea-Breezes here from the S.S.E. to the S.S.W. the Land-Breezes from the N. to the N.E. We coasted along about 20 Leagues, and found it all a streight, bold, even Shore, without Points, Creeks or Inlets for a Ship: And there is no anchoring till within a Mile or a Mile and an half of the Shore. We saw scarce any Opening fit for our Boats; and the fast Land was still barricado'd with Mangroves; So that here was no hope to get Water; nor was it likely that there should be hereabouts any European Settlement, since there was no Sign of a Harbour.

The Land appear'd pleasant enough to the Eye: For the Sides and Tops of the Mountains were cloath'd with Woods mix'd with Savannahs; and there was a Plantation of the Indian Natives, where we saw the Coco-Nuts growing, and could have been glad to have come at some of them. In the

Draught I had with me, a Shoal was laid down hereabouts; but I saw nothing of it, going, or coming; and so have taken no Notice of it in my Map.

Weary of running thus fruitlessly along the South-side of the Island to the Eastward, I resolv'd to return the way I came; and compassing the West-end of the Island, make a Search along the North-side of it. The rather, because the North-North-West Monsoon, which I had design'd to be shelter'd from by coming the way I did, did not seem to be near at Hand, as the ordinary Season of them required; but on the contrary I found the Winds returning again to the South-Eastward; and the Weather was fair, and seem'd likely to hold so; and consequently the North-North-West Monsoon was not like to come in yet. I considered therefore that by going to the Northside of the Island, I should there have the smooth Water, as being the Lee-side as the Winds now were; and hoped to have better riding at Anchor or Landing on that Side, than I could expect here, where the Shore was so lined with Mangroves.

Accordingly, the 18th about Noon I altered my Course, and steered back again towards the South-West-end of the Island. This Day we struck a Dolphin; and the next Day saw two more, but struck none: We also saw a Whale.

In the Evening we saw the Island Rotee, and another Island to the South of it, not seen in my Map; both lying near the South-West-end of Timor. On both these Islands we saw Smoaks by Day, and Fires by Night, as we had seen on Timor ever since we fell in with it. I was told afterwards by the Portugueze, that they had Sugar-works on the Island Rotee; but I knew nothing of that now; and the Coast appearing generally dry and barren, only here and there a Spot of Trees, I did not attempt anchoring there, but stood over again to the Timor Coast.

September the 21st, in the Morning, being near Timor, I saw a pretty large Opening, which immediately I entred with my Ship, sounding as I went in: But had no Ground till I came within the East Point of the Mouth of the Opening, where I anchored in 9 Fathom, a League from the Shore. The Distance from the East-side to the West-side of this Opening, was about 5 Leagues. But whereas I thought this was only an Inlet or large Sound that ran a great way into the Island Timor, I found afterwards that it was a Passage between the West End of Timor and another small Island called Anamabao or Anabao: Into which Mistake I was led by my Sea-Chart, which represented both Sides of the Opening as Parts of the same Coast, and called all of it Timor: See all this rectified, and a View of the whole Passage, as I found it, in a small Map I have made of it. Table VI. N°. 1.

I designed to sail into this Opening till I should come to firm Land; for the Shore was all set thick with Mangroves here by the Sea, on each Side; which were very green, as were also other Trees more within Land. We had now but little Wind; therefore I sent my Boat away, to sound, and to let me know by Signs what Depth of Water they met with, if under 8 Fathom; but if more, I order'd them to go on, and make no Signs. At 11 that Morning, having a pretty fresh Gale, I weighed, and made sail after my Boat; but edg'd over more to the West Shore, because I saw many smaller Openings there, and was in Hopes to find a good Harbour where I might secure the Ship; for then I could with more Safety send my Boats to seek for fresh Water. I had not sailed far before the Wind came to the South-East and blew so strong, that I could not with Safety venture nearer that Side, it being a Lee-shore. Besides, my Boat was on the East-side of the Timor Coast; for the other was, as I found afterwards, the Anabao Shore; and the great Opening I was now in, was the Streight between that Island and Timor; towards which I now tack'd and stood over. Taking up my Boat therefore, I ran under the Timor Side, and at 3 a Clock anchored in 29 Fathom, half a Mile from the Shore. That Part of the South-West Point of Timor, where we anchored in the Morning, bore now South by West, distance 3 Leagues: And another Point of the Island bore North-North-East, distance 2 Leagues.

Not long after, we saw a Sloop coming about the Point last mention'd, with Dutch Colours; which I found, upon sending my Boat aboard, belonged to a Dutch Fort, (the only one thay have in Timor) about 5 Leagues from hence, call'd Concordia. The Governour of the Fort was in the Sloop, and about 40 Soldiers with him. He appear'd to be somewhat surprised at our coming this way; which it seems is a Passage scarce known to any but themselves; as he told the Men I sent to him in my Boat. Neither did he seem willing that we should come near their Fort for Water. He said also, that he did not know of any Water on all that Part of the Island, but only at the Fort; and that the Natives would kill us, if they met us ashore. By the small Arms my Men carried with them in the Boat, they took us to be Pirates, and would not easily believe the Account my Men gave them of what we were, and whence we came. They said that about 2 Years before this, there had been a stout Ship of French Pirates here; and that after

Table VI

Timor

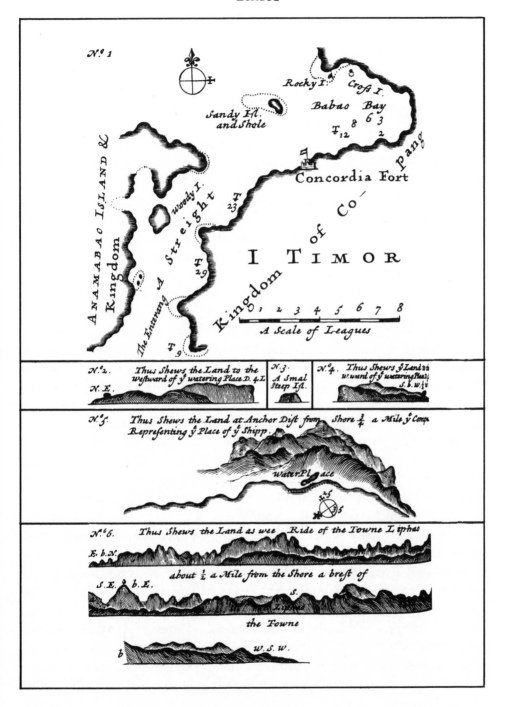

No 1

Rocky I.   Cross I.

Babao   Bay

Sandy Isl.
and Shole
                              8 6 3
                        T 12   2

Concordia Fort

ANAMABAO ISLAND & Kingdom

Woody I.

A Streight

T 23

T 29

The Entrance

T 9

I TIMOR

Kingdom of Co-
Pang

1 2 3 4 5 6 7 8
A Scale of Leagues

No 2. *Thus Shews the Land to the*
westward of y watering Place D. 4 L.
N.E.

No 3.
A Smal
Steep Isl.

No 4. *Thus Shews y Land to*
w.uard of y watering Place
s. b. w. ½ w.

No 5.   *Thus Shews the Land at Anchor Dist from   Shore ¾ a Mile y Comp.*
Representing y Place of y Shipp.

waterPlace

No 6.   *Thus Shews the Land as wee   Ride of the Towne L iphao*
E. b. N.

about ½ a Mile from the Shore a brest of
S.E. ½ b. E.   s.

the Towne

b   w. s. w.

having been suffered to Water, and to refresh themselves, and been kindly used, they had on a sudden gone among the Indians, Subjects of the Fort, and plunder'd them and burnt their Houses. And the Portugueze here told us afterwards, that those Pirates, whom they also had entertain'd, had burnt their Houses, and had taken the Dutch Fort, (though the Dutch car'd not to own so much,) and had driven the Governour and Factory among the wild Indians their Enemies. The Dutch told my Men further, that they could not but think we had of several Nations (as is usual with Pirate Vessels) in our Ship, and particularly some Dutch Men, though all the Discourse was in French; (for I had not one who could speak Dutch:) Or else, since the common Draughts make no Passage between Timor and Anabao, but lay down both as one Island; they said they suspected we had plundered some Dutch Ship of their particular Draughts, which they are forbid to part with.

With these Jealousies the Sloop returned towards their Fort, and my Boat came back with this News to me: But I was not discouraged at this News; not doubting but I should perswade them better, when I should come to talk with them. So the next Morning I weighed, and stood towards the Fort. The Winds were somewhat against us, so that we could not go very fast, being obliged to tack 2 or 3 Times: And coming near the farther End of the Passage between Timor and Anabao, we saw many Houses on each Side not far from the Sea, and several Boats lying by the Shore. The Land on both Sides was pretty high, appearing very dry and of a reddish Colour, but highest on the Timor Side. The Trees on either Side were but small, the Woods thin, and in many Places the Trees were dry and withered.

The Island Anamabao or Anabao, is not very big, not exceeding 10 Leagues in length, and 4 in Breadth; yet it has 2 Kingdoms in it, viz. that of Anamabao on the East-side towards Timor, and the North-East-end; and that of Anabao, which contains the South-West-end and the West-side of the Island; but I know not which of them is biggest. The Natives of both are of the Indian kind, of a swarthy Copper-colour, with black lank Hair. Those of Anamabao are in League with the Dutch, as these afterwards told me, and with the Natives of the Kingdom of Copang in Timor, over-against them, in which the Dutch Fort Concordia stands: But they are said to be inveterate Enemies to their Neighbours of Anabao. Those of Anabao, besides managing their small Plantations of Roots and a few Coco-nuts, do fish, strike Turtle, and hunt Buffalo's; killing them with Swords, Darts, or Lances. But I know not how they get their Iron; I suppose, by Traffick with the Dutch or Portugueze, who send now and then a Sloop and trade thither, but well-arm'd; for the Natives would kill them, could they surprize them. They go always armed themselves; And when they go a fishing or a hunting, they spend 4 or 5 Days or more in ranging about, before they return to their Habitation. We often saw them, after this, at these Employments; but they would not come near us. The Fish or Flesh that they take, besides what serves for present spending, they dry on a Barbacue or wooden Grate, standing pretty high over the Fire, and so carry it home when they return. We came sometimes afterwards to the Places where they had Meat thus a drying, but did not touch any of it.

But to proceed; I did not think to stop any where till I came near the Fort; which yet I did not see: But coming to the End of this Passage, I found that if I went any farther I should be open again to the Sea. I therefore stood in close to the Shore, on the East-side, and anchored in 4 Fathom Water, sandy Ground; a Point of Land still hindring me from seeing the Fort. But I sent my Boat to look about for it; and in a short Time she returned, and my Men told me they saw the Fort, but did not go near it; and that it was not above 4 or 5 Miles from hence. It being now late, I would not send my Boat thither till the next Morning: Mean while about 2 or 300 Indians, Neighbours of the Fort, and sent probably from thence, came to the sandy Bay just against the Ship; where they staid all Night, and made good Fires. They were armed with Lances, Swords and Targets, and made a great Noise all the Night: We thought it was to scare us from landing, should we attempt it: But we took little Notice of them.

The next Morning, being September the 23d, I sent my Clerk ashore in my Pinnace to the Governour, to satisfy him that we were English Men: and in the King's ship, and to ask Water of him; sending a young Man with him, who spake French. My Clerk was with the Governour pretty early; and in Answer to his Queries about me, and my Business in these Parts, told him that I had the King of England's Commission, and desired to speak with him. He beckned to my Clerk to come ashore; but assoon as he saw some small Arms in the Stern-Sheets of the Boat, he commanded him into the Boat again, and would have him be gone. My Clerk sollicited him that he would allow him to speak with him; and at last the Governour consented that he should come ashore; and sent his Lieutenant and 3 Merchants, with a Guard of about a hundred of the Native Indians to receive him. My Clerk said that we were in much want of Water, and hop'd they wou'd allow us to come to their Watering-place, and fill. But the Governour replied, that he had Orders not to supply any Ships but their own East-India Company; neither must they allow any Europeans to come the Way that we came; and wondred how we durst come near their Fort. My Clerk answered him, that had we been Enemies, we must have come ashore among them for Water: But, said the Governour, you are come to inspect into our Trade and Strength; and I will have you therefore be gone with all Speed. My Clerk answered him, that I had no such Design, but, without coming nearer them, would be contented if the Governour would send Water on Board where we lay, about 2 Leagues from the Fort; and that I would make any reasonable Satisfaction for it. The Governour said that we should have what Water we wanted, provided we came no nearer with the Ship: And ordered, that assoon as we pleased, we should send our Boat full of empty Casks, and come to an Anchor with it off the Fort, till he sent Slaves to bring the Casks ashore, and fill them; for that none of our Men must come ashore. The same Afternoon I sent up my Boat as he had directed, with an Officer, and a present of some Beer for the Governour; which he would not accept of; but sent me off about a Ton of Water.

On the 24th in the Morning I sent the same Officer again in my Boat; and about Noon the Boat returned again with the two principal Merchants of the Factory, and the Lieutenant of the Fort; for whose Security they had kept my Officer and one of my Boat's-crew as Hostages, confining them to the Governour's Garden all the Time: For they were very shy of trusting any of them to go into their Fort, as my Officer said: Yet afterwards they were not shy of our Company; and I found that my Officer maliciously endeavour'd to make them shy of me. In the Even I gave the Dutch Officers that came aboard, the best Entertainment I could; and bestowing some Presents on them, sent them back very well pleased; and my Officer and the other Man were returned to me. Next Morning I sent my Boat ashore again with the same Officer; who brought me word from the Governour, that we must pay 4 Spanish Dollars, for every Boat's-load of Water: But in this he spake falsly, as I understood afterwards from the Governour himself, and all his Officers, who protested to me that no such Price was demanded, but left me to give the Slaves what I pleased for their Labour: The Governour being already better satisfied about me, than when my Clerk spoke to him, or than that Officer I sent last would have caused him to be: For the Governour being a civil, genteel and sensible Man, was offended at the Officer for his being so industrious to misrepresent me. I received from the Governour a little Lamb, very fat; and I sent him 2 of the Guinea-hens that I brought from St. Jago, of which there were none here.

I had now 11 Buts of Water on Board, having taken in 7 here, which I would have paid for, but that at present I was afraid to send my Boat ashore again; For my Officer told me, among other of his Inventions, that there were more Guns mounted in the Fort, than when we first came; and that he did not see the Gentlemen that were aboard the Day before; intimating as if they were shy of us; and that the Governour was very rough with him; and I not knowing to the contrary at present, consulted with my other Officers what was best to be done; for by this the Governour should seem to design to quarrel with us. All my other Officers thought it natural to infer so much, and that it was not safe to send the Boat ashore any more, lest it should be seiz'd on; but that it was best to go away, and seek more Water where we could find it. For having now (as I said) 11 Buts aboard; and the Land being promising this way, I did not doubt finding Water in a short Time. But my Officer who occasion'd these Fears in us by his own Forgeries, was himself for going no further; having a Mind, as far as I could perceive, to make every Thing in the Voyage, to which he shew'd himself averse, seem as cross and discouraging to my Men as possible, that he might hasten our Return; being very negligent and backward in most Businesses I had occasion to employ him in; doing nothing well or willingly, though I did all I could to win him to it. He was also industrious to stir up the Sea-men to Mutiny; telling them, among other Things, that any Dutch Ship might lawfully take us in these Seas; but I knew better, and avoided every Thing that could give just Offence.

The rest of my Officers therefore being resolved to go from hence, and having bought some Fish of some Anamabeans, who, seeing our Ship, came purposely to sell some, passing to and fro every Day; I sail'd away on the 26th about 5 in the Afternoon. We pass'd along between a small low sandy Island (over against the Fort), full of Bays and pretty high Trees; sounding as we went along; and had from 25 to 35 Fathom, oasy Ground. See the little Map of this Passage, Table VI. N°. 1.

The 27th in the Morning we anchored in the Middle of the Bay, called Copang Bay, in 12 Fathom, soft Oaze, about 4 Leagues above the Dutch Fort. Their Sloop was riding by the Fort, and in the Night fired a Gun; but for what Reason I know not; and the Governour said afterwards, 'twas the

Skipper's own doing, without his Order. Presently after we had anchored, I went in the Pinnace to search about the Bay for Water, but found none. Then, returning a-board, I weighed, and ran down to the North-Entrance of the Bay, and at 7 in the Evening anchored again, in 37 Fathom, soft Oaze, close by the sandy Island, and about 4 Leagues from the Dutch Fort. The 28th I sent both my Boats ashore on the sandy Island, to cut Wood; and by Noon they both came back laden. In the Afternoon I sent my Pinnace ashore on the North Coast or Point of Copang Bay, which is call'd Babao. Late in the Night they returned, and told me that they saw great Tracks of Buffalo's there, but none of the Buffalo's themselves; neither did they find any fresh Water. They also saw some green Turtle in the Sea, and one Alligator.

The 29th I went out of Copang Bay, designing to Coast it along Shore on the North-side of Timor to the Eastward; as well to seek for Water, as also to acquaint my self with the Island, and to search for the Portugueze Settlements; which we were informed were about forty Leagues to the Eastward of this Place.

We coasted along Shore with Land and Sea-Breezes. The Land by the Shore was of a moderate height, with high and very remarkable Hills farther within the Country; their Sides all spotted with Woods and Savannahs. But these on the Mountains Sides appeared of a rusty Colour not so pleasant and flourishing as those that we saw on the South-side of the Island; for the Trees seemed to be small and withering; and the Grass in the Savannahs also look'd dry, as if it wanted Moisture. But in the Valleys, and by the Sea-side, the Trees look'd here also more green. Yet we saw no good Anchoring-place, or Opening, that gave us any Incouragement to put in; till the 30th Day in the Afternoon.

We were then running along Shore, at about 4 Leagues distance, with a moderate Sea-breeze; when we opened a pretty deep Bay, which appeared to be a good Road to anchor in. There were two large Valleys, and one smaller one, which descending from the Mountains came all into one Valley by the Sea-side against this Bay, which was full of tall green Trees. I presently stood in with the Ship, till within two Leagues of the Shore; and then sent in my Pinnace commanded by my chief Mate, whose great Care, Fidelity, and Diligence, I was well assured of; ordering him to seek for fresh Water; and if he found any, to sound the Bay, and bring me Word what anchoring there was; and to make haste aboard.

An. 1699

As soon as they were gone, I stood off a little, and lay by. The Day was now far spent; and therefore it was late before they got ashore with the Boat; so that they did not come aboard again that Night. Which I was much concern'd at; because in the Evening, when the Sea-Breeze was done and the Weather calm, I perceived the Ship to drive back again to the Westward. I was not yet acquainted with the Tides here; for I had hitherto met with no strong Tides about the Island, and scarce any running in a Stream, to set me along Shore either way. But after this Time, I had pretty much of them; and found at present the Flood set to the Eastward, and the Ebb to the Westward. The Ebb (with which I was now carried) sets very strong, and runs 8 or 9 Hours. The Flood runs but weak, and at most lasts not above 4 hours; and this too is perceived only near the Shore; where checking the Ebb, it swells the Seas, and makes the Water rise in the Bays and Rivers 8 or 9 Foot. I was afterwards credibly informed by some Portugueze, that the Current runs always to the Westward in the Mid-Channel between this Island and those that face it in a Range to the North of it, *viz.* Misicomba (or Omba) Pintare, Laubana, Ende, &c.

We were driven 4 Leagues back again, and took particular Notice of a Point of Land that looked like Flamborough-head, when we were either to the East or West of it; and near the Shore it appeared like an Island. Four or five Leagues to the East of this Point, is another very remarkable bluff Point, which is on the West-side of the Bay that my Boat was in. See two Sights of this Land, Table VI. N°. 2, 3. We could not stem the Tide, till about 3 a Clock in the Afternoon; when the Tide running with us, we soon got abreast of the Bay, and then saw a small Island to the Eastward of us. See a Sight of it Table VI. N°. 4. About 6 we anchored in the Bottom of the Bay, in 25 Fathom, soft Oaze, half a Mile from the Shore.

I made many false Fires in the Night, and now and then fired a Gun, that my Boat might find me; but to no Purpose. In the Morning I found my self driven again by the Tide of Ebb 3 or 4 Leagues to the Westward of the Place where I left my Boat. I had several Men looking out for her; but could not get Sight of her: Besides, I continued still driving to the Westward; for we had but little Wind, and that against us. But by 10 a Clock in the Morning we had the Comfort of seeing the Boat; and at 11 she came aboard, bringing 2 Barrecoes of very good Water.

The Mate told me there was good Anchoring close by the Watering-place; but that there ran a very strong Tide, which near the Shore made several

Races; so that they found much Danger in getting ashore, and were afraid to come off again in the Night, because of the Riplings the Tide made.

We had now the Sea-breeze, and steered away for this Bay; but could hardly stemm the Tide, till about 3 in the Afternoon; when the Tide being turned with us, we went along briskly, and about 6 anchored in the Bay, in 25 Fathom, soft Oaze, half a Mile from the Shore.

The next Morning I went ashore to fill Water, and before Night sent aboard 8 Tons. We fill'd it out of a large Pond within 50 Paces of the Sea. It look'd pale, but was very good, and boiled Pease well. I saw the Tract of an Alligator here. Not far from the Pond, we found the Rudder of a Malayan Proe, 3 great Jars in a small Shed set up against a Tree, and a Barbacue whereon there had been Fish and Flesh of Buffaloes drest, the Bones lying but a little from it.

In 3 Days we fill'd about twenty six Tun of Water, and then had on Board about 30 Ton in all. The 2 following Days we spent in Fishing with the Saine, and the first Morning caught as many as served all my Ship's Company: But afterwards we had not so good Success. The rest of my Men, which could be spared from the Ship, I sent out; Some with the Carpenter's Mate, to cut Timber for my Boats, &c. These went always guarded with 3 or 4 armed Men to secure them: I shewed them what Wood was fitting to cut for our Use, especially the Calabash and Maho; I shewed them also the manner of stripping the Maho-bark, and of making therewith Thread, Twine, Ropes, &c. Others were sent out a Fowling; who brought Home Pidgeons, Parrots, Cackatoos, &c. I was always with one Party or other, my self; especially with the Carpenters, to hasten them to get what they could, that we might be gone from hence.

Our Water being full, I sail'd from hence October the 6th about 4 in the Afternoon, designing to coast along Shore to the Eastward, till I came to the Portugueze Settlements. By the next Morning we were driven 3 or 4 Leagues to the West of the Bay; but in the Afternoon, having a faint Sea-breeze, we got again abreast of it. It was the 11th Day at Noon before we got as far as the small Island before-mentioned, which lies about 7 Leagues to the East of the Watering Bay: For what we gained in the Afternoon by the Benefit of the Sea-breezes we lost again in the Evenings and Mornings, while it was calm, in the Interval of the Breezes. But this Day the Sea-breeze blowing fresher than ordinary, we past by the Island and run before Night about 7 Leagues to the East of it.

This Island is not half a Mile long, and not above 100 Yards in breadth, and look'd just like a Barn, when we were by it: It is pretty high, and may be seen from a Ship's Topmast-head about 10 Leagues. The Top, and Part of the Sides, are covered with Trees, and it is about 3 Leagues from Timor; 'tis about Mid-way between the Watering-place and the Portugueze first and main Settlement by the Shore.

In the Night we were again driven back toward the Island, 3 Leagues: But the 12th Day, having a pretty brisk Sea-breeze, we coasted along Shore; and seeing a great many Houses by the Sea, I stood in with my Ship till I was within 2 Miles of them, and then sent in my Boat, and lay by till it returned. I sent an Officer to command the Boat; and a Portugueze Seaman that I brought from Brazil, to speak with the Men that we saw on the Bay; there being a great many of them, both Foot and Horse. I could not tell what Officer there might be amongst them; but I ordered my Officer to tell the Chief of them that we were English, and came hither for Refreshment. As soon as the Boat came ashore, and the Inhabitants were informed who we were, they were very glad, and sent me Word that I was welcome, and should have any thing that the Island afforded; and that I must run a little farther about a small Point, where I should see more Houses; and that the Men would stand on the Bay, right against the Place where I must anchor. With this News the Boat immediately returned; adding withal, that the Governour lived about 7 Miles up in the Country; and that the chief Person here was a Lieutenant, who desired me, as soon as the Ship was at Anchor, to send ashore one of my Officers to go to the Governour, and certify him of our Arrival. I presently made Sail towards the Anchoring-place, and at 5 a Clock anchored in Laphao Bay, in 20 Fathom, soft Oaze, over against the Town. A description of which, and of the Portugueze Settlement there, shall be given in the following Chapter.

Assoon as I came to Anchor, I sent my Boat ashore with my second Mate, to go to the Governour. The Lieutenant that lived here, had provided Horses and Guides for him, and sent 4 Soldiers with him for his Guard, and, while he was absent, treated my Men with Arack at his own House, where he and some others of the Townsmen shew'd them many broad thin Pieces of Gold; telling them that they had Plenty of that Metal, and would willingly traffick with them for any Sort of European Commodities. About 11 a Clock my Mate returned on Board, and told me he had been in the Country, and was kindly received by the Gentleman he went to wait upon;

who said we were welcome, and should have any thing the Island afforded; and that he was not himself the Governour, but only a Deputy. He asked why we did not salute their Fort when we anchored; My Mate answer'd, that we saw no Colours flying, and therefore did not know there was any Fort till he came ashore and saw the Guns; and if we had known that there was a Fort, yet that we could not have given any Salute till we knew that they would answer it with the like Number of Guns. The Deputy said, it was very well; and that he had but little Powder; and therefore would gladly buy some of us, if we had any to spare; which my Mate told him, we had not.

The 13th the Deputy sent me aboard a Present of 2 young Buffaloes, 6 Goats, 4 Kids, 140 Coco-nuts, 300 ripe Mangoes, and 6 ripe Jacks. This was all very acceptable; and all the Time we lay here, we had fresh Provision, and Plenty of Fruits; so that those of my Men that were sick of the Scurvy, soon recover'd and grew lusty. I staid here till the 22d, went ashore several Times, and once purposely to see the Deputy; who came out of the Country also on purpose to see and talk with me. And then indeed there were Guns fired for Salutes, both aboard my Ship and at the Fort. Our Interview was in a small Church, which was fill'd with the better Sort of People; the poorer Sort thronging on the Outside, and looking in upon us: For the Church had no Wall but at the East-end; the Sides and the West-end being open, saving only that it had Boards about 3 or 4 Foot high from the Ground. I saw but 2 white Men among them all; One was a Padre that came along with the Lieutenant; the other was an Inhabitant of the Town. The rest were all Copper-colour'd, with black lank Hair. I staid there about 2 Hours, and we spoke to each other by an Interpreter. I asked particularly about the Seasons of the Year, and when they expected the North-North-West Monsoon. The Deputy told me, that they expected the Wind to shift every Moment; and that some Years the North-North-West Monsoon set in in September, but never failed to come in October; and for that Reason desir'd me to make what haste I could from hence; for 'twas impossible to ride here when those Winds came. I asked him if there was no Harbour hereabouts, where I might be secured from the Fury of these Winds at their first coming. He told me, that the best Harbour in the Island was at a Place called Babao, on the North-side of Copang Bay; that there were no Inhabitants there, but Plenty of Buffaloes in the Woods, and Abundance of Fish in the Sea; that there was also fresh Water: That there was another

Place, call'd Port Sesiall, about 20 Leagues to the Eastward of Laphao; that there was a River of fresh Water there, and Plenty of Fish, but no Inhabitants: Yet that, if I would go thither, he would send People with Hogs, Goats and Buffaloes, to truck with me for such Commodities as I had to dispose of.

I was afterwards told, that on the East-end of the Island Ende there was also a very good Harbour, and a Portugueze Town; that there was great Plenty of Refreshments for my Men, and Dammer for my Ship; that the Governour or Chief of that Place, was call'd Captain More; that he was a very courteous Gentleman, and would be very glad to entertain an English Ship there; and if I designed to go thither, I might have Pilots here that would be willing to carry me, if I could get the Lieutenant's Consent. That it was dangerous going thither without a Pilot, by Reason of the violent Tides that run between the Islands Ende and Solor. I was told also, that at the Island Solor there were a great many Dutchmen banisht from other Places for certain Crimes. I was willing enough to go thither, as well to secure my Ship in a good Harbour, where I might careen her, (there being Dammer also, which I could not get here, to make use of instead of Pitch, which I now wanted,) and where I might still be refreshing my Men and supporting them, in order to my further Discoveries; as also to inform my self more particularly concerning these Places as yet so little known to us. Accordingly I accepted the Offer of a Pilot and two Gentlemen of the Town, to go with me to Larentucka on the Island Ende: And they were to come on Board my Ship the Night before I sailed. But I was hindred of this Design by some of my Officers, who had here also been very busie in doing me all the Injury they could underhand.

But to proceed. While I staid here, I went ashore every Day, and my Men took there Turns to go ashore and traffick for what they had Occasion for; and were now all very well again: And to keep themselves in Heart, every Man bought some Rice, more or less, to recruit them after our former Fatigues. Besides, I order'd the Purser to buy some for them, to serve them instead of Pease, which were now almost spent. I fill'd up my Water-Casks again here, and cut more Wood; and sent a Present to the Lieutenant, Alexis Mendosa, designing to be gone; for while I lay here, we had some Tornadoes and Rain, and the Sky in the North-West looked very black Mornings and Evenings, with Lightning all Night from that Quarter, which made me very uneasy and desirous to depart hence; because this Road lay expos'd to the North-North-West and North Winds, which were now daily expected, and which are commonly so violent, that 'tis impossible for any Ship to ride them out: Yet, on the other Hand, it was absolutely necessary for me to spend about 2 Months Time longer in some Place here-abouts, before I could prosecute my Voyage farther to the Eastward; for Reasons which I shall give hereafter in its proper Place in the ensuing Discourse. When therefore I sent the Present to the Governour, I desired to have a Pilot to Larentucka on the Island Ende; where I desir'd to spend the Time I had to spare. He now sent me Word that he could not well do it, but would send me a Letter to Port Sesiall for the Natives, who would come to me there and supply me with what Provision they had.

I staid 3 Days, in hopes yet to get a Pilot for Larentucka, or at least the Letter from the Governour to Port Sesiall. But seeing neither, I sail'd from hence the 22d of October, coasting to the Eastward, designing for Sesiall; and before Night, was about 10 Leagues to the East of Laphao. I kept about 3 Leagues off Shore, and my Boat ranged along close by the Shore, looking into every Bay and Cove; and at Night returned on Board. The next Morning, being 3 or 4 Leagues farther to the Eastward, I sent my Boat ashore again to find Sesiall. At Noon they returned, and told me they had been at Sesiall, as they guess'd; that there were two Portugueze Barks in the Port, who threatned to fire at them, but did not; telling them this was *Porto del Roy de Portugal.* They saw also another Bark, which ran and anchor'd close by the Shore; and the Men ran all away for fear: But our Men calling to them in Portugueze, they at last came to them, and told them that Sesiall was the Place which they came from, where the 2 Barks lay: Had not these Men told them, they could not have known it to be a Port, it being only a little bad Cove, lying open to the North; having 2 Ledges of Rocks at its Entrance, one on each Side; and a Channel between, which was so narrow, that it would not be safe for us to go in. However I stood in with the Ship, to be better satisfied; and when I came near it, found it answer my Men's Description. I lay by a-while, to consider what I had best do; for my Design was to lye in a Place where I might get fresh Provisions if I could: For though my Men were again pretty well recruited; and those that had been sick of the Scurvy, were well again; yet I design'd, if possible, to refresh them as much and as long as I could, before I went farther. Besides, my Ship wanted cleaning; and I was resolved to clean her, if possible.

At last after much Consideration, I thought it safer to go away again for

Babao; and accordingly stood to the Westward. We were now about 60 Leagues to the East of Babao. The Coast is bold all the way, having no Sholes, and but one Island which I saw and describ'd coming to the Eastward. The Land in the Country is very mountainous; but there are some large Valleys towards the East-end. Both the Mountains and Valleys on this Side, are barren; some wholly so; and none of them appear so pleasant as the Place where I watered. It was the 23d Day in the Evening when I stood back again for Babao. We had but small Sea and Land-breezes. On the 27th we came into Copang Bay; and the next Day having sounded Babao Road, I ran in and came to an Anchor there, in 20 Fathom, soft Oaze, 3 Mile from the Shore. One Reason, as I said before, of my coming hither, was to ride secure, and to clean my Ship's Bottom; as also to endeavour by Fishing and Hunting of Buffaloes, to refresh my men and save my salt Provision. It was like to be some Time before I could clean my Ship, because I wanted a great many Necessaries, especially a Vessel to careen by. I had a Long-Boat in a Frame, that I brought out of England, by which I might have made a Shift to do it; but my Carpenter was uncapable to set her up. Besides, by that Time the Ship's-sides were calk'd, my Pitch was almost spent; which was all owing to the Carpenter's wilful Waste and Ignorance; so that I had nothing to lay on upon the Ship's Bottom. But instead of this, I intended to make Lime here, which with Oyl would have made a good Coat for her. Indeed had it been adviseable, I would have gone in between Cross Island and Timor, and have hal'd my Ship ashore; for there was a very convenient Place to do it in; but my Ship being sharp, I did not dare to do it: Besides, I must have taken every thing out of her; and I had neither Boats to get my Things ashore, nor Hands to look after them when they were there; for my men would have been all employed; and though here are no Indians living near, yet they come hither in Companies when Ships are here, on Purpose to do any Mischief they can to them; and 'twas not above 2 Years since a Portugueze Ship riding here, and sending her Boat for Water to one of the Galleys, the Men were all killed by the Indians. But to secure my Men, I never suffer'd them to go ashore unarmed; and while some were at Work, others stood to guard them.

We lay in this Place from October the 28th, till December the 12th. In which Time we made very good Lime with Shells, of which here are plenty. We cut Palmeto-leaves to burn the Ship's-sides; and giving her as good a Heel as we could, we burned her Sides, and paid them with Lime and

Water for want of Oyl to mix with it. This stuck on about 2 Months, where 'twas well burned. We did not want fresh Provisions all the Time we lay here, either of Fish or Flesh. For there were fair sandy Bays on the Point of Babao, where in 2 or 3 Hours in a Morning we used with our Sain to drag ashore as much Fish as we could eat all the Day; and for a Change of Diet, when we were weary of Fish, I sent 10 or 11 armed Men a hunting for Buffaloes; who never came empty home. They went ashore in the Evening or early in the Morning, and before Noon always returned with their Burdens of Buffalo, enough to suffice us 2 Days; by which Time we began to long for Fish again.

On the 11th of November, the Governour of Concordia sent one of his Officers to us, to know who we were. For I had not sent thither, since I came to Anchor last here. When the Officer came aboard, he ask'd me why we fired so many Guns the 4th and 5th Days; (which we had done in Honour of King William, and in Memory of the Deliverance from the Powder-Plot:) I told him the occasion of it; and he replied that they were in some Fear at the Fort that we had been Portugueze, and that we were coming with Soldiers to take their Fort; He asked me also why I did not stay and fill my Water at their Fort, before I went away from thence? I told him the Reason of it, and withal offered him Money; bidding him take what he thought reasonable: He took none, and said he was sorry there had been such a Misunderstanding between us; and knew that the Governour would be much concerned at it. After a short Stay, he went ashore; and the next Morning came aboard again, and told me the Governour desired me to come ashore to the Fort and dine with him; and, if I doubted any thing, he would stay aboard till I returned. I told him I had no Reason to mistrust any thing against me, and would go ashore with him; so I took my Clerk and my Gunner, and went ashore in my Pinnace: The Gunner spoke very good French, and therefore I took him to be my Interpreter, because the Governour speaks French: He was an honest Man, and I found him always diligent and obedient. It was pretty late in the Afternoon before we came ashore; so that we had but little Time with the Governour. He seem'd to be much dissatisfied at the Report my Officer had made to me; (of which I have before given an Account;) and said it was false, neither would he now take any Money of me; but told me I was welcome; as indeed I found by what he provided. For there was plenty of very good Victuals, and well drest; and the Linnen was white and clean; and all the Dishes and Plates, of Silver or

fine China. I did not meet any where with a better Entertainment, while I
was abroad; nor with so much Decency and Order. Our Liquor was Wine,
Beer, Toddy, or Water, which we liked best after Dinner. He shew'd me
some Drawers full of Shells, which were the strangest and most curious that
I had ever seen. He told me, before I went away, that he could not supply
me with any Naval Stores; but if I wanted any fresh Provision, he would
supply me with what I had occasion for. I thank'd him, and told him I
would send my Boat for some Goats and Hogs, though afterwards on second
Thoughts I did not do it: For 'twas a great way from the Place where we lay,
to the Fort; and I could not tell what Mischief might befall any of my Men,
when there, from the Natives; especially if incouraged by the Dutch, who
are Enemies to all Europeans but such as are under their own Government.
Therefore I chose rather to fish and hunt for Provisions, than to be beholden
to the Dutch, and pay dearly for it too.

We found here, as I said before, Plenty of Game; so that all the Time we
lay at this Place, we spent none or very little of our Salt-provisions; having
Fish or fresh Buffaloe every Day. We lay here 7 Weeks; and although the
North-North-West Monsoon was every Day expected when I was at Laphao,
yet it was not come, so that if I had prosecuted my Voyage to the Eastward
without staying here, it had been but to little Advantage. For if I had gone
out, and beaten against the Wind a whole Month, I should not have got far;
it may be 40, 50, or 60 Leagues; which was but 24 Hours run for us with a
large Wind; besides the Trouble and Discontent, which might have arisen
among my Men in beating to Windward to so little Purpose, there being
nothing to be got at Sea; but here we lived and did eat plentifully every Day
without Trouble. The greatest Inconveniency of this Place, was want of
Water; this being the latter Part of the dry Season, because the Monsoon was
very late this Year. About 4 Days before we came away, we had Tornadoes,
with Thunder, Lightning and Rain, and much Wind; but of no long Continuance; at which Time we filled some Water. We saw very black Clouds,
and heard it thunder every Day for near a Month before, in the Mountains;
and saw it rain, but none came near us: And even where we hunted, we saw
great Trees torn up by the Roots, and great Havock made among the Woods
by the Wind; yet none touched us.

CHAP. II

An. 1699 The Island Timor, as I have said in my *Voyage round the World*, is about seventy Leagues long, and fourteen or sixteen broad. It lies nearly North-East and South-West. The Middle of it lies in about 9 d. South Lat. It has no Navigable Rivers, nor many Harbours; but abundance of Bays, for Ships to ride in at some Seasons of the Year. The Shore is very bold, free from Rocks, Shoals or Islands; excepting a few which are visible, and therefore easily avoided. On the South-side there is a Shole laid down in our Draughts, about thirty Leagues from the South-West-end; I was fifteen or twenty Leagues further to the East than that distance, but saw nothing of the Shole; neither could I find any Harbour. It is a pretty even Shore, with Sandy Bays and low Land for about three or four Miles up; and then 'tis mountainous. There is no Anchoring but with half a League or a League at farthest from the Shore; and the low Land that bounds the Sea, hath nothing but red Mangroves, even from the Foot of the Mountains till you come within a hundred and fifty or two hundred paces of the Sea; and then you have Sandbanks, cloath'd with a sort of Pine; so that there is no getting Water on this side, because of the Mangroves.

At the South-West end of Timor, is a pretty high Island, called Anabao. It is about ten or twelve Leagues long, and about four broad; near which the Dutch are settled. It lies so near Timor, that 'tis laid down in our Draughts as part of that Island; yet we found a narrow deep Channel fit for any Ships to pass between them. This Channel is about ten Leagues long, and in some places not above a League wide. It runs North-East and South-West, so deep that there is no Anchoring but very nigh the Shore. There is but little tide; the Flood setting North, and the Ebb to the Southward. At the North-East-end of this Channel, are two Points of Land, not above a League asunder; one on the South-side upon Timor, called Copang; the other on the North-side, upon the Island Anabao. From this last point, the Land trends away Northerly two or three Leagues, opens to the Sea, and then bends in again to the Westward.

Being past these Points, you open a Bay of about eight Leagues long, and four wide. This Bay trends in on the South-side North-East by East from the South-point before mentioned; making many small Points or little Coves. About a League to the East of the said South-point, the Dutch have a small Stone Fort, situated on a firm Rock close by the Sea: This Fort they call Concordia. On the East-side of the Fort, there is a small River of fresh Water, which has a broad boarded Bridge over it, near to the Entry into the Fort. Beyond this River is a small sandy Bay, where the Boats and Barks land and convey their Traffick in or out of the Fort. About an hundred Yards from the Sea-side, and as many from the Fort, and forty Yards from the Bridge on the East-side, the Company have a fine Garden, surrounded with a good Stone-Wall; In it is plenty of all sorts of Sallads, Cabbages, Roots for the Kitchen; in some parts of it are Fruit-trees, as Jaca's, Pumplenose, Oranges, sweet Lemons, &c. and by the Walls are Coco-nut and Toddy-trees in great plenty. Besides these, they have Musk and Water-Melons, Pine-Apples, Pomecitrons, Pome-granates, and others sorts of Fruits. Between this Garden and the River, there is a Penn for black Cattle, whereof they have plenty. Beyond the Companies Ground, the Natives have their Houses, in number about fifty or sixty. There are forty or fifty Soldiers belonging to this Fort, but I know not how many Guns they have; For I had only opportunity to see one Bastion, which had in it four Guns. Within the Walls there is a neat little Church or Chapel.

Beyond Concordia the Land runs about seven Leagues to the bottom of the Bay; then it is not above a League and half from side to side, and the Land trends away Northerly to the North-Shore, then turns about again to the Westward, making the South-side of the Bay. About three Leagues and a half from the bottom of the Bay on this side, there is a small Island about a Musket-shot from the Shore; and a Riff of Rocks that runs from it to the Eastward about a mile. On the West-side of the Island is a Channel of three Fathom at low Water, of which depth it is also within, where Ships may haul in and careen. West from this Island the Land rounds away in a Bite or Elbow, and at last ends in a low point of Land, which shoots forth a Ledge of Rocks a mile into the Sea, which is dry at Low-Water. Just against the low Point of Land, and to the West of the Ledge of Rocks, is another pretty high and rocky, yet woody Island, about half a mile from the low Point;

which Island hath a Ledge of corally Rocks running from it all along to the other small Island, only leaving one Channel between them. Many of these Rocks are to be seen at Low-Water, and there seldom is Water enough for a Boat to go over them till quarter Flood or more. Within this Ledge there is two or three Fathom Water, and without it no less than ten or twelve Fathom close to the Rocks. A League without this last Rocky Island, is another small low sandy Island, about four Miles from the low Point, three Leagues from the Dutch-Fort Concordia, and three Leagues and a half from the South-West-point of the Bay. Ships that come in this way, must pass between this low Isle and the low Point, keeping near the Isle.

In this Bay there is any depth of Water from thirty to three Fathom, very good oazy holding Ground. This affords the best Shelter against all Winds of any place about the Island Timor. But from March to October, while either the Southerly Winds or only Land and Sea-breezes hold, the Concordia Side is best to ride in; but when the more violent Northerly Winds come, then the best riding is between the two rocky Islands in nineteen or twenty Fathom. If you bring the Westermost Island to bear South-West by West about a League distance, and the low Point West by South; then the Body of the sandy Island will bear South-West half West, distance two Leagues; and the Ledges of Rocks shooting from each, make such a Bar, that no Sea can come in. Then you have the Land from West by South to East-North-East, to defend you on that Side: And other Winds do not here blow violently. But if they did, yet you are so Land-lock'd, that there can be no Sea to hurt you. This Anchoring place is call'd Babao, about five Leagues from Concordia. The greatest Inconveniency in it, is the multitude of Worms. Here is fresh Water enough to be had in the wet Season; every little Gull discharging fresh Water into the Sea. In the dry Season you must search for it in standing Ponds or Gulls, where the wild Buffaloes, Hogs, &c. resort every Morning and Evening to drink; where you may lye and shoot them, taking care that you go strong enough and well-armed against the Natives upon all occasions. For though there are no Inhabitants near this place; yet the Malayans come in great Companies when Ships are here; and if they meet with any Europeans, they kill them, of what Nation soever they be, not excepting the Portugueze themselves. 'Tis but two Years since a Portugueze Ship riding here, had all the Boats crew cut off as they were watering; as I was inform'd by the Dutch. Here likewise is plenty of Fish of several sorts, which may be catch'd with a Sain; also Tortoise and Oysters.

From the North-East-point of this Bay, on the North-side of the Island, the Land trends away North-North-East for four or five Leagues; afterward North-East or more Easterly; And when you are fourteen or fifteen Leagues to the Eastward of Babao, you come up with a Point that makes like Flamborough-Head, if you are pretty nigh the Land; but if at a distance from it on either side, it appears like an Island. This point is very remarkable, there being none other like it in all this Island. When you are abreast of this Point, you will see another Point about four Leagues to the Eastward; and when you are abreast of this latter Point, you will see a small Island bearing East or East by North (according to your distance from the Land,) just rising out of the Water: When you see it plain, you will be abreast of a pretty deep sandy Bay, which hath a point in the Middle, that comes sloaping from the Mountains, with a curious Valley on each side: The sandy Bay runs from one Valley to the other. You may sail into this Bay, and anchor a little to the Eastward of the Point in twenty Fathom Water, half a Mile from the Shore, soft Oaze. Then you will be about two Leagues from the West-point of the Bay, and about eight Leagues from the small Island before mentioned, which you can see pretty plain bearing East-North-East a little Northwardly. Some other Marks are set down in the foregoing Chapter. In this sandy Bay you will find fresh Water in two or three places. At Spring-tides you will see many Riplings, like Sholes; but they are only Eddies caused by the two Points of the Bay.

We saw Smoaks all Day up in the Mountains, and Fires by Night, at certain places, where we supposed the Natives lived, but saw none of them.

The Tides ran between the two Points of the Bay, very strong and uncertain: Yet it did not rise and fall above nine Foot upon a Spring-tide: But it made great Riplings and a roaring Noise; whirling about like Whirlpools. We had constantly eddy Tides under the Shore, made by the Points on each side of the Bay.

When you go hence to the Eastward, you may pass between the small Island, and Timor; and when you are five or six Leagues to the Eastward of the small island, you will see a large Valley to the Eastward of you; then running a little further, you may see Houses on the Bay: You may luff in, but anchor not till you go about the next Point. Then you will see more Houses, where you may run into twenty or thirty Fathom, and anchor right against the Houses, nearest the West-end of them. This place is called Laphao. It is a Portugueze Settlement, about sixteen Leagues from the Watering-bay.

There are in it about forty or fifty Houses, and one Church. The Houses are mean and low, the Walls generally made of Mud or watled, and their Sides made up with Boards: They are all thatch'd with Palm or Palmeto-Leaves. The Church also is very small: The East-end of it is boarded up to the Top; but the Sides and the West-end are only boarded three or four foot high; the rest is all open: There is a small Altar in it, with two Steps to go up to it, and an Image or two; but all very mean. 'Tis also thatch'd with Palm or Palmeto-Leaves. Each House has a Yard belonging to it, fenced about with wild Canes nine or ten Foot high. There is a Well in each Yard, and a little Bucket with a String to it to draw Water withal. There is a Trunk of a Tree made hollow, placed in each Well, to keep the Earth from falling in. Round the Yards there are many Fruit-trees planted; as Coco-nuts, Tamarins and Toddy-trees.

They have a small Hovel by the Sea-side, where there are six small old Iron Guns standing on a decayed Platform, in rotten Carriages. Their Vents are so big, that when they are fired, the strength of the Powder flying out there, they give but a small Report, like that of a Musket. This is their Court of Guard; and here were a few armed-men watching all the time we lay here.

The Inhabitants of the Town, are chiefly a sort of Indians, of a Copper-colour, with black lank Hair: They speak Portugueze, and are of the Romish Religion; but they take the Liberty to eat Flesh when they please. They value themselves on the account of their Religion and descent from the Portugueze; and would be very angry, if a Man should say they are not Portugueze; Yet I saw but three White Men here, two of which were Padres. There are also a few Chinese living here. It is a place of pretty good Trade and Strength, the best on this Island, Porta-Nova excepted. They have three or four small Barks belonging to the place; with which they trade chiefly about the Island with the Natives, for Wax, Gold, and Sandall-wood. Sometimes they go to Batavia, and fetch European Commodities, Rice, &c.

The Chinese trade hither from Macao; and I was informed that about twenty Sail of small Vessels come from thence hither every Year. They bring coarse Rice, adulterated Gold, Tea, Iron, and Iron-tools, Porcellane, Silks, &c. They take in exchange pure Gold, as 'tis gathered in the Mountains, Bees-wax, Sandall-wood, Slaves, &c. Sometimes also here comes a Ship from Goa. Ships that trade here, begin to come hither the latter-end of March; and none stay here longer than the latter-end of August. For should they be here while the North-North-West Monsoon blows, no Cables nor Anchors would hold them; but they would be driven ashore and dash'd in pieces presently. But from March till September, while the South-South-East Monsoon blows, Ships ride here very secure; For then, though the Wind often blows hard, yet 'tis off Shore; so that there is very smooth Water, and no fear of being driven ashore; And yet even then they moor with three Cables; two towards the Land, Eastward and Westward; and the third right off to Seaward.

As this is the second place of Traffick, so 'tis in Strength the second place the Portugueze have here, though not capable of resisting a hundred Men: For the Pirates that were at the Dutch Fort, came hither also; and after they had fill'd their Water, and cut Fire-wood, and refresh'd themselves, they plunder'd the Houses, set them on fire, and went away. Yet I was told, that the Portugueze can draw together five or six hundred Men in twenty four Hours time, all armed with Hand-Guns, Swords and Pistols; but Powder and Bullets are scarce and dear. The chief Person they have on the Island, is named Antonio Henriquez; They call him usually by the Title of Captain More or Maior. They say he is a white Man, and that he was sent hither by the Vice-Roy of Goa. I did not see him; for he lives, as I was informed, a great way from hence, at a place call'd Porta Nova, which is at the East-end of the Island, and by report is a good Harbour; but they say, that this Captain More goes frequently to Wars in Company with the Indians that are his Neighbours and Friends, against other Indians that are their Enemies. The next Man to him is Alexis Mendosa; he is a Lieutenant, and lives six or seven Miles from hence, and rules this part of the Country. He is a little Man of the Indian-Race, Copper-coloured, with black lank Hair. He speaks both the Indian and Portugueze Languages; is a Roman Catholick, and seems to be a civil brisk Man. There is another Lieutenant at Laphao; who is also an Indian; speaks both his own and the Portugueze Language very well; is old and infirm, but was very courteous to me.

They boast very much of their Strength here, and say they are able at any time to drive the Dutch away from the Island, had they Permission from the King of Portugal so to do. But though they boast thus of their Strength, yet really they are very weak; for they have but a few small Arms, and but little Powder: They have no Fort, nor Magazine of Arms; nor does the Vice-Roy of Goa send them any now: For though they pretend to be under the King of Portugal, they are a sort of lawless People, and are under no

An.1699 Government. It was not long since the Vice-Roy of Goa sent a Ship hither, and a Land-Officer to remain here: But Captain More put him in Irons, and sent him aboard the Ship again; telling the Commander, that he had no occasion for any Officers; and that he could make better Officers here, than any that could be sent him from Goa: and I know not whether there has been any other Ship sent from Goa since: So that they have no Supplies from thence: Yet they need not want Arms and Ammunition, seeing they trade to Batavia. However, they have Swords and Lances as other Indians have; and tho' they are ambitious to be called Portugueze, and value themselves on their Religion, yet most of the Men and all the Women that live here, are Indians; and there are very few right Portugueze in any part of the Island. However, of those that call themselves Portugueze, I was told there are some thousands; and I think their Strength consists more in their Numbers than in good Arms or Discipline.

The Land from hence trends away East by North about 14 Leagues, making many Points and sandy Bays, where Vessels may Anchor.

Fourteen Leagues East from Laphao, there is a small Harbour called Ciccale by the Portugueze, and commended by them for an excellent Port; but it is very small, has a narrow Entrance, and lies open to Northerly Winds: Though indeed there are two Ledges of Rocks, one shooting out from the West Point, and the other from the East Point, which break off the Sea; for the Rocks are dry at low Water. This Place is about 60 Leagues from the South-west-end of the Island.

The whole of this Island Timor, is a very uneven rough Country, full of Hills and small Valleys. In the Middle of it there runs a Chain of high Mountains, almost from one end to the other. It is indifferently well watered (even in the dry times) with small Brooks and Springs, but no great Rivers; the Island being but narrow, and such a Chain of Mountains in the middle, that no Water can run far; but, as the Springs break out on one side or other of the Hills, they make their nearest Course to the Sea. In the wet Season, the Valleys and low Lands by the Sea are overflown with Water; and then the small Drills that run into the Sea, are great Rivers; and the Gulleys, which are dry for 3 or 4 Months before, now discharge an impetuous Torrent. The low Land by the Sea-side, is for the most part friable, loose, sandy Soil; yet indifferently fertile and cloathed with Woods. The Mountains are checquered with Woods, and some Spots of Savannahs: Some of the Hills are wholly covered with tall, flourishing Trees; others but thinly; and these few Trees that are on them, look very small, rusty and withered; and the Spots of Savannahs among them, appear rocky and barren. Many of the Mountains are rich in Gold, Copper or both: The Rains wash the Gold out of Mountains, which the Natives pick up in the adjacent Brooks, as the Spaniards do in America: How they get the Copper, I know not.

The Trees that grow naturally here, are of divers Sorts; many of them wholly unknown to me; but such as I have seen in America or other places, and grow here likewise, are these, *viz.* Mangrove, white, red and black; Maho. Calabash, several Sorts of the Palm-kind: The Cotton-trees are not large, but tougher than those in America: Here are also Locust-trees of 2 or 3 Sorts, bearing Fruit, but not like those I have formerly seen; these bear a large white Blossom, and yield much Fruit, but it is not sweet.

Cana-fistula-trees, are very common here; the Tree is about the Bigness of our ordinary Apple-Trees; their Branches not thick, nor full of Leaves. These and the before-mentioned, blossom in October and November; the Blossoms are much like our Apple-Tree Blossoms, and about that Bigness: At first they are red; but before they fall off, when spread abroad, they are white; so that these Trees in their Season appear extraordinarily pleasant, and yield a very fragrant Smell. When the Fruit is ripe, it is round, and about the Bigness of a Man's Thumb; of a dark brown Colour, inclining to red, and about 2 Foot or 2 Foot and half long. We found many of them under the Trees, but they had no Pulp in them. The Partitions in the Middle, are much at the same Distance with those brought to England, of the same Substance, and such small flat Seed in them: But whether they be the true Cana-fistula or no, I cannot tell, because I found no black Pulp in them.

The Calabashes here are very prickly: The Trees grow tall and tapering; whereas in the West-Indies they are low and spread much abroad.

Here are also wild Tamarind-trees, not so large as the true; though much resembling them both in the Bark and Leaf.

Wild Fig-trees here are many, but not so large as those in America. The Fruit grows, not on the Branches singly, like those in America, but in Strings and Clusters, 40 or 50 in a Cluster, about the Body and great Branches of the Tree, from the very Root up to the Top. These Figs are about the Bigness of a Crab-Apple, of a greenish Colour, and full of small white Seeds; they smell pretty well, but have no Juice or Taste; they are ripe in November.

Here likewise grows Sandal-wood, and many more Sorts of Trees fit for
any Uses. The tallest among them, resemble our Pines; they are streight and
clear-bodied, but not very thick; the Inside is reddish near the Heart, and
hard and ponderous.

Of the Palm-kind there are 3 or 4 Sorts; two of which Kinds I have not
seen any where but here. Both Sorts are very large, and tall. The first Sort
had Trunks of about 7 or eight Foot in Circumference, and about 80 or 90
Foot high. These had Branches at the Top like Coco-nut-Trees, and their
Fruit like Coco-nuts, but smaller: The Nut was of an oval Form, and about
the Bigness of a Duck's Egg: The Shell black and very hard. 'Twas almost
full of Kernel, having only a small empty Space in the Middle, but no
Water as Coco-nuts have. The Kernel is too hard to be eaten. The Fruit
somewhat resembles that in Brazil formerly mentioned. The Husk or
Outside of the Fruit, was very yellow, soft and pulpy, when ripe; and full of
small Fibres; and when it fell down from the Tree, would mash and smell
unsavoury.

The other Sort was as big and tall as the former; the Body growing
streight up without Limbs, as all Trees of the Palm-kind do: But instead of
a great many long green Branches growing from the Head of the Tree, these
had short Branches about the Bigness of a Man's Arm, and about a Foot
long; each of which spread it self into a great many small tough Twigs, that
hung full of Fruit like so many Ropes of Onions. The Fruit was as big as a
large Plumb; and every Tree had several Bushels of Fruit. The Branches
that bore this Fruit, sprouted out at about 50 or 60 Foot heighth from the
Ground. The Trunk of the Tree was all of one Bigness, from the Ground to
that Heighth; but from thence it went tapering smaller and smaller to the
Top, where it was no bigger that a Man's Leg, ending in a Stump: And
there was no Green about the Tree, but the Fruit; so that it appeared like a
dead Trunk.

Besides Fruit-Trees, here were many Sorts of tall streight-bodied Timber-
Trees; one Sort of which, was like Pine. These grow plentifully all round
the Island by the Sea-side, but not far within Land. 'Tis hard Wood, of a
reddish Colour, and very ponderous.

The Fruits of this Island, are Guavoes, Mangoes, Jaca's, Coco-nuts,
Plantains, Bonanoes, Pine-Apples, Citrons, Pome-granates, Oranges,
Lemons, Limes, Musk-Melons, Water-Melons, Pumpkins, &c. Many of
these have been brought hither by the Dutch and Portugueze; and most of

them are ripe in September and October. There were many other excellent Fruits, but not now in Season; as I was inform'd both by Dutch and Portugueze.

Here I met with an Herb, which in the West-Indies we call Calalaloo. It grows wild here. I eat of it several Times, and found it as pleasant and wholesome as Spinage. Here are also Parsly, Sampier, &c. Indian Corn thrives very well here, and is the common Food of the Islanders; though the Portugueze and their Friends sow some Rice, but not half enough for their Subsistence.

The Land-Animals are Buffaloes, Beeves, Horses, Hogs, Goats, Sheep, Monkeys, Guanoes, Lizards, Snakes, Scorpions, Centumpees, &c. Beside the tame Hogs and Buffaloes, there are many wild all over the Country, which any may freely kill. As for the Beeves, Horses, Goats and Sheep, it is probable they were brought in by the Portugueze or Dutch; especially the Beeves; for I saw none but at the Dutch Fort Concordia.

We also saw Monkeys, and some Snakes. One Sort yellow, and as big as a Man's Arm, and about 4 Foot long: Another Sort no bigger than the Stem of a Tobacco-pipe, about 5 Foot long, green all over his Body, and with a flat red Head as big as a Man's Thumb.

The Fowls are wild Cocks and Hens, Eagles, Hawks, Crows, 2 Sorts of Pidgeons, Turtle-doves, 3 or 4 Sorts of Parrots, Parrakites, Cockatoes, Black-birds; besides a Multitude of smaller Birds of divers Colours, whose charming Musick makes the Woods very pleasant. One Sort of these pretty little Birds my Men call'd the Ringing-bird; because it had 6 Notes, and always repeated all his Notes twice one after another; beginning high and shrill, and ending low. This Bird was about the Bigness of a Lark, having a small sharp black Bill and blue Wings; the Head and Breast were of a pale red, and there was a blue Streak about its Neck. Here are also Sea or Water-Fowls, as Men of War-Birds, Boobies, Fishing-hawks, Herons, Goldens, Crab-catchers, &c. The tame Fowl are Cocks, Hens, Ducks, Geese; the 2 last Sorts I only saw at the Dutch Fort; of the other Sort there are not many but among the Portugueze: The Woods abound with Bees, which make much Honey and Wax.

The Sea is very well stock'd with Fish of divers Sorts, *viz.* Mullets, Bass, Breames, Snooks, Mackarel, Parracoots, Gar-fish, Ten-pounders, Scuttle-fish, String-rays, Whip-rays, Rasperages, Cockle-merchants, or Oyster-crackers, Cavallies, Conger-Eels, Rock-fish, Dog-fish, &c. The Rays are so plentiful, that I never drew the Sain but I catch'd some of them; which we salted and dryed. I caught one whose Tail was 13 Foot long. The Cockle-Merchants are shaped like Cavallies, and about their Bigness. They feed on Shell-fish, having 2 very hard, thick, flat Bones in their Throat, with which they break in Pieces the Shells of the Fish they swallow. We always find a great many Shells in their Maws, crushed in Pieces. The Shell-fish, are Oysters of 3 Sorts, *viz.* Long-Oysters, Common Oysters, growing upon Rocks in great Abundance, and very flat; and another Sort of large Oysters, fat and crooked; the Shell of this, not easily to be distinguished from a Stone. Three or four of these roasted, will suffice a Man for one Meal. Cockles, as big as a Man's Head; of which 2 or 3 are enough for a Meal; they are very fat and sweet. Craw-fish, Shrimps, *&c.* Here are also many green Turtle, some Alligators and Grandpisces, *&c.*

The Original Natives of this Island, are Indians, they are of a middle Stature, streight-bodied, slender-limb'd, long-visag'd; their Hair black and lank; their Skins very swarthy. They are very dextrous and nimble, but withal lazy in the highest Degree. They are said to be dull in every Thing but Treachery and Barbarity. Their Houses are but low and mean, their Cloathing only a small Cloath about their Middle; but some of them for Ornament have Frontlets of Mother of Pearl, or thin Pieces of Silver or Gold, made of an oval Form, of the Breadth of a Crown-piece, curiously notched round the Edges; Five of these placed one by another a little above the Eye-brows, making a sufficient Guard and Ornament for their Fore-head. They are so thin, and placed on their Fore-heads so artificially, that they seem riveted thereon: And indeed the Pearl-Oyster-shells make a more splendid Show, than either Silver or Gold. Others of them have Palmeto-caps made in divers Forms.

As to their Marriages, they take as many Wives as they can maintain; and sometimes they sell their Children to purchase more Wives. I enquir'd about their Religion, and was told they had none. Their common Subsistence is by Indian Corn, which every Man plants for himself. They take but little Pains to clear their Land; for in the dry Time they set Fire to the withered Grass and Shrubs, and that burns them out a Plantation for the next wet Season. What other Grain they have, beside Indian Corn, I know not. Their Plantations are very mean; for they delight most in hunting; and here are wild Buffaloes and Hogs enough, though very shy, because of their so frequent hunting.

They have a few Boats and some Fishermen. Their Arms are Lances, thick round short Truncheons and Targets; with these they hunt and kill their Game, and their Enemies too; for this Island is now divided into many Kingdoms, and all of different Languages; though in their Customs and Manner of living, as well as Shape and Colour, they seem to be of one Stock.

The chiefest Kingdoms are Cupang, Amabie, Lortribie, Pobumbie, Namquimal; the Island also of Anamabao or Anabao, is a Kingdom. Each of these hath a Sultan who is supreme in his Province and Kingdom, and hath under him several Raja's and other inferiour Officers. The Sultans for the most Part are Enemies to each other; which Enmities are fomented and kept up by the Dutch, whose Fort and Factory is in the Kingdom of Cupang; and therefore the Bay near which they are settled, is commonly called Cupang-Bay. They have only as much Ground as they can keep within Reach of their Guns; yet this whole Kingdom is at Peace with them; and they freely trade together; as also with the Islanders on Anabao, who are in Amity as well with the Natives of Cupang, as with the Dutch residing there; but they are implacable Enemies to those of Amabie, who are their next Neighbours, and in Amity with the Portugueze: as are also the Kingdoms of Pobumbie, Namquimal and Lortribie. It is very probable, that these 2 European Settlements on this Island, are the greatest Occasion of their continued Wars. The Portugueze vaunt highly of their Strength here, and that they are able at Pleasure to rout the Dutch, if they had Authority so to do from the King of Portugal; and they have written to the Vice-roy of Goa about it: And though their Request is not yet granted, yet (as they say) they live in Expectation of it. These have no Forts, but depend on their Alliance with the Natives: And indeed they are already so mixt, that it is hard to distinguish whether they are Portugueze or Indians. Their Language is Portugueze; and the Religion they have, is Romish. They seem in Words to acknowledge the King of Portugal for their Sovereign; yet they will not accept of any Officers sent by him. They speak indifferently the Malayan and their own native Languages, as well as Portugueze; and the chiefest Officers that I saw, were of this Sort; neither did I see above 3 or 4 white Men among them; and of these, 2 were Priests. Of this mixt Breed there are some thousands; of whom some have small Arms of their own, and know how to use them. The chiefest Person (as I before said) is called Captain More or Maior: He is a white Man, sent hither by the Vice-Roy of Goa, and seems to have great Command here. I did not see him; for he seldom comes down. His Residence is at a Place called Porta Nova; which the People at Laphao told me was a great way off; but I could not get any more particular Account. Some told me that he is most commonly in the Mountains, with an Army of Indians, to guard the Passes between them and the Cupangayans, especially in the dry Times. The next Man to him is Alexis Mendosa: He is a right Indian, speaks very good Portugueze, and is of the Romish Religion. He lives 5 or 6 Miles from the Sea, and is called the Lieutenant. (This is he whom I call'ed Governour, when at Laphao.) He commands next to Captain More, and hath under him another at this Fort (at the Seaside) if it may be so called. He also is called Lieutenant, and is an Indian Portugueze.

Besides this Mungrel-Breed of Indians and Portugueze, here are also some China-Men, Merchants from Maccao: They bring hither coarse Rice, Gold, Tea, Iron-work, Porcelane, and Silk both wrought and raw: They get in Exchange pure Gold as it is here gather'd, Bees-wax, Sandall-Wood, Coire, &c. It is said there are about 20 small China Vessels come hither every Year from Maccao; and commonly one Vessel a Year from Goa, which brings European Commodities and Callicoes, Muslins, &c. Here are likewise some small Barks belonging to this Place, that trade to Batavia, and bring from thence both European and Indian Goods and Rice. The Vessels generally come here in March, and stay till September.

The Dutch, as I before said, are setled in the Kingdom of Cupang, where they have a small neat Stone Fort. It seems to be pretty strong; yet, as I was informed, had been taken by a French Pirate about 2 Years ago: The Dutch were used very barbarously, and ever since are very jealous of any Strangers that come this Way; which I my self experienced. These depend more on their own Strength than on the Natives their Friends; having good Guns, Powder, and Shot enough on all Occasions, and Soldiers sufficient to manage the Business here, all well disciplin'd and in good Order; which is a Thing the Portugueze their Neighbours are altogether destitute of, they having no European Soldiers, few Arms, less Ammunition, and their Fort consisting of no more than 6 bad Guns planted against the Sea, whose Touch-holes (as was before observed) are so enlarg'd by Time, that a great Part of the Strength of the Powder flies away there; and having Soldiers in pay, the Natives on all Occasions are hired; and their Government now is so loose, that they will admit of no more Officers from Portugal or Goa. They have also little or no Supply of Arms or Ammunition from thence, but buy it as often as they can, of the Dutch, Chinese, &c. So that upon the whole it seems improbable that they should ever attempt to drive out the Dutch, for fear of loosing themselves, notwithstanding their boasted Prowess and Alliance with the Natives: And indeed, as far as I could hear, they have Business enough to keep their own present Territories from the Incursions of the Cupangayans; who are Friends to the Dutch, and whom doubtless the Dutch have ways enough to preserve in their Friendship; besides that they have an inveterate Malice to their Neighbours, insomuch that they kill all they meet, and bring away their Heads in Triumph. The great Men of Cupang stick the Heads of those they have killed, on Poles; and set them on the Tops of their Houses; and these they esteem above all their other Riches. The inferiour Sort bring the Heads of those they kill, into Houses made for that Purpose; of which there was one at the Indian Village near the Fort Concordia, almost full of Heads, as I was told. I know not what Encouragement they have for their Inhumanity.

The Dutch have always 2 Sloops belonging to their Fort; in these they go about the Island, and trade with the Natives, and, as far as I could learn, they trade indifferently with them all. For though the Inland People are at war with each other, yet those by the Sea-side seem to be little concerned; and, generally speaking the Malayan Language, are very sociable and easily induced to trade with those that speak that Language; which the Dutch here always learn; Besides, being well acquainted with the Treachery of these People, they go well arm'd among them, and are very vigilant never to give them an Opportunity to hurt them; and it is very probable that they supply them with such Goods, as the Portugueze cannot.

The Malayan Language, as I have before said, is generally spoken amongst all the Islands hereabouts. The greater the Trade is, the more this Language is spoken: In some it is become their only Language; in others it is but little spoken, and that by the Sea-side only. With this Language the Mahometan Religion did spread it self, and was got hither before any European Christians came: But now, though the Language is still used, the Mahometan Religion falls, where-ever the Portugueze or Dutch are settled; unless they be very weak, as at Solor and Ende, where the chief Language is Malayan, and the Religion Mahometanism; though the Dutch are settled at Solor, and the Portugueze at the East-end of the Island Ende, at a Place called Lorantuca; which, as I was informed, is a large Town, hath a pretty strong Fort and safe Harbour. The chief Man there (as at Timor) is called

Captain More, and is as absolute as the other. These 2 principal Men are Enemies to each other; and by their Letters and Messages to Goa, inveigh bitterly against each other; and are ready to do all the ill Offices they can; yet neither of them much regards the Vice-Roy of Goa, as I was inform'd.

L'Orantuca is said to be more populous than any Town on Timor; the Island Ende affording greater Plenty of all manner of Fruit, and being much better supplied with all Necessaries, than Laphao; especially with Sheep, Goats, Hogs, Poultry, &c. but it is very dangerous getting into this Harbour, because of the violent Tides, between the Islands Ende and Solor. In the middle Channel between Timor and the Range of Islands to the Northward of it, whereof Ende and Solor are 2, there runs a constant Current all the Year to the Westward; though near either Shore there are Tides indeed; but the Tide of Flood, which sets West, running 8 or 9 Hours, and the Ebb not exceeding 3 or 4 Hours, the Tide in some Places riseth 9 or 10 Foot on a Spring.

The Seasons of the Year here at Timor, are much the same as in other Places in South Latitude. The fair Weather begins in April or May, and continues to October, then the Tornadoes begin to come, but no violent bad Weather till the Middle of December. Then there are violent West or North-West Winds, with Rain, till towards the Middle of February. In May the Southerly Winds set in, and blow very strong on the North-side of the Island, but fair. There is great Difference of Winds on the 2 Sides of the Island: For the Southerly Winds are but very faint on the South-side, and very hard on the North-side; and the bad Weather on the South-side comes in very violent in October, which on the North-side comes not till December. You have very good Sea and Land-breezes, when the Weather is fair; and may run indifferently to the East or West, as your Business lies. We found from September to December the Winds veering all round the Compass gradually in 24 Hours Time; but such a constant Western Current, that it's much harder getting to the East than West at or near Spring Tides: Which I have more than once made Tryal of. For weighing from Babao at 6 a Clock in the Morning on the 12th Instant, we kept plying under the Shore till the 20th, meeting with such a Western Current, that we gain'd very little. We had Land and Sea-breezes; but so faint, that we could hardly stem the Current; and when it was calm between the Breezes, we drove a-Stern faster than ever we sailed a-Head.

CHAP. III

On the 12th of December 1699, we sailed from Babao, coasting along the Island Timor to the Eastward, towards New Guinea. It was the 20th before we got as far as Laphao, which is but forty Leagues. We saw black Clouds in the North-West, and expected the Wind from that Quarter above a Month sooner.

That Afternoon we saw the opening between the Islands Omba and Fetter, but feared to pass through in the Night. At two a Clock in the Morning, it fell calm; and continued so till Noon, in which time we drove with the Current back again South-West six or seven Leagues.

On the 22d, steering to the Eastward to get through between Omba and Fetter, we met a very strong Tide against us, so that we, although we had a very fresh Gale, yet made way very slowly; yet before Night, got through. By a good Observation we found that the South-East-point of Omba lies in Latitude 8 d. 25 m. In my Draughts it's laid down in 8 deg. 10 min. My true Course from Babao, is East, 25 deg. North, distance one hundred eighty three miles. We sounded several times when near Omba, but had no ground. On the North-East point of Omba we saw four or five Men, and a little further three pretty Houses on a low Point, but did not go ashore.

At five this Afternoon, we had a Tornado, which yielded much Rain, Thunder and Lightning; yet we had but little Wind. The 24th in the Morning we catched a large Shark, which gave all the Ships Company a plentiful Meal.

The 27th we saw the burning Island, it lies in Latitude 6 deg. 36 min. South; it is high, and but small. It runs from the Sea a little sloaping towards the Top; which is divided in the Middle into two Peaks, between which issued out much Smoak: I have not seen more from any Vulcano. I saw no Trees; but the North-side appeared green, and the rest look'd very barren.

An. 1699   Having past the burning Island, I shap'd my Course for two Islands
called Turtle Isles, which lye North-East by East a little Easterly, and
distant about fifty Leagues from the burning Isle. I fearing the Wind might
veer to the Eastward of the North, steered 20 Leagues North-East, then
North-East by East. On the 28th we saw two small low Islands, called
Luca-parros, to the North of us. At Noon I accounted my self 20 Leagues
short of the Turtle Isles.

The next Morning, being in the Latitude of the Turtle Islands, we look'd
out sharp for them, but saw no appearance of any Island, till 11 a Clock;
when we saw an Island at a great distance. At first we supposed it might be
one of the Turtle Isles: But it was not laid down true, neither in Latitude
nor Longitude from the burning Isle, nor from the Luca-parros, which last
I took to be a great help to guide me, they being laid down very well from
the Burning Isle, and that likewise in true Latitude and distance from
Omba: So that I could not tell what to think of the Island now in sight; we
having had fair Weather, so that we could not pass by the Turtle Isles
without seeing them; and This in sight was much too far off for them. We
found Variation 1 deg. 2 min. East. In the Afternoon I steered North-East
by East for the Islands that we saw. At 2 a Clock I went and look'd over the
Fore-yard, and saw 2 Islands at much greater distance than the Turtle
Islands are laid down in my Draughts; one of them was a very high peak'd
Mountain, cleft at Top, and much like the burning Island that we past by,
but bigger and higher; the other was a pretty long high flat Island. Now I
was certain that these were not the Turtle Islands, and that they could be no
other than the Bande-Isles; yet we steered in, to make them plainer. At 3 a
Clock we discovered another small flat Island to the North-West of the
others, and saw a great deal of Smoak rise from the Top of the high Island;
At 4 we saw other small Islands, by which I was now assured that these were
the Bande-Isles there. At 5 I altered my Course and steered East, and at 8
East-South-East; because I would not be seen by the Inhabitants of those
Islands in the Morning. We had little Wind all Night: and in the Morning
as soon as 'twas Light, we saw another high peak'd Island: At 8 it bore
South-South-East half East, distance 8 Leagues. And this I knew to be Bird-
Isle. 'Tis laid down in our Draughts in Latitude 5 deg. 9 min. South, which
is too far Southerly by 27 Miles according to our Observation; And the like
Error in laying down the Turtle-Islands, might be the Occasion of our
missing them.

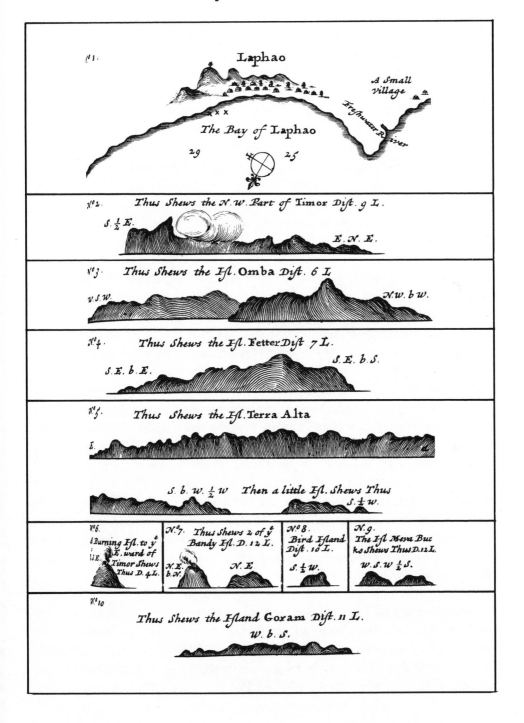

Nº 1.

Laphao

A Small Village

Freſhwater River

The Bay of Laphao

29   25

Nº 2.   *Thus Shews the N. W. Part of Timor Diſt. 9 L.*

S. ½ E.   E. N. E.

Nº 3.   *Thus Shews the Iſl. Omba Diſt. 6 L*

v. s. w.   N. w. b w.

Nº 4.   *Thus Shews the Iſl. Fetter Diſt. 7 L.*

S. E. b. E.   S. E. b. S.

Nº 5.   *Thus Shews the Iſl. Terra Alta*

E.

S. b. w. ½ w   *Then a little Iſl. Shews Thus*

S. ¼ w.

Nº 6.   A Burning Iſl. to yᵉ E. ward of Timor Shews Thus D. 4 L.

S. E.

Nº 7. *Thus Shews 2 of yᵉ Bandy Iſl. D. 12 L.*

N. E. b. N.   N. E.

Nº 8. *Bird Iſland Diſt. 10 L.*

S. ¼ w.

Nº 9. *The Iſl. Meva Buc ko Shews Thus D. 12 L.*

w. s. w ½ S.

Nº 10

Thus Shews the Iſland Goram Diſt. 11 L.

w. b. S.

An. 1699   At night I shortned Sail, for fear of coming too nigh some Islands, that stretch away bending like a half Moon from Ceram towards Timor, and which in my Course I must of necessity pass through. The next Morning betimes, I saw them; and found them to be at a farther distance from Bird-Island, than I expected. In the Afternoon it fell quite calm; and when we had a little Wind, it was so unconstant, flying from one Point to another, that I could not without difficulty get through the Islands where I designed: Besides, I found a Current setting to the Southward; so that it was betwixt 5 and 6 in the Evening, before I past through the Islands; and then just weathered little Waiela, whereas I thought to have been 2 or 3 Leagues more Northerly. We saw the day before, betwixt 2 and 3, a Spout but a small distance from us. It fell down out of a black Cloud, that yielded great store of Rain, Thunder and Lightning: This Cloud hovered to the Southward of us for the space of three Hours, and then drew to the Westward a great pace; at which time it was that we saw the Spout, which hung fast to the Cloud till it broke; and then the Cloud whirl'd about to the South-East, then to East-North-East; where meeting with an Island, it spent it self and so dispersed; and immediately we had a little of the Tail of it, having had none before. Afterward we saw a Smoak on the Island Kosiway, which continued till Night.

An. 1700   On New-years-day we first described the Land of New-Guinea, which appear'd to be high Land; And the next day we saw several high Islands on the Coast of New-Guinea, and ran in with the main Land. The Shore here lies along East-South-East and West-North-West. It is high even land, very well cloathed with tall flourishing Trees, which appear'd very green and gave us a very pleasant Prospect. We ran to the Westward of four mountainous Islands; and in the Night had a small Tornado, which brought with it some Rain and a fair Wind. We had fair Weather for a long time; only when near any Land, we had some Tornadoes; but off, at Sea, commonly clear Weather; though if in sight of Land, we usually saw many black Clouds hovering about it.

On the 5th and 6th of January, we plied to get in with the Land; designing to anchor, fill Water, and spend a little time in searching the Country, till after the change of the Moon; For I found a strong Current setting against us. We anchor'd in 38 Fathom Water, good oazie Ground. We had an Island of a League long without us, about 3 Miles distant; and we rode from the Main about a Mile. The Eastermost Point of Land seen,

Table VIII   **New Guinea**

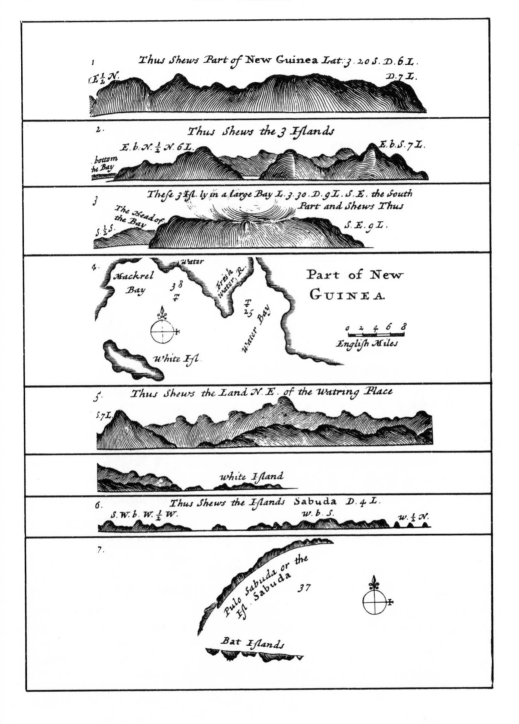

1. *Thus Shews Part of New Guinea Lat: 3. 20 S. D. 6 L.*
.E ½ N.   *D. 7 L.*

2. *Thus Shews the 3 Islands*
E. b. N. ½ N. 6 L.   E. b. S. 7 L.
.bottom the Bay

3. *These 3 Isl. ly in a large Bay L. 3. 30. D. 9 L. S. E. the South*
Part and Shews Thus
The Head of the Bay
S. ½ S.   S. E. 9 L.

4. Mackrel Bay   water   Fresh water R.
3 8   7
T 25
Water Bay
White Isl.

Part of New
GUINEA.

0 2 4 6 8
English Miles

5. *Thus Shews the Land N. E. of the Watring Place*
S. 7 L.

white Island

6. *Thus Shews the Islands Sabuda D. 4 L.*
S. W. b. W. ½ W.   w. b. S.   w. ½ N.

7.
Pulo Sabuda or the Isl. Sabuda   37

Bat Islands

bore East by South half South, distance 3 Leagues: And the Westermost, West-South-West half South, distance 2 leagues. So soon as we anchor'd, we sent the Pinnace to look for Water, and try if they could catch any Fish. Afterwards we sent the Yawle another way to see for Water. Before Night the Pinnace brought on board several sorts of Fruits, that they found in the Woods, such as I never saw before. One of my Men killed a stately Land-Fowl, as big as the largest Dunghil-Cock. It was of a Sky-colour; only in the middle of the Wings was a white Spot, about which were some reddish Spots: On the Crown it had a large Bunch of long Feathers, which appear'd very pretty. His Bill was like a Pidgeons; he had strong Legs and Feet, like Dunghil-Fowls; only the Claws were reddish. His Crop was full of small Berries. It lays an Egg as big as a large Hen's Egg; for our Men climb'd the Tree where it nested, and brought off one Egg. They found Water; and reported that the Trees were large, tall and very thick; and that they saw no sign of People. At night the Yawle came aboard, and brought a wooden *Fissgigg, very ingeniously made; the Matter of it was a small Cane; They found it by a small Barbecue, where they also saw a shatter'd Canoa.

The next Morning I sent the Boatswain ashore a fishing, and at one Haul he catcht 352 Mackarels, and about 20 other Fishes; which I caused to be equally divided among all my Company. I sent also the Gunner and chief Mate, to search about if they could find convenient anchoring nearer a Water-ing-place: By night they brought word that they had found a fine Stream of good Water, where the Boat could come close to, and it was very easie to be fill'd; and that the Ship might anchor as near to it as I pleas'd: So I went thither. The next Morning therefore we anchor'd in 25 Fathom Water, soft oazie Ground, about a Mile from the River: We got on board 3 Tun of Water that Night; and caught 2 or 3 Pike-fish, in shape much like a Parracota, but with a longer Snout, something resembling a Garr, yet not so long. The next day I sent the Boat again for Water, and before night all my Casks were full.

Having fill'd here about 15 Tuns of Water, seeing we could catch but little Fish, and had no other Refreshments, I intended to sail next day; but finding that we wanted Wood, I sent to cut some; and going ashore to hasten it, at some distance from the place where our Men were, I found a small Cove, where I saw two Barbecues, which appear'd not to be above 2 Months

*   Fish-spear.

standing: The Sparrs were cut with some sharp Instrument; so that, if done by the Natives, it seems that they have Iron. On the 10th, a little after 12 a-Clock, we weighed and stood over to the North-side of the Bay; and at 1 a-Clock stood out with the Wind at North and North-North-West. At 4 we past out by a White Island, which I so named from its many white Cliffs, having no name in our Draughts. It is about a League long, pretty high, and very woody: 'Tis about 5 Miles from the Main, only at the West-end it reaches within 3 Miles of it. At some distance off at Sea, the West-point appears like a Cape-land; The North-side trends away North-North-West, and the East-side East-South-East. This Island lies in Latitude 3 degrees 4 min. South; and the Meridian Distance from Babao, 500 and 12 Miles East. After we were out to Sea, we plied to get to the Northward; but met with such a strong Current against us, that we got but little. For if the Wind favour'd us in the night, that we got 3 or 4 Leagues; we lost it again, and were driven as far astern next Morning; so that we plyed here several Days.

The 14th, being past a point of Land that we had been 3 Days getting about, we found little or no Current; so that having the Wind at North-West by West and West-North-West, we stood to the Northward, and had several Soundings: At 3 a-Clock, 38 Fathom; the nearest part of New-Guinea being about 3 Leagues distance: At 4, 37; at 5, 36; at 6, 36; at 8, 33 Fathom; Then the Cape was about 4 Leagues distant; so that as we ran off, we found our Water shallower. We had then some Islands to the Westward of us, at about four Leagues distance.

A little after noon we saw Smokes on the Islands to the West of us; and having a fine Gale of Wind, I steered away for them: At 7 a-Clock in the Evening we anchored in 35 Fathom, about two Leagues from an Island, good soft oazie Ground. We lay still all night, and saw Fires ashore. In the Morning we weighed again, and ran farther in, thinking to have shallower Water; but we ran within a Mile, of the Shore, and came to in 38 Fathom, good soft holding Ground. While we were under Sail, 2 Canoes came off within call of us: They spoke to us, but we did not understand their Language, nor Signs. We wav'd to them to come aboard, and I call'd to them in the Malayan Language to do the same; but they would not; yet they came so nigh us, that we could shew them such Things as we had to truck with them; Yet neither would this entice them to come aboard; but they made Signs for us to come ashore, and away they went. Then I went after them in my Pinnace, carrying with me Knives, Beads, Glasses, Hatchets,

&c. When we came near the Shore, I called to them in the Malayan Language: I saw but 2 Men at first, the rest lying in Ambush behind the Bushes; but assoon as I threw ashore some Knives and other Toys, they came out, flung down their Weapons, and came into the Water by the Boat's Side, making Signs of Friendship by pouring Water on their Heads with one Hand, which they dipt into the Sea. The next Day in the Afternoon several other Canoes came aboard, and brought many Roots and Fruits, which we purchas'd.

This Island has no Name in our Draughts, but the Natives call it Pulo Sabuda. It is about 3 Leagues long, and 2 Miles wide, more or less. It is of a good Heighth, so as to be seen 11 or 12 Leagues. It is very Rocky; yet above the Rocks, there is good yellow and black Mould; not deep, yet producing plenty of good tall Trees, and bearing any Fruits or Roots which the Inhabitants plant. I do not know all its Produce; but what we saw, were Plantains, Coco-Nuts, Pine-Apples, Oranges, Papaes, Potatoes, and other large Roots. Here are also another sort of wild Jaca's, about the bigness of a Mans two Fists, full of Stones or Kernels, which eat pleasant enough when roasted. The Libby Tree grows here in the Swampy Valleys, of which they make Sago Cakes: I did not see them make any, but was told by the Inhabitants that it was made of the Pith of the Tree, in the same Manner I have described in my *Voyage round the World.* They shew'd me the Tree whereof it was made, and I bought about 40 of the Cakes. I bought also 3 or 4 Nutmegs in their Shell, which did not seem to have been long gathered; but whether they be the Growth of this Island or not, the Natives would not tell whence they had them, and seem'd to prize them very much. What Beasts the Island affords, I know not: But here are both Sea and Land-Fowl. Of the first, Boobies and Men of War-Birds are the chief; some Goldens, and small Milk-white Crab-catchers. The Land-fowls are Pidgeons, about the Bigness of Mountain-Pidgeons in Jamaica; and Crows about the Bigness of those in England, and much like them; but the inner Part of their Feathers are white, and the Outside black; so that they appear all black, unless you extend the Feathers. Here are large Sky-colour'd Birds, such as we lately kill'd on New Guinea; and many other small Birds, unknown to us. Here are likewise Abundance of Bats, as big as young Coneys; their Necks, Head, Ears and Noses, like Foxes; their Hair rough; that about their Necks, is of a whitish yellow, that on their Heads and Shoulders black; their Wings are 4 Foot over, from Tip to Tip: They smell like Foxes. The Fish

are Bass, Rock-fish, and a Sort of Fish like Mullets, Old-wives, Whip-rays,
and some other Sorts that I know not, but no great Plenty of any; for 'tis
deep Water till within less than a Mile of the Shore; then there is a Bank of
Coral Rocks, within which you have Shoal Water, white clean Sand: So
there is no good Fishing with the Sain.

This Island lies in Latitude 2 deg. 43 min. South, and Meridian distance
from Port Babao on the Island Timor, 486 Miles. Besides this Island, here
are 9 or 10 other small Islands, as they are laid down in the Draughts.

The Inhabitants of this Island are a Sort of very tawny Indians, with long
black Hair; who in their Manners differ but little from the Mindanayans,
and others of these Eastern Islands. These seem to be the chief; for besides
them we saw also shock curl-pated New-Guinea Negroes; many of which are
Slaves to the others, but I think not all. They are very poor, wear no
Cloaths, but have a Clout about their Middle, made of the Rinds of the
Tops of Palmeto Trees; but the Women had a Sort of Callicoe-Cloaths.
Their chief Ornaments are Blue and Yellow-Beads, worn about their
Wrists. The Men arm themselves with Bows and Arrows, Lances, broad
Swords like those of Mindanao; their Lances are pointed with Bone. They
strike Fish very ingeniously with wooden Fiss-gigs, and have a very
ingenious way of making the Fish rise: For they have a Piece of Wood
curiously carv'd and painted much like a Dolphin (and perhaps other
Figures;) these they let down into the Water by a Line with a small Weight
to sink it; when they think it low enough, they haul the Line into their Boats
very fast, and the Fish rise up after this Figure; and they stand ready to
strike them when they are near the Surface of the Water. But their chief
Livelihood is from their Plantations. Yet they have large Boats, and go over
to New-Guinea, where they get Slaves, fine Parrots, &c. which they carry to
Goram and exchange for Callicoes. One Boat came from thence a little
before I arriv'd here; of whom I bought some Parrots; and would have
bought a Slave, but they would not barter for any Thing but Callicoes,
which I had not. Their Houses on this Side were very small, and seem'd
only to be for Necessity; but on the other Side of the Island we saw good
large Houses. Their Proes are narrow with Outlagers on each Side, like
other Malayans. I cannot tell of what Religion these are; but I think they are
not Mahometans, by their drinking Brandy out of the same Cup with us
without any Scruple. At this Island we continued till the 20th Instant,
having laid in Store of such Roots and Fruits as the Island afforded.

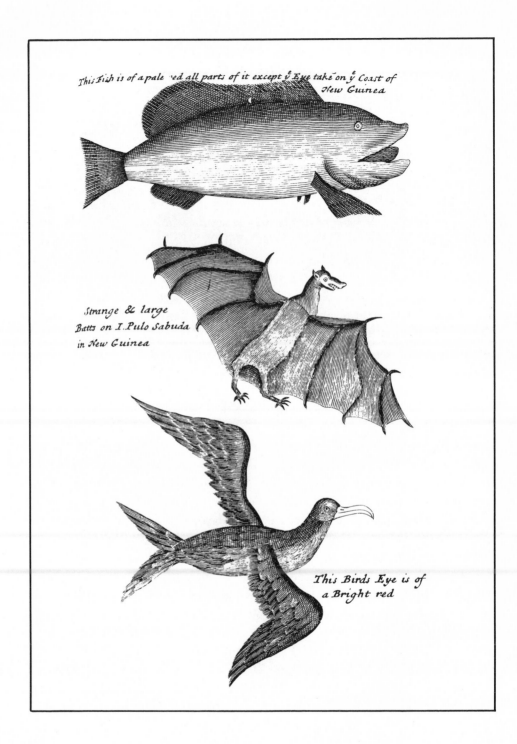

This Fish is of a pale _red_ all parts of it except _y_ Eye take on _y_ Coast of
New Guinea

Strange & large
Batts on I. Pulo Sabuda
in New Guinea

This Birds Eye is of
a Bright red

Table IX   New Guinea

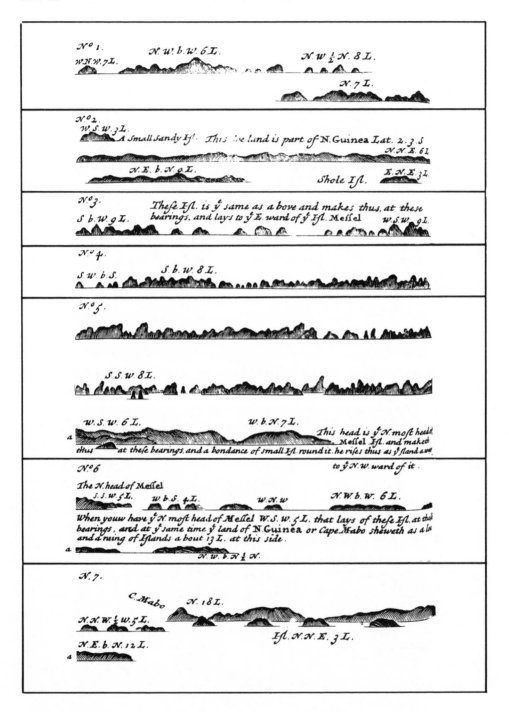

On the 20th, at half Hour after 6 in the Morning, I weigh'd, and standing out we saw a large Boat full of Men lying at the North-point of the Island. As we passed by, they rowed towards their Habitations, where we supposed they had withdrawn themselves for fear of us (tho' we gave them no Cause of Terrour,) or for some Differences among themselves.

We stood to the Northward till 7 in the Evening; then saw a Ripling; and the Water being discoloured, we sounded, and had but 22 Fathom. I went about and stood to the Westward till 2 next Morning, then tack'd again, and had these several Soundings: At 8 in the Evening, 22; at 10, 25; at 11, 27; at 12, 28 Fathom; at 2 in the Morning 26; at 4, 24; at 6, 23; at 8, 28; at 12, 22.

We passed by many small Islands, and among many dangerous Shoals, without any remarkable Occurrence, till the 4th of February, when we got within 3 Leagues of the North-West Cape of New-Guinea, called by the Dutch Cape Mabo. Off this Cape there lies a small woody Island, and many Islands of different Sizes to the North and North-East of it. This Part of New Guinea is high Land, adorn'd with tall Trees that appeared very green and flourishing. The Cape it self is not very high, but ends in a low sharp Point; and on either Side there appears another such Point at equal Distances, which makes it resemble a Diamond. This only appears when you are abreast of the middle Point; and then you have no Ground within 3 Leagues of the Shore.

In the Afternoon we past by the Cape, and stood over for the Islands. Before it was dark, we were got within a League of the Westermost; but had no Ground with 50 Fathom of Line. However fearing to stand nearer in the dark, we tack'd and stood to the East, and plyed all Night. The next Morning we were got 5 or 6 Leagues to the Eastward of that Island; and having the Wind Easterly, we stood in to the Northward among the Islands; sounded, and had no Ground. Then I sent in my Boat to sound, and they had Ground with 50 Fathom near a Mile from the Shore. We tack'd before the Boat came aboard again, for fear of a Shoal that was about a Mile to the East of that Island the Boat went to; from whence also a Shoal-point stretched out it self till it met the other: They brought with them such a Cockle, as I have mentioned in my *Voyage round the World*, found near Celebes; and they saw many more, some bigger than that which they brought aboard, as they said; and for this Reason I named it Cockle-Island. I sent them to sound again ordering them to fire a Musquet if they found good anchoring; we were then standing to the Southward, with a fine Breeze. Assoon as they fired, I tack'd and stood in: They told me they had 50 Fathom when they fired. I tack'd again, and made all the Sail I could to get out, being near some Rocky Islands and Shoals to Leeward of us. The Breeze increased, and I thought we were out of Danger; but having a Shoal just by us, and the Wind falling again, I ordered the Boat to tow us, and by their Help we got clear from it. We had a strong Tide setting to the Westward.

At 1 a-Clock, being past the Shoal, and finding the Tide setting to the Westward, I anchor'd in 35 Fathom, coarse Sand, with small Coral and Shells. Being nearest to Cockle-Island, I immediately sent both the Boats thither; one to cut Wood, and the other to fish. At 4 in the Afternoon, having a small Breeze at South-South-West, I made a Sign for my Boats to come aboard. They brought some Wood, and a few small Cockles, none of them exceeding 10 Pound weight; whereas the Shell of the great one weighed 78 Pound; but it was now high Water, and therefore they could get no bigger. They also brought on Board some Pidgeons, of which we found Plenty on all the Islands where we touch'd in these Seas. Also in many Places we saw many large Batts, but kill'd none, except those I mention'd at Pulo Sabuda. As our Boats came aboard, we weigh'd and made Sail, steering East-South-East, as long as the Wind held; In the Morning we found we had got 4 or 5 Leagues to the East of the Place where we weighed. We stood to and fro till 11; and finding that we lost Ground, anchor'd in 42 Fathom, coarse gravelly Sand, with some Coral. This Morning we thought we saw a Sail.

In the Afternoon I went ashore on a small woody Island, about 2 Leagues from us. Here I found the greatest Number' of Pidgeons that ever I saw either in the East or West-Indies, and small Cockles in the Sea round the Island, in such Quantities that we might have laden the Boat in an Hour's Time: These were not above 10 or 12 Pound Weight. We cut some Wood, and brought off Cockles enough for all the Ship's Company; but having no small Shot, we could kill no Pidgeons. I return'd about 4 a-Clock; and then my Gunner and both Mates went thither, and in less than 3 quarters of an Hour they kill'd and brought off 10 Pidgeons. Here is a Tide: The Flood sets West and the Ebb East; but the latter is very faint, and but of small Continuance. And so we found it ever since we came from Timor. The Winds we found Easterly, between North-East and East-South-East; so that if these continue, it is impossible to beat farther to the Eastward on this Coast against Wind and Current. These Easterly Winds encreased from the Time we were in the Latitude of about 2 deg. South; and as we drew nigher the Line, they hung more Easterly. And now being to the North of the Continent of New Guinea, where the Coast lies East and West, I find the Trade-wind here at East; which yet in higher Latitudes is usually at North-North-West and North-West; and so I did expect them here, it being to the South of the Line.

The 7th in the Morning I sent my Boat ashore on Pidgeon-Island, and staid still Noon. In the Afternoon my Men returned, brought 22 Pidgeons, and many Cockles, some very large, some small: They also brought one empty Shell, that weigh'd 258 Pound.

At 4 a-Clock we weigh'd, having a small Westerly Wind, and a Tide with us; at 7 in the Evening we anchor'd in 42 Fathom, near King William's Island, where I went ashore the next Morning, drank his Majesty's Health, and honour'd it with his Name. It is about 2 Leagues and a half in length, very high, and extraordinarily well cloathed with Woods. The Trees are of divers Sorts, most unknown to us, but all very green and flourishing; many of them had Flowers, some white, some purple, others yellow; all which smelt very fragrantly. The Trees are generally tall and streight-bodied, and may be fit for any Uses. I saw one of a clean Body, without Knot or Limb, 60 or 70 Foot high by Estimation. It was 3 of my Fathoms about, and kept its Bigness without any sensible Decrease even to the Top. The Mould of the Island is black, but not deep; it being very rocky. On the Sides and Top of the Island, are many Palmeto-Trees, whose Heads we could discern over all the other Trees, but their Bodies we could not see.

About 1 in the Afternoon we weighed and stood to the Eastward, between the Main and King William's Island; leaving the island on our Larboard side, and sounding till we were past the Island; and then we had no Ground. Here we found the Flood setting East by North, and the Ebb West by South. There were Shoals and small Islands between us and the Main, which caused the Tide to set very inconstantly, and make many Whirlings in the Water; yet we did not find the Tide to set strong any way, nor the Water to rise much.

On the 9th, being to the Eastward of King William's Island, we plied all Day between the Main and other Islands, having Easterly Winds and fair

An. 1700

Weather till 7 the next Morning. Then we had very hard Rain till 8, and saw many Shoals of Fish. We lay becalm'd off a pretty deep Bay on New-Guinea, about 12 or 14 Leagues wide, and 7 or 8 Leagues deep, having low Land near its Bottom, but high Land without. The Eastermost Part of New-Guinea seen, bore East by South, distant 12 Leagues: Cape Mabo West-South-West half South, distant 7 Leagues.

At 1 in the Afternoon it began to rain, and continu'd till 6 in the Evening; so that having but little Wind and most Calms, we lay still off the foremention'd Bay, having King William's Island still in Sight, though distant by Judgment 15 or 16 Leagues West. We saw many Shoals of small Fish, some Sharks, and 7 or 8 Dolphins; but catcht none. In the Afternoon, being about 4 Leagues from the Shore, we saw an Opening in the Land, which seem'd to afford good Harbour: In the Evening we saw a large Fire there; and I intended to go in (if Winds and Weather would permit) to get some Acquaintance with the Natives.

Since the 4th Instant that we passed Cape Mabo, to the 12th, we had small Easterly Winds and Calms, so that we anchor'd several Times; where I made my Men cut Wood, that we might have a good Stock when a Westerly Wind should present; and so we ply'd to the Eastward, as Winds and Currents would permit; having not got in all above 30 Leagues to the Eastward of Cape Mabo. But on the 12th, at 4 in the Afternoon, a small Gale sprung up at North-East by North, with Rain: At 5 it shuffled about to North-West, from thence to the South-West, and continued between those 2 Points a pretty brisk Gale; so that we made Sail and steered away North-East, till the 13th in the Morning, to get about the Cape of Good Hope. When 'twas Day, we steer'd North-East half East, then North-East by East till 7 a-Clock; and being then 7 or 8 Leagues off Shore, we steer'd away East; the Shore trending East by South. We had very much Rain all Night, so that we could not carry much Sail; yet we had a very steddy Gale. At 8 this Morning the Weather clear'd up, and the Wind decreas'd to a fine Top-gallant Gale, and settled at West by South. We had more Rain these 3 Days past, than all the Voyage in so short Time. We were now about 6 Leagues from the Land of New-Guinea, which appear'd very high; and we saw 2 Head-lands, about 20 Leagues asunder; the one to the East, and the other to the West, which last is called the Cape of Good Hope. We found Variation East 4 deg.

The 15th in the Morning between 12 and 2 a-Clock, it blew a very brisk

Table X   New Guinea &c.

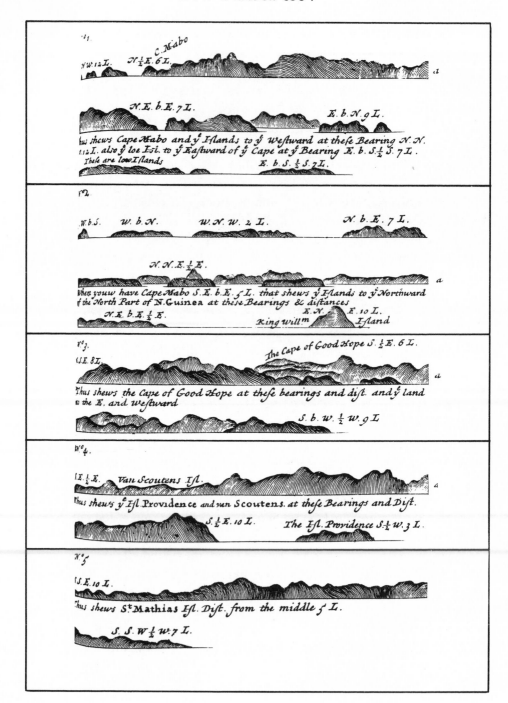

N°1.
N.W. 12 L. N ½ E. 6 L.   C. Mabo   a
N.E. b. E. 7 L.   E. b. N. 9 L.
Thus shews Cape Mabo and y⁰ Islands to y⁰ Westward at these Bearing N.N.
W. 12 L. also y⁰ loe Isl. to y⁰ Eastward of y⁰ Cape at y⁰ Bearing E. b. S. ½ S. 7 L.
These are low Islands   E. b. S. ½ S. 7 L.

N°2.
W. b. S.   W. b. N.   W. N. W. 2 L.   N. b. E. 7 L.
N. N. E. ½ E.   a
When youw have Cape Mabo S. E. b. E. 5 L. that shews y⁰ Islands to y⁰ Northward
of the North Part of N. Guinea at these Bearings & distances
N. E. b. E. ½ E.   E. N.   E. 10 L.
                    King willᵐ   Island

N°3.   The Cape of Good Hope S. ½ E. 6 L.
S.E. 8 L.   a
Thus shews the Cape of Good Hope at these bearings and dist. and y⁰ land
to the E. and Westward
                              S. b. W. ½ W. 9 L.

N°4.
S.E. ½ E.   Van Scoutens Isl.   a
Thus shews y⁰ Isl. Providence and van Scoutens. at these Bearings and Dist.
              S. ½ E. 10 L.   The Isl. Providence S. ¼ W. 3 L.

N°5.
S.E. 10 L.
Thus shews St Mathias Isl. Dist. from the middle 5 L.
        S. S. W. ½ W. 7 L.

Gale at North-West, and look'd very black in the South-West. At 2 it flew about at once to the South-South-West, and rained very hard. The Wind settled sometime at West-South-West, and we steered East-North-East till 3 in the Morning: Then the Wind and Rain abating, we steered East half North for fear of coming near the Land. Presently after, it being a little clear, the Man at the Bowsprit-end, call'd out, *Land on our Starboard Bow.* We lookt out and saw it plain. I presently sounded, and had but 10 Fathom soft Ground. The Master, being somewhat scar'd, came running in haste with this News, and said it was best to anchor: I told him no, but sound again; then we had 12 Fathom; the next Cast, 13 and a half; the 4th, 17 Fathom; and then no Ground with 50 Fathom Line. However we kept off the Island, and did not go so fast but that we could see any other Danger before we came nigh it. For here might have been more Islands not laid down in my Draughts besides This. For I search'd all the Draughts I had, if perchance I might find any Island in the one, which was not in the others; but I could find none near us. When it was Day, we were about 5 Leagues off the Land we saw; but, I believe, not above 5 Mile or at most 2 Leagues off it, when we first saw it in the Night.

This is a small Island, but pretty high; I named it Providence. About 5 Leagues to the Southward of this, there is another Island, which is called William Scouten's Island, and laid down in our Draughts: It is a high Island, and about 20 Leagues long.

It was by mere Providence that we miss'd the small Island. For had not the Wind come to West-South-West, and blown hard, so that we steered East-North-East; we had been upon it by our Course that we steered before, if we could not have seen it. This Morning we saw many great Trees and Logs swim by us; which it's probable came out of some great Rivers on the Main.

On the 16th we crossed the Line, and found Variation 6 deg. 26 min. East. The 18th by my Observation at Noon, we found that we had had a Current setting to the Southward, and probably that drew us in so nigh Scouten's Island. For this 24 Hours we steered East by North with a large Wind, yet made but an East by South half South Course; though the Variation was not above 7 deg. East.

The 21st we had a Current setting to the Northward, which is against the true Trade Monsoon, it being now near the full Moon. I did expect it here, as in all other Places. We had Variation 8 deg. 45 min. East. The 22d we

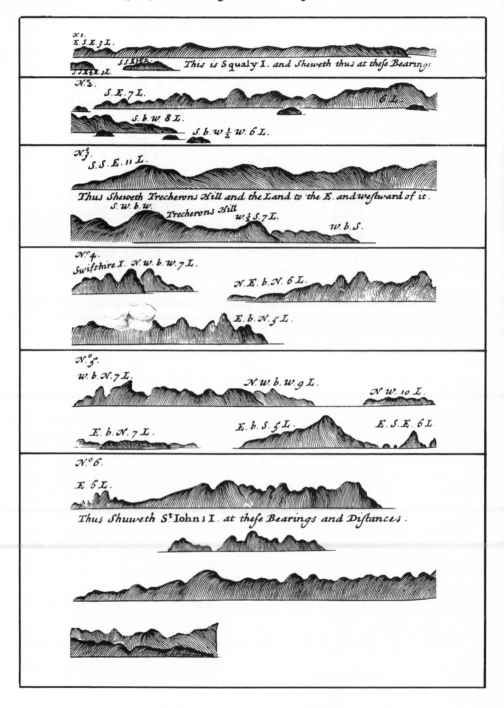

N.1.
E.S.E. 3 L.

This is Squaly I. and Sheweth thus at these Bearings
S.S.E 3 L.
S.S.E½E. 3 L.

N.2.
S.E. 7 L.

S.b.w. 8 L.
S.b.w.½.w. 6 L.

N.3.
S.S.E. 11 L.

Thus Sheweth Trecherons Hill and the Land to the E. and westward of it.
S.W.b.w.   Trecherons Hill   w.½.S. 7 L.   w.b.S.

N.º 4.
Swifſhire I. N.w.b.w. 7 L.

N.E. b.N. 6 L.

E.b.N. 5 L.

N.º 5.
w.b.N. 7 L.

N.w.b.w. 9 L.

N.W. 10 L.

E.b.N. 7 L.

E.b.S. 5 L.

E.S.E. 6 L.

N.º 6.

E. 6 L.

Thus Shuweth St Iohns I. at these Bearings and Diſtances.

found but little Current; if any, it set to the Southward.　　　　

On the 23d in the Afternoon we saw 2 Snakes; and the next Morning another, passing by us, which was furiously assaulted by 2 Fishes, that had kept us Company 5 or 6 Days. They were shaped like Mackarel, and were about that Bigness and Length, and of a yellow greenish Colour. The Snake swam away from them very fast, keeping his Head above Water; the Fish snapp'd at his Tail; but when he turn'd himself, that Fish would withdraw, and another would snap; so that by Turns they kept him employed; yet he still defended himself, and swam away a great Pace, till they were out of Sight.

The 25th betimes in the Morning, we saw an Island to the Southward of us, at about 15 Leagues distance. We steer'd away for it, supposing it to be that which the Dutch call Wishart's Island; but finding it otherwise, I called it Matthias; it being that Saint's Day. This Island is about 9 or 10 Leagues long, mountainous and woody, with many Savannah's, and some Spots of Land which seem'd to be clear'd.

At 8 in the Evening we lay by, intending, if I could, to anchor under Matthias Isle. But the next Morning seeing another Island, about 7 or 8 Leagues to the Eastward of it, we steer'd away for it; at Noon we came up fair with its South-West-end, intending to run along by it, and anchor on the South-East-side: But the Tornadoes came in so thick and hard, that I could not venture in. This Island is pretty low and plain, and cloath'd with Wood; the Trees were very green, and appear'd to be large and tall, as thick as they could stand one by another. It is about 2 or 3 Leagues long, and at the South-West-point there is another small low woody Island, about a Mile round, and about a Mile from the other. Between them there runs a Riff of Rocks, which joyns them. (The biggest, I named Squally Island.)

Seeing we could not anchor here, I stood away to the Southward, to make the Main. But having many hard Squalls and Tornadoes, we were often forced to hand all our Sails and steer more Easterly to go before it. On the 26th at 4 a Clock it clear'd up to a hard Sky, and a brisk settled Gale; then we made as much Sail as we could. At 5 it clear'd up over the Land, and we saw, as we thought, Cape Solomaswer bearing South-South-East distance 10 Leagues. We had many great Logs and Trees swimming by us all this Afternoon, and much Grass; we steered in South-South-East till 6, then the Wind slackned, and we stood off till 7, having little Wind; then we lay by till 10, at which Time we made Sail, and steer'd away East all Night. The

An. 1700 next Morning, as soon as it was light, we made all the Sail we could, and steer'd away East-South-East, as the Land lay; being fair in Sight of it, and not above 7 Leagues distance. We past by many small low woody Islands which lay between us and the Main, not laid down in our Draughts, We found Variation 9 deg. 50 min. East.

The 28th we had many violent Tornadoes, Wind, Rain, and some Spouts; and in the Tornadoes the Wind shifted. In the Night we had fair Weather, but more Lightning than we had seen at any Time this Voyage. This Morning we left a large high Island on our Larboard-side, called in the Dutch Draughts Wishart's Isle, about 6 Leagues from the Main; and seeing many Smoaks upon the Main, I therefore steer'd towards it.

Fishes taken on the Coast of New Guinea

This Fish fins & tail are blew on ẏ edges & red in the
middle with blew spots all over ẏ Body. but ẏ Belly white.

A Pike Fish Conger on ẏ Coast of New Guinea

This Fish is a pale red with blew spots on ẏ body the
long Tail blew in ẏ midle & white on ẏ side.

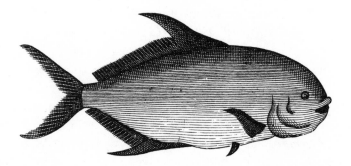

CHAP. IV

The main Land, at this place, is high and mountainous, adorn'd with tall flourishing Trees; The Sides of the Hills had many large Plantations and Patches of clear'd Land; which, together with the Smoaks we saw, were certain Signs of its being well inhabited; and I was desirous to have some Commerce with the Inhabitants. Being nigh the Shore, we saw first one Proe; a little after, 2 or 3 more; and at last a great many Boats came from all the adjacent Bays. When they were 46 in Number, they approach'd so near us, that we could see each others Signs, and hear each other speak; though we could not understand them, nor they us. They made Signs for us to go in towards the Shore, pointing that way; it was squally Weather, which at first made me cautious of going too near; but the Weather beginning to look pretty well, I endeavoured to get into a Bay a-head of us, which we could have got into well enough at first; but while we lay by, we were driven so far to leeward, that now it was more difficult to get in. The Natives lay in their Proes round us; to whom I shew'd Beads, Knives, Glasses, to allure them to come nearer; but they would not come so nigh, as to receive any thing from us. Therefore I threw out some things to them, *viz.* a Knife fastned to a piece of Board, and a Glass-bottle corked up with some Beads in it, which they took up and seemed well pleased. They often struck their left Breast with their right Hand, and as often held up a black Truncheon over their Heads, which we thought was a Token of Friendship; Wherefore we did the like. And when we stood in towards their Shore, they seem'd to rejoyce; but when we stood off, they frown'd, yet kept us Company in their Proes, still pointing to the Shore. About 5 a-Clock, we got within the Mouth of the Bay, and sounded several times, but had no Ground though within a mile of the Shore. The Bason of this Bay was above 2 Miles within us, into which we might have gone; but as I was not assured of Anchorage there, so I thought it not Prudence to run in at this time; it being near Night, and seeing a black Tornado rising in the West, which I most fear'd: Besides, we had near 200 Men in Proes close by us. And the Bays on the Shore were lined with men from one end to the other, where there could not be less than 3 or 400 more. What Weapons they had, we know not, nor yet their Design. Therefore I had, at their first coming near us, got up all our small Arms, and made several put on Cartouch Boxes to prevent Treachery. At last I resolved to go out again: Which when the Natives in their Proes perceived, they began to fling Stones at us as fast as they could, being provided with Engines for that purpose; (wherefore I named this place Slinger's Bay:) But at the Firing of one Gun they were all amaz'd, drew off and flung no more Stones. They got together, as if consulting what to do; for they did not make in towards the Shore, but lay still, though some of them were killed or wounded; and many more of them had paid for their Boldness, but that I was unwilling to cut off any of them; which if I had done, I could not hope afterwards to bring them to treat with me.

The next day we sailed close by an Island, where we saw many Smoaks, and Men in the Bays; out of which came 2 Canoas, taking much pains to overtake us, but they could not, though we went with an easy Sail; and I could not now stay for them. As I past by the South-East-Point, I sounded several times within a Mile of the Sandy Bays, but had no Ground: About 3 Leagues to the Northward of the South-East Point, we opened a large deep Bay, secur'd from West-North-West and South-West Winds. There were 2 other Islands that lay to the North-East of it, which secur'd the Bay from North-East Winds; One was but small, yet woody; the other was a League long, inhabited and full of Coco-Nut Trees. I endeavoured to get into this Bay; but there came such Flaws off from the high Land over it, that I could not; Besides, we had many hard Squalls, which deterr'd me from it; and Night coming on, I would not run any hazard, but bore away to the small inhabited Island, to see if we could get Anchoring on the East-side of it. When we came there, we found the Island so narrow, that there could be no Shelter; therefore I tack'd and stood toward the greater Island again: And being more than Mid-way between both, I lay by, designing to endeavour for Anchorage next Morning. Between 7 and 8 at Night, we spied a Canoa close by us; and seeing no more, suffered her to come aboard. She had 3 Men in her, who brought off 5 Coco-Nuts, for which I gave each of them a Knife and a String of Beads, to encourage them to come off again in the Morning: But before these went away, we saw 2 more Canoas coming;

therefore we stood away to the Northward from them, and then lay by again till Day. We saw no more Boats this Night; neither design'd to suffer any to come aboard in the dark.

By nine a-Clock the next Morning, we were got within a League of the great Island, but were kept off by violent Gusts of Wind. These Squalls gave us warning of their Approach, by the Clouds which hung over the Mountains, and afterwards descended to the Foot of them; and then it is we expect them speedily.

On the 3d of March, being about 5 Leagues to Leeward of the great Island, we saw the Main Land a-head; and another great high Island to Leeward of us, distance about 7 Leagues; which we bore away for. It is called in the Dutch Draughts, Garret Dennis Isle. It is about 14 or 15 Leagues round; high and mountainous, and very woody: Some Trees appeared very large and tall; and the Bays by the Sea-side are well stored with Coco-nut-Trees; where we also saw some small Houses. The Sides of the Mountains are thick set with Plantations; and the Mould in the new clear'd Land, seem'd to be of a brown reddish Colour. This Island is of no regular Figure, but is full of Points shooting forth into the Sea; between which are many Sandy Bays, full of Coco-nut-Trees. The middle of the Isle lies in 3 deg. 10 min. South Latitude. It is very populous; The Natives are very black, strong, and well-limb'd People; having great round Heads, their Hair naturally curl'd and short, which they shave into several Forms, and dye it also of diverse Colours, *viz.* Red, White and Yellow. They have broad round Faces with great bottle Noses, yet agreeable enough, till they disfigure them by Painting, and by wearing great things through their Noses as big as a Man's Thumb and about four Inches long; these are run clear through both Nostrils, one end coming out by one Cheek-Bone, and the other end against the other; and their Noses so stretched, that only a small slip of them appears about the Ornament. They have also great Holes in their Ears, wherein they wear such stuff as in their Noses. They are very dextrous active Fellows in their Proes, which are very ingeniously built. They are narrow and long, with Out-lagers on one side; the Head and Stern higher than the rest, and carved into many Devices, *viz.* some Fowl, Fish, or a Man's Head, painted or carv'd: And though it's but rudely done, yet the Resemblance appears plainly, and shews an ingenious Fancy. But with what Instruments they make their Proes or carved Work, I know not; for they seem to be utterly ignorant of Iron. They have very neat Paddles, with which they manage their Proes dextrously, and make great way through the Water. Their Weapons are chiefly Lances, Swords and Slings, and some Bows and Arrows: They have also wooden Fissgigs, for striking Fish. Those that came to assault us in Slingers-Bay on the Main, are in all Respects like these; and I believe these are alike treacherous. Their Speech is clear and distinct; the Words they used most, when near us, were *Vacousee Allamais*, and then they pointed to the Shore. Their Signs of Friendship, are either a great Truncheon, or Bough of a Tree full of Leaves, put on their Heads; often striking their Heads with their Hands.

The next Day, having a fresh Gale of Wind, we got under a high Island, about 4 or 5 Leagues round, very woody, and full of Plantations upon the Sides of the Hills; and in the Bays by the Water-side, are Abundance of Coco-nut-Trees. It lies in the Latitude of 3 deg. 25 min. South, and Meridian Distance from Cape Mabo 1316 m. On the South-East part of it are 3 or 4 other small woody Islands; one high and peek'd, the other low and flat; all bedeck'd with Coco-nut-Trees and other Wood. On the North there is another Island of an indifferent Heighth, and of a somewhat larger Circumference than the great high Island last mentione'd. We past between this and the high Island. The high Island is called in the Dutch Draughts Anthony Cave's Island. As for the flat low Island, and the other small one, it is probable they were never seen by the Dutch; nor the Islands to the North of Garret Dennis's Island. As soon as we came near Cave's Island, some Canoas came about us, and made Signs for us to come ashore, as all the rest had done before; probably thinking we could run the Ship a-ground any where, as they did their Proes; for we saw neither Sail nor Anchor among any of them, though most Eastern Indians have both. These had Proes made of one Tree, well dug, with Outlagers on one side: They were but small yet well shap'd. We endeavour'd to anchor, but found no Ground within a Mile of the Shore: We kept close along the North-side, still sounding till we came to the North-East-end, but found no Ground; the Canoas still accompanying us; and the Bays were covered with Men going along as we sail'd: Many of them strove to swim off to us, but we left them astern. Being at the North-East Point, we found a strong Current setting to the North-West; so that though we had steer'd to keep under the high Island, yet we were driven towards the flat one. At this time 3 of the Natives came aboard: I gave each of them a Knife, a Looking-Glass, and a String of Beads. I shew'd them Pumpkins and Coco-nut-shells, and made Signs to them to bring some aboard, and had presently 3 Coco-nuts out of one of the Canoas. I shewed them Nutmegs, and by their Signs I guess'd they had some on the Island. I also shew'd them some Gold-Dust, which they seem'd to know, and call'd out *Manneel, Manneel*, and pointed towards the Land. A while after these Men were gone, 2 or 3 Canoas came from the flat Island, and by Signs invited us to their Island; at which the others seem'd displeas'd, and us'd very menacing Gestures and (I believe) Speeches to each other. Night coming on, we stood off to Sea; and having but little Wind all Night, were driven away to the North-West. We saw many great Fires on the flat Island. These last Men that came off to us, were all black, as those we had seen before, with frizled Hair: They were very tall, lusty, well-shap'd Men; They wear great things in their Noses, and paint as the others, but not much; They make the same Signs of Friendship, and their Language seems to be one: But the others had Proes, and these Canoas. On the Sides of some of these, we saw the Figures of several Fish neatly cut; and these last were not so shy as the others.

Steering away from Cave's Island South-South-East, we found a strong Current against us, which set only in some places in Streams; and in them we saw many Trees and Logs of Wood, which drove by us. We had but little Wood aboard; wherefore I hoisted out the Pinnace, and sent her to take up some of this Drift-wood. In a little time she came aboard with a great Tree in a tow, which we could hardly hoist in with all our Tackles. We cut up the Tree and split it for Fire-wood. It was much worm-eaten, and had in it some live Worms above an Inch long, and about the bigness of a Goose-quill, and having their Heads crusted over with a thin Shell.

After this we passed by an Island, called by the Dutch St. John's Island, leaving it to the North of us. It is about 9 or 10 Leagues round, and very well adorn'd with lofty Trees. We saw many Plantations on the Sides of the Hills, and Abundance of Coco-nut-Trees about them; as also thick Groves on the Bays by the Sea-side. As we came near it, 3 Canoas came off to us, but would not come aboard. They were such as we had seen about the other Islands: They spoke the same Language, and made the same Signs of Peace; and their Canoas were such, as at Cave's Island.

We stood along by St. John's Island, till we came almost to the South-East-Point; and then seeing no more Islands to the Eastward of us, nor any likelihood of anchoring under this, I steer'd away for the Main of New-Guinea; we being now (as I suppos'd) to the East of it, on this North-side.

My Design of seeing these Islands as I past along, was to get Wood and Water, but could find no Anchor-Ground, and therefore could not do as I purpos'd. Besides, these Islands are all so populous, that I dar'd not send my Boat ashore, unless I could have anchor'd pretty nigh. Wherefore I rather chose to prosecute my Design on the Main, the Season of the Year being now at hand; for I judg'd the Westerly Winds were nigh spent.

On the 8th of March, we saw some Smoaks on the Main, being distant from it 4 or 5 Leagues. 'Tis very high, woody Land, with some Spots of Savannah. About 10 in the Morning 6 or 7 Canoas came off to us: Most of them had no more than one Man in them; they were all black, with short curl'd Hair; having the same Ornaments in their Noses, and their Heads so shav'd and painted, and speaking the same Words, as the Inhabitants of Cave's Island before-mentioned.

There was a Head-land to the Southward of us, beyond which seeing no Land, I supposed that from thence the Land trends away more Westerly. This Head-land lies in the Latitude of 5 deg. 2 min. South, and Meridian distance from Cape Mabo, 1290 Miles. In the Night we lay by, for fear of over-shooting this Head-land. Between which and Cape St. Maries, the Land is high, Mountainous and Woody; having many Points of Land shooting out into the Sea, which make so many fine Bays. The Coast lies North-North-East and South-South-West.

The 9th in the Morning a huge black Man came off to us in a Canoa, but would not come aboard. He made the same signs of Friendship to us, as the rest we had met with; yet seem'd to differ in his Language, not using any of those Words which the others did. We saw neither Smoaks nor Plantations near this Head-land. We found here Variation 1 deg. East.

In the Afternoon, as we plied near the Shore, 3 Canoas came off to us; one had 4 Men in her, the others 2 apiece. That with the 4 Men, came pretty nigh us, and shew'd us a Coco-nut and Water in a Bamboo, making Signs that there was enough ashore where they lived; they pointed to the place where they would have us go, and so went away. We saw a small round pretty high Island, about a League to the North of this Head-land, within which there was a large deep Bay, whither the Canoas went; and we strove to get thither before Night, but could not; wherefore we stood off, and saw Land to the Westward of this Head-Land, bearing West by South half South, distance about 10 Leagues; and, as we thought, still more Land bearing South-West by South, distance 12·or 14 Leagues: But being

Table XII   Nova Brittannia .

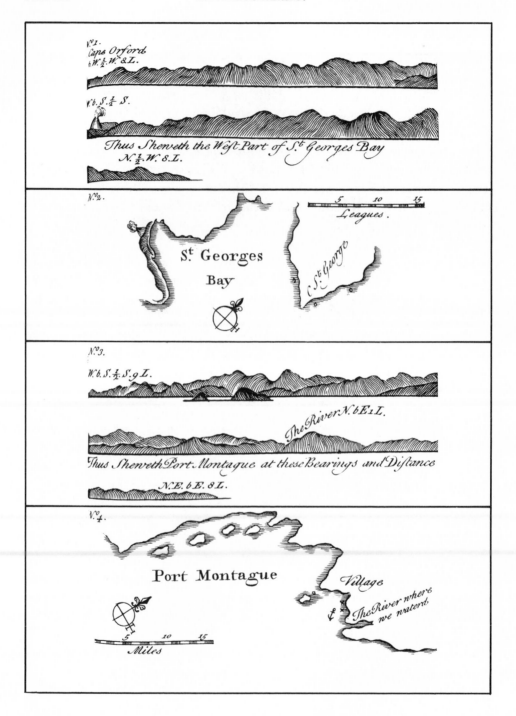

Nᵒ 1.
Cape Orford
b.W.¼.W° 8 L.

Vᵗ b. S. ¼ S.

Thus Sheweth the West Part of Sᵗ Georges Bay
N.½.W. 8 L.

Nᵒ 2.

5   10   15
Leagues .

Sᵗ Georges
Bay

C. Sᵗ George

Nᵒ 3.

W. b. S. ¼ S. 9 L.

The River N. b E 1 L.

Thus Sheweth Port Montague at these Bearings and Distance
N.E. b E. 8 L.

Nᵒ 4.

Port Montague

Village

The River where
we watered

5   10   15
Miles

clouded, it disappeared, and we thought we had been deceived. Before Night we opened the Head-Land fair, and I named it Cape St. George. The Land from hence trends away West-North-West about 10 Leagues, which is as far as we could see it; and the Land that we saw to the Westward of it in the Evening, which bore West by South half South, was another Point about 10 Leagues from Cape St. George; between which there runs in a deep Bay for 20 Leagues or more. We saw some high Land in Spots like Islands, down in that Bay at a great distance; but whether they are Islands, or the Main closing there, we know not. The next Morning we saw other Land to the South-East of the Westermost Point, which till then was clouded; it was very high Land, and the same that we saw the day before, that disappear'd in a Cloud. This Cape St. George lies in the Latitude of 5 deg. 5 min. South; and Meridian distance from Cape Mabo 1290 Miles. The Island off this Cape, I called St. George's Isle; and the Bay between it and the West-Point, I named St. George's Bay. *Note*, No Dutch Draughts go so far as this Cape, by 10 Leagues. On the 10th in the Evening, we got within a League of the Westermost Land seen, which is pretty high and very woody, but no Appearance of Anchoring. I stood off again, designing (if possible) to ply to and fro in this Bay, till I found a Conveniency to Wood and Water. We saw no more Plantations, nor Coco-nut-Trees; yet in the Night we discerned a small Fire right against us. The next Morning we saw a Burning Mountain in the Country. It was round, high, and peaked at top (as most Vulcano's are,) and sent forth a great Quantity of Smoak. We took up a Log of drift Wood, and split it for Firing; in which we found some small Fish.

The Day after, we past by the South-West Cape of this Bay, leaving it to the North of us: When we were abreast of it, I called my Officers together, and named it Cape Orford, in Honour of my noble *Patron; drinking his Lordship's Health. This Cape bears from Cape St. George South-West about 18 Leagues. Between them there is a Bay about 25 Leagues deep, having pretty high Land all round it, especially near the Capes, though they themselves are not high. Cape Orford lies in the Latitude of 5 deg. 24 min. South, by my Observation; and Meridian distance from Cape St George, 44 Miles West. The Land trends from this Cape North-West by West into the Bay, and on the other Side South-West per Compass, which is South-West 9 deg. West, allowing the Variation which is here 9 deg. East. The Land on

* Edward Russel, Lord Orford 1653–1727. Lord High Admiral.

each Side of the Cape, is more Savannah than Wood-Land, and is highest on the North-West-side. The Cape it self is a Bluff-point, of an indifferent Heighth, with a flat Table Land at Top. When we were to the South-West of the Cape, it appeared to be a low Point shooting out; which you cannot see when a-breast of it. This Morning we struck a Log of Drift-wood with our Turtle-Irons, hoisted it in and split it for Firewood. Afterwards we struck another, but could not get it in. There were many Fish about it.

We steer'd along South-West as the Land lies, keeping about 6 Leagues off the Shore; and being desirous to cut Wood and fill Water, if I saw any Conveniency, I lay by in the Night, because I would not miss any Place proper for those Ends, for fear of wanting such Necessaries as we could not live without. This Coast is high and mountainous, and not so thick with Trees as that on the other side of Cape Orford.

On the 14th, seeing a pretty deep Bay a-head, and some Islands where I thought we might ride secure, we ran in towards the Shore and saw some Smoaks. At 10 a-Clock we saw a Point, which shot out pretty well into the Sea, with a Bay within it, which promised fair for Water; and we stood in, with a moderate Gale. Being got into the Bay within the Point, we saw many Coco-nut-Trees, Plantations, and Houses. When I came within 4 or 5 Mile of the Shore, 6 small Boats came off to view us, with about 40 Men in them all. Perceiving that they only came to view us, and would not come aboard, I made Signs and waved to them to go ashore; but they did not or would not understand me; therefore I whistled a Shot over their Heads out of my Fowling-piece, and then they pull'd away for the Shore, as hard as they could. These were no sooner ashore, but we saw 3 Boats, coming from the Islands to Leeward of us, and they soon came within call; for we lay becalm'd. One of the Boats had about 40 Men in her, and was a large well built Boat; the other 2 were but small. Not long after, I saw another Boat coming out of that Bay where I intended to go: She likewise was a large Boat, with a high Head and Stern painted, and full of Men; this I thought came off to fight us, as 'tis probable they all did; therefore I fired another small Shot over the great Boat that was nigh us, which made them leave their Babling and take to their Paddles. We still lay becalm'd; and therefore they rowing wide of us, directed their Course toward the other great Boat that was coming off: When they were pretty near each other, I caus'd the Gunner to fire a Gun between them which he did very dextrously; it was loaden with round and Partridge-shot; the last dropt in the Water somewhat short of them, but the round Shot went between both Boats, and grazed about 100 Yards beyond them; this so affrighted them, that they rowed away for the Shore as fast as they could, without coming near each other; and the little Boats made the best of their Way after them: And now having a gentle Breeze at South-South-East, we bore into the Bay after them. When we came by the Point, I saw a great Number of Men peeping from under the Rocks: I ordered a Shot to be fired close by, to scare them. The Shot graz'd between us and the Point; and mounting again, flew over the Point, and graz'd a 2d Time just by them. We were obliged to sail along close by the Bays; and seeing Multitudes setting under the Trees, I ordered a 3d Gun to be fired among the Coco-nut-Trees, to scare them; for my Business being to Wood and Water, I thought it necessary to strike some Terrour into the Inhabitants, who were very numerous, and (by what I saw now, and had formerly experienc'd,) treacherous. After this I sent my Boat to sound; they had first 40, then 30, and at last 20 Fathom Water. We followed the Boat, and came to anchor about a quarter of a Mile from the Shore, in 26 Fathom Water, fine black Sand and Oaze. We rode right against the Mouth of a small River, where I hoped to find fresh Water. Some of the Natives standing on a small Point at the River's Mouth, I sent a small Shot over their Heads to fright them; which it did effectually. In the Afternoon I sent my Boat ashore to the Natives who stood upon the Point by the River's Mouth with a Present of Coco-nuts; when the Boat was come near the Shore, they came running into the Water, and put their Nuts into the Boat. Then I made a Signal for the Boat to come aboard, and sent both it and the Yawl into the River to look for fresh Water, ordering the Pinnace to lye near the River's Mouth, while the Yawl went up to search. In an Hour's time they return'd aboard with some Barrecoes full of fresh Water, which they had taken up about half a Mile up the River. After which, I sent them again with Casks; ordering one of them to fill Water, and the other to watch the Motion of the Natives, lest they should make any Opposition; but they did not, and so the Boats return'd a little before Sun-set with a Tun and half of Water; and the next Day by Noon brought aboard about 6 Tun of Water.

I sent ashore Commodities to purchase Hogs, &c. being informed that the Natives have plenty of them, as also of Yamms and other good Roots; But my Men returned without getting any thing that I sent them for; the Natives being unwilling to trade with us: Yet they admir'd our Hatchets and Axes; but would part with nothing but Coco-nuts; which they us'd to climb the Trees for; and so soon as they gave them our Men, they beckon'd to them to be gone; for they were much afraid of us.

The 18th, I sent both Boats again for Water, and before Noon they had filled all my Casks. In the Afternoon I sent them both to cut Wood; but seeing about 40 Natives standing on the Bay at a small Distance from our Men, I made a Signal for them to come aboard again; which they did, and brought me Word that the Men which we saw on the Bay were passing that way, but were afraid to come nigh them. At 4 a Clock I sent both the Boats again for more Wood, and they return'd in the Evening. Then I called my Officers to consult whether it were convenient to stay here longer, and en- deavour a better Acquaintance with these People; or go to Sea. My Design of tarrying here longer, was, if possible, to get some Hogs, Goats, Yamms and other Roots; as also to get some Knowledge of the Country and its Product. My Officers unanimously gave their Opinions for staying longer here. So the next Day I sent both Boats ashore again, to fish and to cut more Wood. While they were ashore about 30 or 40 Men and Women past by them; they were a little afraid of our People at first; but upon their making signs of Friendship, they past by quietly; the Men finely bedeck'd with Feathers of divers Colours about their Heads, and Lances in their Hands; the Women had no Ornament about them, nor any Thing to cover their Nakedness, but a Bunch of small green Boughs, before and behind, stuck under a String which came round their Wastes. They carried large Baskets on their Heads, full of Yamms. And this I have observ'd amongst all the wild Natives I have known, that they make their Women carry the Burdens, while the Men walk before, without any other Load than their Arms and Ornaments. At Noon our Men came aboard with the Wood they had cut, and had catch'd but 6 Fishes at 4 or 5 Hauls of the Sain, though we saw Abundance of Fish leaping in the Bay all the Day long.

In the afternoon I sent the Boats ashore for more Wood; and some of our men went to the Natives Houses, and found they were now more shy than they us'd to be; had taken down all the Coco-nuts from the Trees, and driven away their Hogs. Our People made Signs to them to know what was become of their Hogs, &c. The Natives pointing to some Houses in the Bottom of the Bay, and imitating the Noise of those Creatures, seem'd to intimate that there were both Hogs and Goats of several Sizes, which they express'd by holding their Hands abroad at several Distances from the Ground.

An. 1700

At Night our Boats came aboard with Wood; and the next Morning I went my self with both Boats up the River to the Watering-place, carrying with me all such Trifles and Iron-work as I thought most proper to induce them to a Commerce with us; but I found them very shy and roguish. I saw but 2 Men and a Boy: One of the Men by some Signs was perswaded to come to the Boat's Side, where I was; to him I gave a Knife, a String of Beads, and a Glass-bottle; the Fellow call'd out, *Cocos, Cocos*, pointing to a Village hard by, and signified to us that he would go for some; but he never return'd to us. And thus they had frequently of late served our Men. I took 8 or 9 Men with me, and marched to their Houses, which I found very mean; and their Doors made fast with Withes.

I visited 3 of their Villages; and finding all the Houses thus abandon'd by the Inhabitants, who carried with them all their Hogs, *&c*. I brought out of their Houses some small Fishing-nets in Recompence for those Things they had receiv'd of us. As we were coming away, we saw 2 of the Natives; I shewed them the Things that we carried with us, and called to them, *Cocos, Cocos*, to let them know that I took these Things because they had not made good what they had promis'd by their Signs, and by their calling out *Cocos*. While I was thus employ'd, the men in the Yawl filled 2 Hogsheads of Water, and all the Barrecoes. About 1 in the Afternoon I came aboard, and found all my Officers and Men very importunate to go to that Bay where the Hogs were said to be. I was loath to yield to it, fearing they would deal too roughly with the Natives. By 2 a-Clock in the Afternoon many black Clouds gather'd over the land, which I thought would deter them from their Enterprize; but they sollicited me the more to let them go. At last I consented, sending those Commodities I had ashore with me in the Morning, and giving them a strict Charge to deal by fair means, and to act cautiously for their own Security. The Bay I sent them to was about 2 Miles from the Ship. Assoon as they were gone, I got all Things ready, that, if I saw Occasion, I might assist them with my great Guns. When they came to Land, the Natives in great Companies stood to resist them; shaking their Lances, and threatning them; and some were so daring, as to wade into the Sea, holding a Target in one Hand and a Lance in the other. Our Men held up to them such Commodities as I had sent, and made Signs of Friendship; but to no Purpose; for the Natives waved them off. Seeing therefore they could not be prevailed upon to a friendly Commerce, my Men, being resolved to have some Provision among them, fired some Muskets to scare them away; which had the desired Effect upon all but 2 or 3, who stood still in a menacing Posture, till the boldest dropt his Target and ran away; they suppos'd he was shot in the Arm: He and some others felt the Smart of our Bullets, but none were kill'd; our Design being rather to fright than to kill them. Our Men landed, and found Abundance of tame Hogs running among the Houses. They shot down 9, which they brought away, besides many that ran away wounded. They had but little Time; for in less than an Hour after they went from the Ship, it began to rain: Wherefore they got what they could into the Boats; for I had charg'd them to come away if it rain'd. By that Time the Boat was aboard, and the Hogs taken in, it clear'd up; and my Men desir'd to make another Trip thither before Night; this was about 5 in the Evening; and I consented, giving them Order to repair on Board before Night. In the Close of the Evening they returned accordingly, with 8 Hogs more, and a little live Pig; and by this Time the other Hogs were jerk'd and salted. These that came last, we only drest and corn'd till Morning; and then sent both Boats ashore for more Refreshments, either of Hogs or Roots: But in the Night the Natives had convey'd away their Provisions of all Sorts. Many of them were now about the Houses, and none offer'd to resist our Boats landing, but on the contrary were so amicable, that one Man brought 10 or 12 Coco-nuts, left them on the Shore after he had shew'd them to our Men, and went out of Sight. Our People finding nothing but Nets and Images, brought some of them away; which 2 of my Men brought aboard in a small Canoa; and presently after, my Boats came off. I order'd the Boatswain to take care of the Nets, till we came at some place where they might be disposed of for some Refreshment for the Use of all the Company: The Images I took into my own Custody.

In the Afternoon I sent the Canoa to the Place from whence she had been brought; and in her, 2 Axes, 2 Hatchets (one of them helv'd,) 6 Knives, 6 Looking-glasses, a large Bunch of Beads, and 4 Glass-bottles. Our Men drew the Canoa ashore, placed the Things to the best Advantage in her, and came off in the Pinnace which I sent to guard them. And now being well stock'd with Wood, and all my Water-casks full, I resolv'd to sail the next Morning. All the Time of our Stay here, we had very fair Weather; only sometimes in the Afternoon we had a Shower of Rain, which lasted not above an Hour at most: Also some Thunder and Lightning, with very little Wind. We had Sea and Land-breezes; the former between the South-South-East, and the latter from North-East to North-West.

Fishes taken on the
Coast of New
Guinea.

This Fish his fins & Taill is ▬ Blew. w.th Blew spots all over y.e Body.

This Place I named Port Mountague, in Honour of my noble *Patron. It
lies in the Latitude of 6 deg. 10 min. South, and Meridian distance from
Cape St. George, 151 Miles West. The Country hereabouts is mountainous
and woody, full of rich Valleys and pleasant fresh Water-brooks. The
Mould in the Valleys is deep and yellowish; that on the Sides of the Hills of
a very brown Colour, and not very deep, but rocky underneath; yet excellent
planting Land. The Trees in general are neither very streight, thick, nor
tall; yet appear green and pleasant enough: Some of them bore Flowers,
some Berries, and others big Fruits; but all unknown to any of us. Coco-
nut-Trees thrive very well here; as well on the Bays by the Sea-side, as more
remote among the Plantations. The Nuts are of an indifferent Size, the Milk
and Kernel very thick and pleasant. Here is Ginger, Yamms, and other very
good Roots for the Pot, that our Men saw and tasted. What other Fruits or
Roots the Country affords, I know not. Here are Hogs and Dogs; other
Land-Animals we saw none. The Fowls we saw and knew, were Pidgeons,
Parrots, Cockadores and Crows like those in England; a Sort of Birds about
the Bigness of a Black-Bird, and smaller Birds many. The Sea and Rivers
have Plenty of Fish; we saw Abundance, though we catch'd but few, and
these were Cavallies, Yellow-tails and Whip-rays.

We departed from hence on the 22d of March, and on the 24th in the
Evening we saw some high Land bearing North-West half West; to the
West of which we could see no Land, though there appeared something like
Land bearing West a little Southerly; but not being sure of it, I steered
West-North-West all Night, and kept going on with an easy Sail, intending
to coast along the Shore at a distance. At 10 a Clock I saw a great Fire
bearing North-West by West, blazing up in a Pillar, sometimes very high
for 3 or 4 Minutes, then falling quite down for an equal Space of Time;
sometimes hardly visible, till it blazed up again. I had laid me down having
been indisposed this 3 Days: But upon a Sight of this, my chief Mate called
me; I got up and view'd it for about half an Hour, and knew it to be a
burning Hill by its Intervals: I charg'd them to look well out, having bright
Moon-light. In the Morning I found that the Fire we had seen the Night
before, was a burning Island; and steer'd for it. We saw many other Islands,
one large high Island, and another smaller, but pretty high. I stood near the
Vulcano, and many small low Islands with some Shoals.

* Charles Montagu, Earl of Halifax 1661–1715.

March the 25th 1700, in the Evening we came within 3 Leagues of this Burning-hill, being at the same Time 2 Leagues from the Main. I found a good Channel to pass between them, and kept nearer the Main than the Island. At 7 in the Evening I sounded, and had 52 Fathom fine Sand and Oaze. I stood to the Northward to get clear of this Streight, having but little Wind and fair Weather. The Island all Night vomited Fire and Smoak very amazingly; and at every Belch we heard a dreadful Noise like Thunder, and saw a Flame of Fire after it, the most terrifying that ever I saw. The Intervals between its Belches, were about half a Minute, some more, others less: Neither were these Pulses or Eruptions alike; for some were but faint Convulsions, in Comparison of the more vigorous; yet even the weakest vented a great deal of Fire; but the largest made a roaring Noise, and sent up a large Flame 20 or 30 Yards high; and then might be seen a great Stream of Fire running down to the Foot of the Island, even to the Shore. From the Furrows made by this descending Fire, we could in the Day Time see great Smoaks arise, which probably were made by the sulphureous Matter thrown out of the Funnel at the Top, which tumbling down to the Bottom, and there lying in a Heap, burn'd till either consumed or extinguished; and as long as it burn'd and kept its Heat, so long the Smoak ascended from it; which we perceived to increase or decrease, according to the Quantity of Matter discharged from the Funnel. But the next Night, being shot to the Westward of the Burning-Island, and the Funnel of it lying on the South-side, we could not discern the Fire there, as we did the Smoak in the Day when we were to the Southward of it. This Vulcano lies in the Latitude of 5 deg. 33 min. South, and Meridian distance from Cape St. George, 332 Miles West.

The Eastermost Part of New-Guinea lies 40 Miles to the Westward of this Tract of Land; and by Hydrographers they are made joyning together: But here I found an Opening and Passage between, with many Islands; the largest of which lye on the North-side of this Passage or Streight. The Channel is very good, between the Islands and the Land to the Eastward. The East-part of New-Guinea, is high and mountainous, ending on the North-East with a large Promontory, which I nam'd King William's Cape, in Honour of his present Majesty. We saw some Smoaks on it; and leaving it on our Larboard-side, steer'd away near the East Land; which ends with two remarkable Capes or Heads, distant from each other about 6 or 7 Leagues. Within each Head were two very remarkable Mountains, ascending very gradually from the Sea-side; which afforded a very pleasant and agreeable Prospect. The Mountains and lower Land were pleasantly mixt with Wood-Land and Savannahs. The Trees appeared very green and flourishing; and the Savannahs seem'd to be very smooth and even; no Meadow in England appears more green in the Spring, than these. We saw Smoaks, but did not strive to anchor here; but rather chose to get under one of the Islands, (where I thought I should find few or no Inhabitants,) that I might repair my Pinnace, which was so crazy that I could not venture ashore any where with her. As we stood over to the Islands, we look'd out very well to the North, but could see no Land that way; by which I was well assur'd that we were got through, and that this East-Land does not join to New-Guinea; therefore I named it Nova-Britannia. The North-West Cape, I called Cape *Glocester, and the South-West-point Cape *Anne; and the North-West Mountain, which is very remarkable, I call'd Mount Glocester.

This Island which I called Nova-Britannia, has about 4 deg. of Latitude: The Body of it lying in 4 deg. and the Northermost part in 2 deg. 30 min. and the Southermost in 6 deg. 30 min. South. It has about 5 deg. 18 min. Longitude from East to West. It is generally high, mountainous Land, mixt with large Valleys; which, as well as the Mountains, appeared very fertile; and in most Places that we saw, the Trees are very large, tall and thick. It is also very well inhabited with strong well-limb'd Negroes, whom we found very daring and bold at several Places. As to the Product of it, I know no more than what I have said in my Account of Port Mountague: But it is very probable this Island may afford as many rich Commodities as any in the World; and the Natives may be easily brought to Commerce, though I could not pretend to it under my present Circumstances.

Being near the Island to the Northward of the Vulcano, I sent my Boat to sound, thinking to anchor here; but she return'd and brought me Word that they had no Ground, till they met with a Riff of Coral Rocks about a Mile from the Shore. Then I bore away to the North-side of the Island, where we found no anchoring neither. We saw several People, and some Coco-nut-Trees, but could not send ashore for want of my Pinnace, which was out of order. In the Evening I stood off to Sea, to be at such a distance, that I might not be driven by any Current upon the Shoals of this Island, if it

*   Duke of Gloucester 1689–1700.
*   Princess Anne 1665–1714 became Queen 1702.

Table XIII   Dampiers Paſſage and Iſlands on y̑ Coaſt of N.Guinea

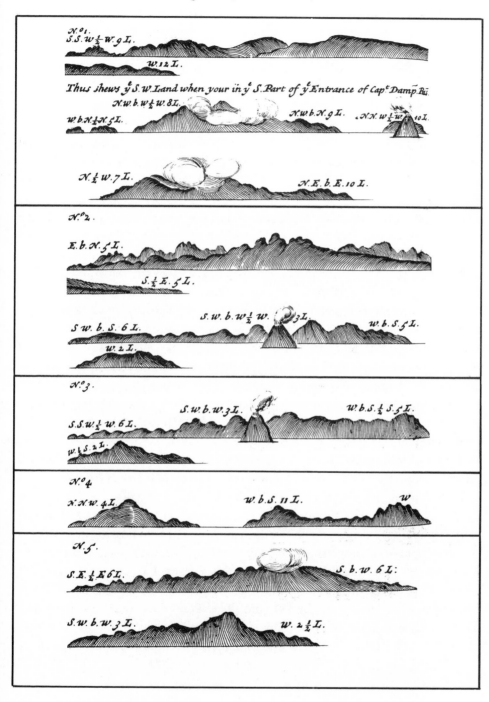

N.º 1.
S.S.W. ½ W. 9 L.

W. 12 L.

Thus ſhews y̑ S.W. Land when your in y̑ S. Part of y̑ Entrance of Capᵉ Damp. Paſ.
N.W. b. W. ½ W. 8 L.
W.b.N. ½ N. 5 L.   N.W. b. N. 9 L.   N.N.W. ½ W. 10 L.

N. ½ W. 7 L.   N.E. b. E. 10 L.

N.º 2.

E. b. N. 5 L.

S. ½ E. 5 L.

S.W. b. W. ½ W.   3 L.
S.W. b. S. 6 L.   W. b. S. 5 L.
W. 2 L.

N.º 3.

S.W. b. W. 3 L.   W. b. S. ½ S. 5 L.
S.S.W. ½ W. 6 L.
W. ½ S. 2 L.

N.º 4

N.N.W. 4 L.   W. b. S. 11 L.   W

N.º 5.

S.E. ½ E. 6 L.   S. b. W. 6 L:

S.W. b. W. 3 L.   W. 2 ½ L.

should prove calm. We had but little Wind, especially the Beginning of the Night; but in the Morning I found my self so far to the West of the Island, that the Wind being at East-South-East, I could not fetch it; wherefore I kept on to the Southward, and stemm'd with the Body of a high Island about 11 or 12 Leagues long, lying to the Southward of that which I before designed for. I named this Island *Sir George Rook's Island.

We also saw some other Islands to the Westward; which may be better seen in my Draught of these Lands, than here described. But seeing a very small Island lying to the North-West of the long Island which was before us, and not far from it; I steer'd away for that; hoping to find anchoring there: And having but little Wind, I sent my Boat before to sound; which, when we were about 2 Miles distance from the Shore, came on Board and brought me Word that there was good anchoring in 30 or 40 Fathom Water, a Mile from the Isle, and within a Riff of the Rocks which lay in a half Moon, reaching from the North-part of the Island to the South-East: so at Noon we got in and anchored in 36 Fathom, a Mile from the Isle.

In the Afternoon I sent my Boat ashore to the Island, to see what Convenience there was to haul our Vessel ashore in order to be mended, and whether we could catch any Fish. My Men in the Boat rowed about the Island, but could not land by Reason of the Rocks and a great Surge running in upon the Shore. We found Variation here, 8 deg. 25 min. West.

I design'd to have stay'd among these Islands till I had got my Pinnace refitted; but having no more than one Man who had skill to work upon her, I saw she would be a long Time in repairing; (which was one great Reason why I could not prosecute my Discoveries further:) And the Easterly Winds being set in, I found I should scarce be able to hold my Ground.

The 31st in the Forenoon we shot in between 2 Islands, lying about 4 Leagues asunder; with Intention to pass between them. The Southermost is a long Island, with a high Hill at each End; this I named Long Island. The Northermost is a round high Island towering up with several Heads or Tops, something resembling a Crown; this I named Crown-Isle, from its Form. Both these Islands appear'd very pleasant, having Spots of green Savannahs mixt among the Wood-land: The Trees appeared very green and flourishing, and some of them looked white and full of Blossoms. We past close by Crown-Isle; saw many Coco-nut-Trees on the Bays and the Sides of

* Admiral Sir George Rooke 1650–1709.

the Hills; and one Boat was coming off from the Shore, but return'd again. We saw no Smoaks on either of the Islands, neither did we see any Plantations; and it is probable they are not very well peopled. We saw many Shoals near Crown-Island, and Riffs of Rocks running off from the Points, a Mile or more into the Sea. My Boat was once over-board, with Design to have sent her ashore; but having little Wind, and seeing some Shoals, I hoisted her in again, and stood off out of Danger.

In the Afternoon, seeing an Island bearing North-West by West, we steer'd away North-West by North, to be to the Northward of it. The next Morning, being about Mid-way from the Islands we left Yesterday, and having this to the Westward of us; the Land of the Main of New Guinea within us to the Southward, appear'd very high. When we came within 4 or 5 Leagues of this Island to the West of us, 4 Boats came off to view us; one came within call, but return'd with the other 3 without speaking to us: So we kept on for the Island; which I named *Sir R. Rich's Island. It was pretty high, woody, and mixt with Savannah's like those formerly mentioned. Being to the North of it, we saw an Opening between it and another Island 2 Leagues to theWest of it, which before appear'd all in One. The Main seemed to be high Land, trending to the Westward.

On Tuesday the 2d of April, about 8 in the Morning, we discovered a high peeked Island to the Westward, which seem'd to smoak at its Top. The next Day we past by the North-side of the Burning Island, and saw a Smoak again at its Top; but the Vent lying on the South-side of the Peek, we could not observe it distinctly, nor see the Fire. We afterwards opened 3 more Islands, and some Land to the Southward, which we could not well tell whether it were Islands or Part of the Main. These Islands are all high, full of fair Trees and Spots of green Savannahs; as well the Burning Isle as the rest; but the Burning Isle was more round and peek'd at Top, very fine Land near the Sea, and for two Thirds up it. We also saw another Isle sending forth a great Smoak at once; but it soon vanished, and we saw it no more. We saw also among these Islands 3 small Vessels with Sails, which the People on Nova Britannia seem wholly ignorant of.

The 11th at Noon, having a very good Observation, I found my self to the Northward of my Reckoning; and thence concluded that we had a Current setting North-West, or rather more Westerly, as the Land lies.

* Sir Robert Rich 1648–1699, a Lord of the Admiralty.

Table XIV Iſlands *on the Coaſt* of N. Guinea

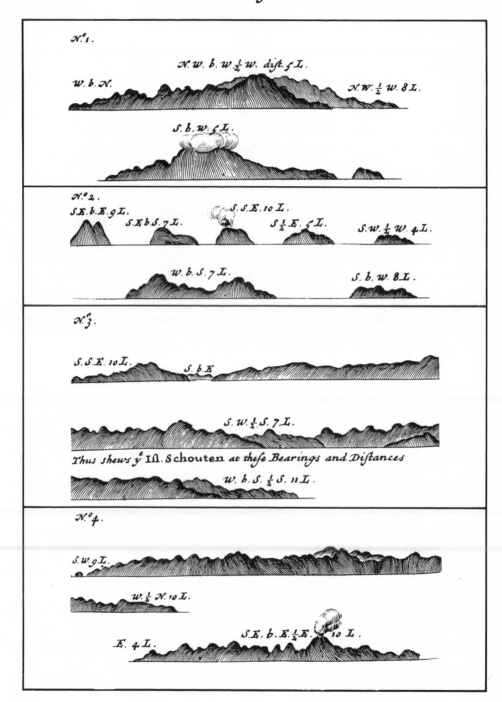

From that Time to the next Morning, we had fair clear Weather, and a fine moderate Gale from South-East to East by North: But at Day-break, the Clouds began to fly, and it lightned very much in the East, South-East, and North-East. At Sun-rising, the Sky look'd very red in the East near the Horizon; and there were many black Clouds both to the South and North of it. About a Quarter of an Hour after the Sun was up, there was a Squall to the Windward of us; when on a sudden one of our Men on the Fore-castle called out that he saw something astern, but could not tell what: I look'd out for it, and immediately saw a Spout beginning to work within a Quarter of a Mile of us, exactly in the Wind. We presently put right before it. It came very swiftly, whirling the Water up in a Pillar about 6 or 7 Yards high. As yet I could not see any pendulous Cloud, from whence it might come; and was in Hopes it would soon lose its Force. In 4 or 5 Minutes Time, it came within a Cable's Length of us, and past away to Leeward; and then I saw a long pale Stream, coming down to the whirling Water. This Stream was about the Bigness of a Rainbow: The upper End seem'd vastly high, not descending from any dark Cloud, and therefore the most strange to me; I never having seen the like before. It past about a Mile to Leeward of us, and then broke. This was but a small Spout, not strong nor lasting; yet I perceived much Wind in it, as it past by us. The Current still continued at North-West a little Westerly, which I allow'd to run a Mile per Hour.

By an Observation the 13th at Noon, I found my self 25 min. to the Northward of my Reckoning; whether occasion'd by bad Steerage, a bad Account, or a Current, I could not determine; but was apt to judge it might be a Complication of all; for I could not think it was wholly the Current, the land here lying East by South, and West by North, or a little more Northerly and Southerly. We had kept so nigh as to see it, and at farthest had not been above 20 Leagues from it, but sometimes much nearer; and it is not probable that any Current should set directly off from a Land. A Tide indeed may; but then the Flood has the same Force to strike in upon the Shore, as the Ebb to strike off from it: But a Current must have set nearly along Shore, either Easterly or Westerly; and if any thing Northerly or Southerly, it could be but very little in Comparison of its East or West Course, on a Coast lying as this doth; which yet we did not perceive. If therefore we were deceiv'd by a Current, it is very probable that the Land is here disjoyn'd, and that there is a Passage through to the Southward, and that the Land from King William's Cape to this Place is an Island, separated from New-Guinea by some Streight, as Nova-Britannia is by that which we came through. But this being at best but a probable Conjecture, I shall insist no farther upon it.

The 14th we passed by Scouten's Island and Providence Island, and found still a very strong Current setting to the North-West. On the 17th we saw a high Mountain on the Main, that sent forth great Quantities of Smoak from its Top: This Vulcano we did not see in our Voyage out. In the Afternoon we discovered King William's Island, and crowded all the Sail we could, to get near it before Night; thinking to lye to the Eastward of it till Day, for fear of some Shoals that lye at the West-end of it. Before Night we got within 2 Leagues of it, and having a fine Gale of Wind and a light Moon, I resolv'd to pass through in the Night; which I hop'd to do before 12 a-Clock, if the Gale continued; but when we came within 2 Miles of it, it fell calm; yet afterwards by the Help of the Current, a small Gale, and our Boat, we got through before Day. In the Night we had a very fragrant Smell from the Island. By Morning-light we were got 2 Leagues to the Westward of it; and then were becalm'd all the Morning; and met such whirling Tides, that when we came into them, the Ship turn'd quite round; and though sometimes we had a small Gale of Wind, yet she could not feel the Helm when she came into these Whirlpools: Neither could we get from amongst them, till a brisk Gale sprung up; yet we drove not much any way, but whirl'd round like a Top. And those Whirlpools were not constant to one Place, but drove about strangely; and sometimes we saw among them large Riplings of the Water, like great Over-falls, making a fearful Noise. I sent my Boat to sound, but found no Ground.

The 18th, Cape Mabo bore S. distance 9 Leagues. By which Account it lies in the Latitude of 50 min. South, and Meridian distance from Cape S. George 1243 Miles. S. John's Isle lies 48 Miles to the East of Cape St. George; which being added to the Distance between Cape St. George and Cape Mabo, makes 1291 Meridional Parts; which was the furthest that I was to the East. In my outward bound Voyage I made Meridian distance between Cape Mabo and Cape St. George, 1290 Miles; and now in my Return, but 1243; which is 47 short of my distance going out. This Difference may probably be occasion'd by the strong Western Current which we found in our Return, which I allowed for after I perceiv'd it; and though we did not discern any Current when we went to the Eastward, except when near the Islands; yet it is probable we had one against us,

though we did not take Notice of it because of the strong Westerly Winds.
King William's Island lies in the Latitude of 21 Min. South, and may be seen distinctly off of Cape Mabo.

In the Evening we past by Cape Mabo; and afterwards steer'd away South-East, half East, keeping along the Shore, which here trends South-easterly. The next Morning seeing a large Opening in the Land, with an Island near the South-side; I stood in, thinking to anchor there. When we were shot in within 2 Leagues of the Island, the Wind came to the West, which blows right into the Opening. I stood to the North Shore; intending, when I came pretty nigh to send my Boat into the Opening, and sound, before I would adventure in. We found several deep Bays, but no Soundings within 2 Miles of the Shore; therefore I stood off again. Then seeing a Ripling under our Lee, I sent my Boat to sound on it; which return'd in half an Hour, and brought me Word that the Ripling we saw was only a Tide, and that they had no Ground there.

CHAP. V

An. 1700 The Wind seeming to incline to East, as might be expected according to the Season of the Year; I rather chose to shape my Course as these Winds would best permit, than strive to return the same way we came; which, for many Leagues, must have been against this Monsoon: Though indeed on the other hand, the Dangers in that way, we already knew; but what might be in this, by which we now proposed to return, we could not tell.

We were now in a Channel about 8 or 9 Leagues wide, having a Range of Islands on the North-side, and another on the South-side, and very deep Water between, so that we had no Ground. The 22d of April in the Morning, I sent my Boat ashore to an Island on the North-side, and stood that way with the Ship. They found no Ground till within a Cable's length of the Shore, and then had Coral Rocks; so that they could not catch any Fish, though they saw a great many. They brought aboard a small Canoa, which they found a-drift. They met with no Game ashore, save only one party-colour'd Parrakite. The Land is of an indifferent Height; very Rocky, yet cloathed with tall Trees, whose bare Roots run along upon the Rocks. Our People saw a Pond of Salt Water, but found no fresh. Near this Island we met a pretty strong Tide, but found neither Tide nor Current off at some distance.

On the 24th, being about 2 Leagues from an Island to the Southward of us, we came over a Shoal, on which we had but 5 Fathom and a half. We did not descrie it, till we saw the Ground under us. In less than half an Hour before, the Boat had been sounding in discoloured Water, but had no Ground. We mann'd the Boat presently, and tow'd the Ship about; and then sounding, had 12, 15 and 17 Fathom, and then no Ground with our Hand-lead. The Shoal was rocky; but in 12 and 15 Fathom we had oazy Ground.

We found here very strange Tides, that ran in Streams, making a great Sea; and roaring so loud, that we could hear them before they came within a

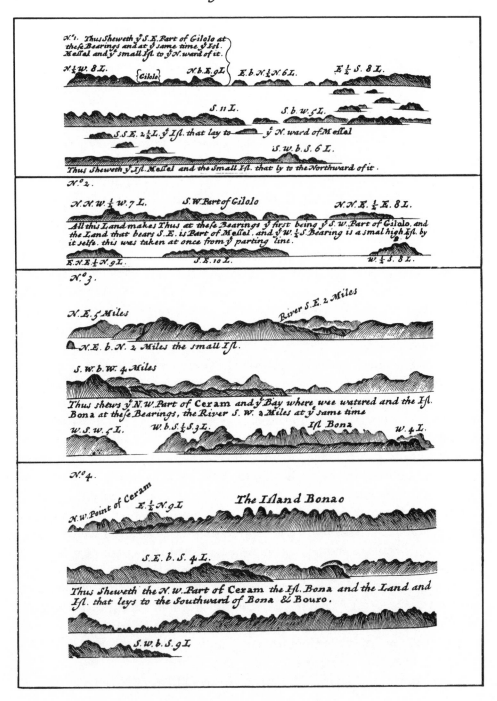

N.°1. Thus Sheweth y.ᵉ S.E. Part of Gilolo at theſe Bearings and at y.ᵉ ſame time y.ᵉ Iſl. Meſſel and y.ᵉ ſmall Iſl. to y.ᵉ N. ward of it.

N.½.W. 8 L.   [Gilolo]   N.b.E. 9 L.   E.b.N.½.N. 6 L.   E.½.S. 8 L.

S. 11 L.   S.b.w. 5 L.

S.S.E. 2½ L. y.ᵉ Iſl. that lay to   y.ᵉ N. ward of Meſſel

S.w.b.S. 6 L.

Thus Sheweth y.ᵉ Iſl. Meſſel and the Small Iſl. that ly to the Northward of it.

N.°2.

N.N.W.¼.w. 7 L.   S.W. Part of Gilolo   N.N.E.½.E. 8 L.

All this Land makes Thus at theſe Bearings y.ᵉ first being y.ᵉ S.w. Part of Gilolo, and the Land that bears S.E. is Part of Meſſel, and y.ᵉ W.¼.S. Bearing is a ſmal high Iſl. by it ſelfe. this was taken at once from y.ᵉ parting line.

E.N.E.½.N. 9 L.   S.E. 10 L.   W.¼.S. 8 L.

N.°3.

N.E. 5 Miles   River S.E. 2 Miles

N.E.b.N. 2 Miles the ſmall Iſl.

S.w.b.w. 4 Miles

Thus ſhews y.ᵉ N.W. Part of Ceram and y.ᵉ Bay where wee watered and the Iſl. Bona at theſe Bearings, the River S.w. 2 Miles at y.ᵉ ſame time

W.S.w. 5 L.   W.b.S.¼.S. 3 L.   Iſl Bona   W. 4 L.

N.°4.

N.W. Point of Ceram   E.½.N. 9 L.   The Iſland Bonao

S.E.b.S. 4 L.

Thus Sheweth the N.W. Part of Ceram the Iſl. Bona and the Land and Iſl. that leys to the Southward of Bona & Bouro.

S.w.b.S. 9 L.

Mile of us. The Sea round about them seem'd all broken, and tossed the Ship so that she would not answer her Helm. These Riplings commonly lasted 10 or 12 minutes, and then the Sea became as still and smooth as a Mill-pond. We sounded often when in the midst of them, and afterwards in the smooth Water; but found no Ground, neither could we perceive that they drove us any way.

We had in one Night several of these Tides, that came most of them from the West; and the Wind being from that Quarter, we commonly heard them a long time before they came; and sometimes lowered our Top-sails, thinking it was a Gust of Wind. They were of great length from North to South, but their breadth not exceeding 200 Yards, and they drove a great pace: For though we had little Wind to move us, yet these would soon pass away, and leave the Water very smooth; and just before we encountred them, we met a great Swell, but it did not break.

The 26th we saw the Island Ceram; and still met some Riplings, but much fainter than those we had the 2 preceeding Days. We sail'd along the Island Ceram to the Westward, edging in withal, to see if peradventure we might find a Harbour to anchor in, where we might water, trim the Ship, and refresh our Men.

In the Morning we saw a Sail to the North of us, steering in for the West-end of Ceram, as we likewise were. In the Evening, being near the Shore on the North-side of the Island, I stood off to Sea with an easy Sail; intending to stand in for the Shore in the Morning, and try to find Anchoring, to fill Water, and get a little Fish for refreshment. Accordingly in the Morning early, I stood in with the North-West-point of Ceram; leaving a small Island, called Bonao, to the West. The Sail we saw the Day before, was now come pretty nigh us, steering in also (as we did) between Ceram and Bonao. I shortned Sail a little for him; and when he got a-breast of us, not above 2 Miles off, I sent my Boat aboard. It was a Dutch Sloop, come from Teranate, and bound for Amboyna: My Men whom I sent in the Boat, bought 5 Bags of new Rice, each containing about 130 pounds, for 6 Spanish Dollars. The Sloop had many rare Parrots aboard for Sale, which did not want price. A Malayan Merchant aboard, told our men, that about 6 Months ago he was at Bencola, and at that time the Governour either dyed or was kill'd, and that the Commander of an English Ship then in that Road succeeded to that Government.

In the Afternoon, having a Breeze at North and North-North-East, I sent my Boat to sound, and standing after her with the Ship, anchored in 30 Fathom Water oazy Sand, half a Mile from the Shore, right against a small River of fresh Water. The next Morning I sent both the Boats ashore to Fish; they return'd about 10 a-Clock, with a few Mullets and 3 or 4 Cavallies, and some Pan-Fish. We found Variation here, 2 deg. 15 min. East.

When the Sea was smooth by the Land-Winds, we sent our Boats ashore for Water; who, in a few Turns, filled all our Casks.

The Land here is low, swampy and woody; the Mould is a dark Grey, friable Earth. Two Rivers came out within a Bow-shot of each other, just opposite to the place where we rode: One comes right down out of the Country; and the other from the South, running along by the Shore, not Musquet-shot from the Sea-side. The Northermost River is biggest, and out of it we filled our Water; our Boats went in and out at any time of Tide. In some places the Land is overflown with fresh Water, at full Sea. The Land hereabouts is full of Trees unknown to us, but none of them very large or high; the Woods yield many wild Fruits and Berries, such as I never saw elsewhere. We met with no Land-Animals. The Fowls we found, were Pidgeons, Parrots, Cockadores, and a great number of small Birds unknown to me. One of the Master's Mates killed 2 Fowls as big as Crows; of a black Colour, excepting that the Tails were all white. Their Necks were pretty long, one of which was of a Saffron-colour, the other Black. They had very large Bills, much like a Rams-horn; their Legs were strong and Short, and their claws like a Pidgeon's; their Wings of an ordinary length: Yet they make a great Noise when they fly, which they do very heavily. They feed on Berries, and perch on the highest Trees. Their Flesh is sweet; I saw some of the same Species at New-Guinea, but no where else.

May the 3d, at 6 in the Morning we weighed, intending to pass between Bonao and Ceram; but presently after we got under Sail, we saw a pretty large Proe coming about the North-West-point of Ceram. Wherefore I stood to the North to speak with her, putting aboard our Ensign. She seeing us coming that way, went into a small Creek, and skulked behind a Point a while: At last discovering her again, I sent my Boat to speak with her; but the Proe row'd away, and would not come nigh it. After this, finding I could not pass between Bonao and Ceram, as I purposed; I steer'd away to the North of it.

This Bonao is a small Island, lying about 4 Leagues from the North-West

This Bird was taken on the
Coast of New Guinea

A Stately Land Fowl found on the
Coast of New Guinea described

A Strange Land
Fowl found on the
Island Ceram

An. 1700

Point of Ceram. I was inform'd by the Dutch Sloop before-mentioned, that notwithstanding its smallness, it hath one fine River, and that the Dutch are there settled. Whether there be any Natives on it, or not, I know not, nor what its Produce is. They further said, that the Ceramers were their mortal Enemies; yet that they were settled on the Westermost Point of Ceram in spite of the Natives.

The next Day, as we approach'd the Island Bouro, there came off from it a very fragrant Scent, much like that from King William's Island; and we found so strong a Current setting to the Westward, that we could scarce stem it. We plied to get to the Southward, intending to pass between Bouro and Keelang.

In the Evening, being near the West-end of Bouro, we saw a Brigantine to the North-West of us, on the North-side of Bouro, standing to the Eastward. I would not stand East or West for fear of coming nigh the Land which was on each side of us, *viz* Bouro on the West, and Keelang on the East. The next Morning we found our selves in Mid-channel between both Islands; and having the Wind at South-West we steer'd South-South-East, which is right through between both. At 11 a-Clock it fell calm; and so continued till Noon; by that time the Brigantine, which we saw a-Stern the Night before, was got 2 or 3 Leagues a-head of us. It is probable she met a strong Land-wind in the Evening, which continued all Night; she keeping nearer the Shore, than I could safely do. She might likewise have a Tide or Current setting Easterly, where she was; though we had a Tide setting Northwardly against us, we being in Mid-channel.

About 8 at Night, the Brigantine which we saw in the Day, came close along by us on our Weather-side: Our Guns were all ready before Night, Matches lighted, and small Arms on the Quarter-Deck ready loaden. She standing one way, and we another; we soon got further asunder. But I kept good watch all the Night, and in the Morning saw her a-Stern of us, standing as we did. At 10 a-Clock, having little Wind, I sent the Yawle aboard of her. She was a Chinese Vessel, laden with Rice, Arrack, Tea, Porcellane, and other Commodities, bound for Amboyna. The Commander said that his Boat was gone ashore for Water, and ask'd our Men if they saw her; for she had been wanting 2 or 3 Days, and they knew not what was become of her. They had their Wives, and Children aboard, and probably came to settle at some new Dutch Factory. The Commander also inform'd us, that the Dutch had lately settled at Ampulo, Menippe, Bonao, and on a

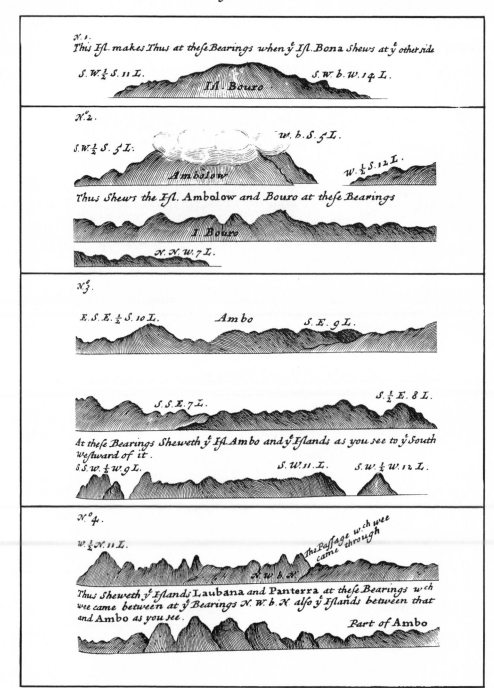

N. 1.
This Iſl. makes Thus at theſe Bearings when ỹ Iſl. Bona Shews at ỹ other ſide

S. W. ½ S. 11 L.   S. W. b. W. 14 L.

Iſl Bouro

N.° 2.

w. b. S. 5 L.

S. W. ½ S. 5 L.   W. ½ S. 12 L.

Ambolow

Thus Shews the Iſl. Ambolow and Bouro at theſe Bearings

I Bouro

N. N. W. 7 L.

N.° 3.

E. S. E. ½ S. 10 L.   Ambo   S. E. 9 L.

S. S. E. 7 L.   S. ½ E. 8 L.

At theſe Bearings Sheweth ỹ Iſl. Ambo and ỹ Iſlands as you ſee to ỹ South
weſtward of it .

S. S. W. ¼ W. 9 L.   S. W. 11 L.   S. W. ¼ W. 12 L.

N.° 4.

w. ½ N. 11 L.   The Paſſage w.ch wee
                                                came through

Thus Sheweth ỹ Iſlands Laubana and Panterra at theſe Bearings w.ch
wee came between at ỹ Bearings N. W. b. N. alſo ỹ Iſlands between that
and Ambo as you ſee .   Part of Ambo

Point of Ceram. The next Day we past out to the Southward between Keelang and Bouro. After this, we had for several Days a Current setting Southerly, and a great tumbling Sea, occasion'd more by the strong Current than by Winds, as was apparent by the jumping of its Waves against each other; and by Observation I found 25 Miles more Southing than our Course gave us.

On the 14th we discovered the Island Misacomby, and the next Day sail'd along to the West on the North-side of the Island. In some Charts it is called Omba; it is a mountainous Island, spotted with Woods and Savannahs; about 20 Leagues long, and 5 or 6 broad. We saw no signs of Inhabitants on it. We fell in nearest to the West-end of it; and therefore I chose to pass on to the Westward, intending to get through to the Southward between this and the next isle to the West of it, or between any other 2 Islands to the West, where I should meet with the clearest Passage; because the Winds were now at North-East and East-North-East, and the Isle lies nearly East and West; so that if the Winds continued, I might be a long time in getting to the East-end of it, which yet I knew to be the best Passage. In the Night, being at the West-end, and seeing no clear Passage, I stood off with an easie Sail, and in the Morning had a fine Land-wind, which would have carried us 5 or 6 Leagues to the East, if we had made the best of it; but we kept on only with a gentle Gale, for fear of a Westerly Current. In the Morning, finding we had not met with any Current as we expected; assoon as it was Light, we made Sail to the Westward again.

After Noon, being near the end of the Isle Pentare, which lies West from Misacomby, we saw many Houses and Plantations in the Country, and many Coco-nut-Trees growing by the Sea-side. We also saw several Boats sailing cross a Bay or Channel at the West-end of Misacomby, between it and Pentare. We had but little Wind, and that at North, which blows right in, with a Swell rowling in withal; wherefore I was afraid to venture in, though probably there might be good Anchoring, and a Commerce with the Natives. I continued steering to the West, because the Night before, at Sun-setting, I saw a small round high Island to the West of Pentare, where I expected a good Passage.

We could not that Day reach the West-end of Pentare, but saw a deep Bay to the West of us, where I thought might be a Passage through, between Pentare and Laubana. But as yet the Lands were shut one within an other, that we could not see any Passage. Therefore I ordered to sail 7 Leagues more Westerly, and lye by till next Day. In the Morning we look'd out for an Opening, but could see none; yet by the distance and bearing of a high round Island called Potoro, we were got to the West of the Opening, but not far from it. Wherefore I tack'd and stood to the East; and the rather, because I had reason to suppose this to be the Passage we came through in the *Cygnet* mentioned in my *Voyage round the World*; but I was not yet sure of it, because we had rainy Weather, so that we could not now see the Land so well as we did then. We then accidentally saw the Opening, at our first falling in with the Islands; which now was a Work of some time and difficulty to discover. However before 10 a Clock we saw the Opening plain; and I was the more confirm'd in my Knowledge of this Passage, by a Spit of Sand and 2 Islands at the North-East part of its Entrance. The Wind was at South-South-West, and we plied to get through before Night; for we found a good Tide helping us to the South. About 7 or 8 Leagues to the West of us we saw a high round piked Mountain, from whose Top a Smoak seem'd to ascend as from a Vulcano. There were 3 other very high piked Mountains, 2 on the East, and 1 on the West of that which smoaked.

In our plying to get through between Pentare and Laubana, we had (as I said) a good Tide or Current setting us to the Southward. And it is to be observed, that near the Shores in these Parts we commonly find a Tide setting Northwardly or Southwardly, as the Land lyes; but the Northwardly Tide sets not above 3 Hours in 12, having little strength; and sometimes it only checks the contrary Current, which runs with great Violence, especially in narrow Passes, such as this, between 2 Islands. It was 12 at Night before we got clear of 2 other small Islands, that lay on the South-side of the Passage; and there we had a very violent Tide setting us through against a brisk Gale of Wind. Notwithstanding which, I kept the Pinnace out, for fear we should be becalm'd. For this is the same place, through which I passed in the Year 1687, mentioned in my *Voyage round the World*, Only then we came out between the Western small Island and Laubana, and now we came through between the two small Islands. We sounded frequently, but had no Ground. I said there, that we came through between Omba and Pentare: For we did not then see the Opening between those 2 Islands; which made me take the West-side of Pentare for the West-end of Omba, and Laubana for Pentare. But now we saw the Opening between Omba and Pentare; which was so narrow that I would not venture through: Besides, I had now discovered my Mistake, and hop'd to meet with the other Passage

An. 1700

again, as indeed we did, and found it to be bold from Side to Side, which in the former Voyage I did not know. After we were through, we made the best of our way to Timor; and on May the 18th in the Morning, we saw it plain, and made the high Land over Laphao the Portugueze Factory, as also the high Peak over our first Watering-place, and a small round Island about mid-way between them.

We coasted along the Island Timor, intending to touch at Babao, to get a little Water and Refreshments. I would not go into the Bay where we first water'd, because of the Currents which there whirl about very strangely, especially at Spring-tides, which were now setting in; besides, the South-East Winds come down in Flaws from the Mountains, so that it would have been very dangerous for us. Wherefore we crowded all the sail we could, to get to Babao before Night, or at least to get Sight of the sandy Island at the Entrance of the Bay; but could not. So we plied all Night; and the next Morning entered the Bay.

There being good Ground all over this Bay, we anchored at 2 a Clock in 30 Fathom Water, soft oazy Ground. And the Morning after I sent my Boat ashore with the Sain to fish. At Noon she return'd and brought enough for all the Ship's Company. They saw an Indian Boat at a round rocky Island about a Mile from them.

On the 22d, I sent my Boat ashore again to fish: At Noon she return'd with a few Fish, which serv'd me and my Officers. They catch'd one Whiteing, the first I had seen in these Seas. Our People went over to the rocky Island, and there found several Jarrs of Turtle, and some hanging up a drying, and some Cloaths; their Boat was about a Mile off, striking Turtle. Our Men left all as they found. In the Afternoon a very large Shark came under our Stern; I never had seen any near so big before. I put a Piece of Meat on a Hook for him, but he went a-Stern and return'd no more. About Midnight, the Wind being pretty moderate, I weigh'd and stood into the Bottom of the Bay, and ran over nearer the South Shore, where I thought to lye and Water, and at convenient Times get Fish for our Refreshment. The next Morning I sent my Pinnace with 2 Hogsheads and 10 Barrecoes for Water; they return'd at Noon with the Casks full of Water; very thick and muddy, but sweet and good. We found Variation, 15 min. West.

This Afternoon, finding that the Breezes were set in here, and that it blew so hard that I could neither fish nor fill Water without much Difficulty and Hazard of the Boat; I resolved to be gone, having good Quantity of Water aboard. Accordingly at half an Hour after 2 in the Morning we weighed with the Wind at East by South, and stood to Sea. We coasted along by the Island Rotte, which is high Land, spotted with Woods and Savannahs. The Trees appear'd small and shrubby, and the Savannahs dry and rusty. All the North-side has sandy Bays by the Sea. We saw no Houses nor Plantations.

The next Day we crowded all the Sail we could to get to the West of all the Isles before Night, but could not; for at 6 in the Evening we saw Land bearing South-West by West. For here are more Islands than are laid down in any Draughts that I have seen. Wherefore I was oblig'd to make a more Westerly Course than I intended, till I judg'd we might be clear of the Land. And when we were so, I could easily perceive by the Ship's Motion. For till then, being under the Lee of the Shore, we had smooth Water; but now we had a troubled Sea which made us dance lustily. This turbulent Sea, was occasion'd in Part by the Current; which setting out slanting against the Wind, was by it raised into short cockling Seas. I did indeed expect a South-West Current here, but not so very strong as we found it.

On the 26th we continued to have a very strong Current setting South-wardly; but on what Point exactly, I know not. Our whole Distance by Log was but 82 Miles, and our Difference of Latitude since Yesterday-noon by Observation 100 Miles, which is 18 Miles more than the whole Distance; and our Course, allowing no Lee-way at all, was South 17 Deg. West, which gives but 76 Miles Difference of Latitude, 24 less than we found by Observation. I did expect (as has been said) we might meet a great Current setting to the South Yesterday, because there is a constant Current setting out from among those Islands we pass'd through between Timor and the Isles to the West of it, and, 'tis probable, in all the other Openings between the Islands, even from the East-end of Java to the End of all that Range that runs from thence, both to the East and West of Timor; but being got so far out to Sea as we were, though there may be a very great Current, yet it does not seem probable to me that it should be of so great Strength as we now found: For both Currents and Tides lose their Force in the open Sea, where they have room to spread; and it is only in narrow Places, or near Head-lands, that their Force is chiefly felt. Besides in my Opinion, it should here rather set to the West than South; being open to the narrow Sea, that divides New-Holland from the Range of Islands before-mentioned.

The 27th, we found that in the last 24 Hours we had gone 9 Miles less South than the Log gave: So that 'tis probable we were then out of the

Southern Current, which we felt so much before. We saw many Tropick-Birds about us. And found Variation 1 deg. 25 min. West.

On June the 1st, we saw several Whales, the first we had at this Time seen on the Coast: But when we were here before, we saw many; at which Time we were nearer the Shore than now. The Variation now, was 5 deg. 38 min. West.

I design'd to have made New-Holland in about the Latitude of 20 deg. and steer'd Courses by day to make it, but in the Night could not be so bold; especially since we had sounding. This Afternoon I steer'd in South-West, till 6 a-Clock; then it blowing fresh, and Night coming on, I steer'd West-South-West, till we had 40 Fathom; and then stood West, which Course carries along Shore. In the Morning again from 6 to 12 I steer'd West-South-West, to have made the Land, but, not seeing it, I judged we were to the West of it. Here is very good Soundings on this Coast. When we past this way to the Eastward, we had, near this Latitude of 19 deg. 50 min. 38 Fathom, about 18 Leagues from the Land: But, this Time, we saw not the Land. The next Morning I saw a great many Scuttle-Fish-bones, which was a Sign that we were not far from the Land. Also a great many Weeds continually floating by us.

We found the Variation increase considerably as we went Westward. For on the 3d, it was 6 deg. 10 min. West; on the 4th, 6 deg. 20 min. and on the 6th, 7 deg. 20 min. That Evening we saw some Fowls like Men of War Birds flying North-East, as I was told; for I did not see them, having been indisposed these 3 or 4 Days.

On the 11th we found the Variation 8 deg. 1 min. West; on the 12th, 6 deg. 0 min. I kept on my Course to the Westward till the 15th, and then altered it. My Design was to seek for the Tryal Rocks; but having been sick 5 or 6 Days, without any fresh Provision or other good Nourishment aboard, and seeing no Likelihood of my Recovery, I rather chose to go to some Port in Time, than to beat here any longer; my People being very negligent, when I was not upon Deck my self: I found the Winds variable, so that I might go any way, East, West, North, or South; wherefore, its probable I might have found the said Rocks, had not Sickness prevented me; which Discovery (when ever made) will be of great use to Merchants trading to these Parts.

From hence nothing material happened, till we came upon the Coast of Java. On the 23d we saw Princes-Isle plain, and the Mouth of the Streights of Sunda. By my Computation, the Distance between Timor and Princes-Isle, is 14 deg. 22 min. The next Day in the Afternoon, being abreast of Crockadore Island, I steer'd away East-North-East for an Island that lies near Mid-way between Sumatra and Java but nearest the Java Shore; which is by English Men called Thwart-the-way. We had but small Winds till about 3 a-Clock, when it freshned, and I was in good Hopes to pass through before Day: But at 9 a Clock the Wind fell, and we got but little. I was then abreast of Thwart-the-way, which is a pretty high long Island; but before 11, the Wind turned, and presently afterward it fell calm. I was then about 2 Leagues from the said Island; and, having a strong Current against us, before Day we were driven astern 4 or 5 Leagues. In the Morning we had the Wind at North-North-West; it look'd black and the Wind unsettled: So that I could not expect to get through. I therefore stood toward the Java Shore, and at 10 anchored in 24 Fathom Water, black oazy Ground, 3 Leagues from the Shore. I sounded in the Night when it was calm, and had 54 Fathom, coarse Sand and Coral.

In the Afternoon before, we had seen many Proes; but none came off to us; and in the Night we saw many Fires ashore. This Day a large Proe came aboard of us, and lay by our Side an Hour. There were only 4 Men in her, all Javians, who spoke the Malayan Language. They ask'd if we were English; I answered, we were; and presently one of them came aboard, and presented me with a small Hen, some Eggs and Coco-nuts; for which I gave some Beads and a small Looking-Glass, and some Glass-Bottles. They also gave me some Sugar-canes, which I distributed to such of my Men as were scorbutick. They told me there were 3 English Ships at Batavia.

The 28th at 2 in the Afternoon we anchored in 26 Fathom Water; presently it fell calm and began to rain very violently, and so continued from 3 till 9 in the Evening. At 1 in the Morning we weigh'd with a fine Land-wind at South-South-East; but presently the Wind coming about at East, we anchored; for we commonly found the Current setting West. If at any Time it turn'd, it was so weak, that it did us little good; and I did not think it safe to venture through without a pretty brisk leading Gale; for the Passage is but narrow, and I knew not what Dangers might be in the way, nor how the Tide sets in the Narrow, having not been this way these 28 Years, and all my People wholly Strangers: We had the Opening fair before us.

While we lay here, 4 Malayan Proes came from the Shore, laden with Coco-nuts, Plantains, Bonanoes, Fowls, Ducks, Tobacco, Sugar, &c. These

An. 1700

were very welcome, and we purchased much Refreshment of them. At 10 a-Clock I dismiss'd all the Boats, and weigh'd with the Wind at North-West. At half an Hour past 6 in the Evening, we anchored in 32 Fathom Water in a coarse Sort of Oaze. We were now past the Island Thwart-the-way, but had still one of the small Islands to pass. The Tide begun to run strong to the West; which obliged me to anchor while I had Soundings, for Fear of being driven back again or on some unknown Sand. I lay still all Night. At 5 a Clock the next Morning, the Tide began to slacken: At 6, I weig'd with the Wind at South-East by East, a handsom Breeze. We just weather'd the Button; and sounding several Times, had still between 30 and 40 Fathom. When we were abreast of the Button, and about 2 Leagues from the Westermost point of Java, we had 34 Fathom, small Peppery Sand. You may either come between this Island and Java, or, if the Wind is Northerly, run out between the Island Thwart-the-way and this last small Island.

The Wind for the most Part being at East and East by South, I was obliged to run over towards the Sumatra Shore, sounding as I went, and had from 34 to 23 Fathom. In the Evening I sounded pretty quick, being got near the Sumatra Shore; and, finding a Current setting to the West, between 8 and 9 a-Clock we anchored in 34 Fathom. The Tide set to the West from 7 in the Evening to 7 this Morning; and then, having a small Gale at West-South-West, I weigh'd and stood over to the Java Shore.

In the Evening having the Wind between East-North-East and South-East by East, we could not keep off the Java Shore. Wherefore I anchored in 27 Fathom Water, about a League and a half off Shore. At the same Time we saw a Ship at anchor near the Shore, about 2 Mile to Leeward of us. We found the Tide setting to the West-ward, and presently after we anchored it fell calm. We lay still all Night, and saw many Fires ashore. At 5 the next Morning, being July the 1st, we weigh'd and stood to the North for a Sea-breeze: At 10 the Wind coming out, I tack'd and had a fine brisk Gale. The Ship we saw at anchor, weigh'd also and stood after us. While we past by Pulo Baby, I kept sounding, and had no less than 14 Fathom. The other Ship coming after us with all the Sail she could make, I shortned Sail on Purpose that she might overtake us, but she did not. A little after 5, I anchored in 13 Fathom good oazy Ground. About 7 in the Evening, the Ship that followed us, past by close under our Stern; she was a Dutch Fly-boat; they told us they came directly from Holland, and had been in their Passage six Months. It was now dark, and the Dutch Ship anchored within a

Mile of us. I order'd to look out sharp in the Morning; that so soon as the Dutch Man began to move, we might be ready to follow him; for I intended to make him my Pilot. In the Morning at half an hour after 5 we weigh'd, the Dutch Man being under Sail before; and we stood directly after him. At 8, having but little Wind, I sent my Boat aboard of him, to see what News he had brought from Europe. Soon after, we spied a Ship coming from the East, plying on a Wind to speak with us, and shewing English Colours. I made a Signal for my Boat, and presently bore away towards her; and being pretty nigh, the Commander and Super-cargoe came aboard, supposing we had been the Tuscany Galley, which was expected then at Batavia. This was a Country Ship, belonging to Fort St. George, having come out from Batavia the Day before, and bound to Bencola. The Commander told me that the *Fleet*-frigat was at Anchor in Batavia Road, but would not stay there long: He told me also, that his Majesty's Ships commanded by Captain Warren were still in India, but he had been a great while from the Coast and had not seen them. He gave me a Draught of these Streights, from the Button and Cap to Batavia, and shew'd me the best way in thither. At 11 a Clock, it being calm, I anchored in 14 Fathom good oazy Ground.

At 2 a Clock we weigh'd again; the Dutch Ship being under Sail before, standing close to Mansheters Island; but finding he could not weather it, he tack'd and stood off a little while, and then tack'd again. In the mean Time I stood pretty nigh the said Island, sounding, but could not weather it. Then I tack'd and stood off, and the Dutch stood in towards the Island; and weathered it. I being desirous to have room enough, stood off longer, and then went about, having the Dutch Ship 4 Points under my Lee. I kept after him; but as I came nearer the Island, I found a Tide setting to the West, so that I could not weather it. Wherefore at 6 in the Evening I anchored in 7 Fathom oazy Ground, about a Mile from the Island: The Dutch Ship went about 2 Miles further, and anchored also; and we both lay still all Night. At 5 the next Morning we weigh'd again, and the Dutch Ship stood away between the Island Cambusses and the Main; but I could not follow, because we had a Land-wind. Wherefore I went without the Cambusses, and by Noon we saw the Ships that lay at the careening Island near Batavia. After the Land-wind was spent, which we had at South-East and South-South-East; the Sea-breeze came up at East. Then we went about; and the Wind coming after-ward at East-North-East, we had a large Wind to run us into Batavia Road: And at 4 in the Afternoon, we anchored in 6 Fathom soft Oaze.

CHAP. VI

We found in Batavia Road a great many Ships at anchor, most Dutch, and but one English Ship named the *Fleet*-frigat, commanded by one Merry. We rode a little without them all. Near the Shore lay a stout China Junk, and a great many small Vessels, *viz* Brigantines, Sloops and Malayan Proes in abundance. Assoon as I anchored, I sent my Boat aboard the *Fleet*-frigat, with orders to make them strike their Pendant, which was done soon after the Boat went aboard. Then my Clerk, whom I sent in the Boat, went for the Shore, as I had directed him; to see if the Government would answer my Salute: But it was now near Night, and he had only time to speak with the Ship-bander, who told him that the Government would have answered my Salute with the same number of Guns, if I had fired as soon as I anchored; but that now it was too late. In the Evening my Boat came aboard, and the next Morning I my self went ashore, visited the Dutch General, and desir'd the Priviledge of buying such Provision and Stores, as I now wanted; which he granted me.

I lay here till the 17th of October following, all which time we had very fair Weather, some Tornadoes excepted. In the mean time I supplied the Carpenter with such Stores as were necessary for refitting the Ship; which prov'd more leaky after he had caulk'd Her, then she was before: So that I was obliged to carreen her, for which purpose I hired Vessels to take in our Guns, Ballast, Provision and Stores.

The English Ships that arriv'd here from England, were first the *Liampo*, commanded by Captain Monk, bound for China; next, the *Panther* commanded by Captain Robinson; then the *Mancel*-Frigat, commanded by Captain Clerk. All these brought good Tidings from England. Most of them had been unfortunate in their Officers; especially Captain Robinson, who said that some of them had been conspiring to ruin him and his Voyage. There came in also several English Country Vessels; first a Sloop from Ben-

jarr, commanded by one Russel, bound to Bengale; next, the *Monsoon*, be-
longing to Bengale: She had been at Malacca at the same time that his
Majesty Ship the *Harwich* was there: Afterwards came in also another small
Ship from Bengale.

While we stay'd here, all the forenamed English Ships sailed hence; the 2
Bengale Ships excepted. Many Dutch Ships also came in here, and departed
again before us. We had several Reports concerning our Men of War in
India, and much talk concerning Rovers who had committed several Spoils
upon the Coast, and in the Streights of Malacca. I did not hear of any Ships
sent out to quash them. At my first coming in, I was told that 2 Ships had
been sent from Amboyna in quest of me; which was lately confirm'd by one
of the Skippers, whom I by accident met with here. He told me they had 3
Protests against me; that they came to Pulo-Sabuda on the Coast of New-
Guinea 28 Days after my departure thence, and went as far as Scouten's
Island, and hearing no further News of me, return'd. Something likewise to
this purpose Mr. Merry, Commander of the *Fleet*-frigat, told me at my first
arrival here; and that the General at Batavia had a Copy of my Commission
and Instructions; but I look'd upon it as a very improbable thing.

While we lay here, the Dutch held several Consultations about sending
some Ships for Europe sooner than ordinary: At last the 16th of October was
agreed upon for the Day of Sailing, which is 2 Months sooner than usual.
They lay ready 2 or 3 Days before, and went out on the 10th. Their Names
were, the *Ostresteen*, bound to Zealand; the *Vanheusen*, for Enchiehoust; and
the 3 *Crowns*, for Amsterdam, commanded by Skipper Jacob Uncright, who
was Commadore over all the rest. I had by this time finished my Business
here, *viz.* fitted the Ship, recruited my self with Provision, filled all my
Water; and the time of the Year to be going for Europe being now at hand,
I prepar'd to be gone also.

Accordingly on the 17th of October, at half an Hour after 6 in the
Morning, I weigh'd Anchor from Batavia, having a good Land-wind at
South, and fair Weather: And by the 19th at Noon, came up with the 3
Dutch Ships before-mentioned. The 29th of November in the Morning we
saw a small Hawk flying about the Ship till she was quite tired. Then she
rested on the Mizen-Top-Sail-Yard, where we catch'd her. It is probable she
was blown off from Madagascar by the violent Northerly Winds; that being
the nighest Land to us, though distance near 150 Leagues.

The 30th of December, we arrived at the Cape of Good Hope; and departed again on the 11th of January, 1701. About the end of the Month, we saw abundance of Weeds or Blubber swim by us, for I cannot determine which. It was all of one Shape and Colour. As they floated on the Water, they seem'd to be of the breadth of the Palm of a Man's Hand, spread out round into many Branches about the Bigness of a Man's Finger. They had in the middle a little Knob, no bigger than the Top of a Mans Thumb. They were of a Smoak-colour; and the Branches, by their pliantness in the Water, seem'd to be more simple than Gellies, I have not seen the like before.

The 2d of February, we anchored in St. Helena Road, and set sail again from thence on the 13th.

On the 21st we made the Island of Ascension, and stood in towards it. The 22d between 8 and 9 a-Clock, we sprung a Leak, which increased so that the Chain-pump could not keep the Ship free. Whereupon I set the Hand-pump to work also, and by 10 a-Clock suck'd her: Then wore the Ship, and stood to the Southward, to try if that would ease her; and then the Chain-pump just kept her free. At 5 the next Morning we made Sail and stood in for the Bay; and at 9 anchored in 10 and a half Fathom, sandy Ground. The South-point bore South-South-West distance 2 Miles, and the North-point of the Bay, North-East half North, distance 2 Miles. As soon as we anchored, I ordered the Gunner to clear his Powder-room, that we might there search for the Leak, and endeavour to stop it within board if possible; for we could not heel the Ship so low, it being within 4 Streaks of the Keel; neither was there any convenient place to haul her ashore. I ordered the Boatswain to assist the Gunner; and by 10 a-Clock the Powder-room was clear. The Carpenter's Mate, Gunner, and Boatswain went down; and soon after I followed them my self, and ask'd them whether they could come at the Leak: They said they believed they might, by cutting the Cieling; I told the Carpenter's Mate (who was the only Person in the Ship that understood any Thing of Carpenters-work,) that if he thought he could come at the Leak by cutting the Cieling without weakening the Ship, he might do it for he had stopp'd one Leak so before; which though not so big as this, yet having seen them both, I thought he might as well do this as the other. Wherefore I left him to do his best. The Ceiling being cut, they could not come at the Leak; for it was against one of the Foot-hook-Timbers, which the Carpenter's Mate said he must first cut, before it could be stopp'd. I went down again to see it, and found the Water to come in very violently. I told them I never had known any such thing as cutting Timbers to stop Leaks; but if they who ought to be best Judges in such Cases, thought they could do any good, I bid them use their utmost Care and Diligence, promising the Carpenter's Mate that I would always be a Friend to him if he could and would stop it: He said, by 4 a-Clock in the Afternoon he would make all well, it being then about 11 in the Forenoon. In the Afternoon my Men were all employ'd, pumping with both Pumps; except such as assisted the Carpenter's Mate. About one in the Afternoon I went down again, and the Carpenter's Mate was cutting the After-part of the Timber over the Leak. Some said it was best to cut the Timber away at once; I bid them hold their Tongue, and let the Carpenter's Mate alone; for he knew best, and I hop'd he would do his utmost to stop the Leak. I desir'd him to get every thing ready for stopping the violence of the Water, before he cut any further; for fear it should over-power us at once. I had already ordered the Carpenter to bring all the Oakam he had, and the Boatswain to bring all the waste Cloaths, to stuff in upon Occasion; and had for the same purpose sent down my own Bed-cloaths. The Carpenter's Mate said he should want short Stantions, to be placed so that the upper-end should touch the Deck, and the under-part rest on what was laid over the Leak; and presently took a Length for them. I ask'd the Master-Carpenter what he thought best to be done: He replied till the Leak was all open, he could not tell. Then he went away to make a Stantion, but it was too long: I ordered him to make many of several Lengths, that we might not want of any Size. So, once more desiring the Carpenter's Mate to use his utmost Endeavours, I went up, leaving the Boatswain and some others there. About 5 a Clock the Boatswain came to me, and told me the Leak was increased, and that it was impossible to keep the Ship above Water; when on the contrary I expected to have had the News of the Leak's being stopt. I presently went down, and found the Timber cut away, but nothing in Readiness to stop the Force of the Water from coming in. I asked them why they would cut the Timber, before they had got all Things in Readiness: The Carpenter's Mate answered, they could do nothing till the Timber was cut that he might take the Dimensions of the Place; and that there was a Chaulk which he had lined out, preparing by the Carpenter's Boy. I ordered them in the mean Time to stop in Oakam, and some Pieces of Beef; which accordingly was done, but all to little Purpose: For now the Water gush'd in with such Violence, notwithstanding all our Endeavours to check it, that it flew in over the Cieling; and for want of

An.1701

Passage out of the Room overflow'd it above 2 Foot deep. I ordered the Bulkhead to be cut open, to give Passage to the Water that it might drain out of the Room; and withal ordered to clear away abaft the Bulk-head, that we might bail: So now we had both Pumps going, and as many bailing as could; and by this Means the Water began to decrease; which gave me some Hope of Saving the Ship. I ask'd the Carpenter's Mate, what he thought of it; He said, *Fear not; for by 10 a Clock at Night I'll engage to stop the Leak.* I went from him with a heavy Heart; but putting a good Countenance upon the Matter, encouraged my Men, who pump'd and bail'd very briskly; and, when I saw Occasion, I gave them some Drams to comfort them. About 11 a Clock at Night, the Boatswain came to me, and told me, that the Leak still encreased; and that the Plank was so rotten, it broke away like Dirt; and that now it was impossible to save the Ship; for they could not come at the Leak, because the Water in the Room was got above it. The rest of the Night we spent in Pumping and Bailing. I worked my self to encourage my Men, who were very diligent; but the Water still encreas'd, and we now thought of nothing but saving our Lives. Wherefore I hoisted out the Boat, that, if the Ship should sink, yet we might be saved: And in the Morning we weighed our Anchor, and warp'd in nearer the Shore; yet did but little good.

In the Afternoon, with the Help of a Sea-breeze, I ran into 7 Fathom, and anchored; then carried a small Anchor ashore, and warp'd in till I came into 3 Fathom and a half. Where having fastned her, I made a Raft to carry the Men's Chests and Bedding ashore; and, before 8 at Night, most of them, were ashore. In the Morning I ordered the Sails to be unbent, to make Tents; and then my self and Officers went ashore. I had sent ashore a Puncheon, and a 36 Gallon Cask of Water, with one Bag of Rice for our common use: But great Part of it was stolen away, before I came ashore; and many of my Books and Papers lost.

On the 26th following, we, to our great Comfort, found a Spring of fresh Water, about 8 Miles from our Tents, beyond a very high Mountain, which we must pass over: So that now we were, by God's Providence, in a Condition of subsisting some Time; having Plenty of very good Turtle by our Tents, and Water for the fetching. The next Day I went up to see the Watering-place, accompanied with most of my Officers. We lay by the way all Night, and next Morning early got thither; where we found a very fine Spring on the South-East-side of the high Mountain, about half a Mile from

An.1701 its Top: But the continual Fogs make it so cold here, that it is very un-wholsome living by the Water. Near this Place, are Abundance of Goats and Land-crabs. About 2 Mile South-East from the Spring, we found 3 or 4 shrubby Trees, upon one of which was cut an Anchor and Cable, and the Year 1642. About half a Furlong from these, we found a convenient Place for sheltering Men in any Weather. Hither many of our Men resorted; the hollow Rocks affording convenient Lodging; the Goats, Land-crabs, Men of War Birds, and Boobies, good Food; and the Air was here exceeding wholsome.

About a Week after our coming ashore, our Men that liv'd at this new Habitation, saw 2 Ships making towards the Island. Before Night they brought me the News; and I ordered them to turn about a Score of Turtle, to be in Readiness for their Ships if they should touch here: But before Morning they were out of Sight, and the Turtle were releas'd again. Here we continued without seeing any other Ship till the second of April; when we saw 11 Sail to Windward of the Island: But they likewise past by. The Day after appear'd 4 Sail, which came to anchor in this Bay. They were his Majesty's Ships the *Anglesey, Hastings* and *Lizard*; and the *Canterbury* East-India Ship. I went on board the *Anglesey* with about 35 of my Men; and the rest were dispos'd of into the other 2 Men of War.

We sail'd from Ascension, the 8th; and continued aboard till the 8th of May: At which Time the Men of War having miss'd St. Jago, where they design'd to Water, bore away for Barbadoes: But I being desirous to get to England as soon as possible, took my Passage in the Ship *Canterbury*, ac-companied with my Master, Purser, Gunner, and 3 of my superiour Officers.

INDEX

This index is taken directly from the 1729 edition, but has been condensed and edited for the purposes of this publication

PART I

PART II